FREDDIE MERCURY

FREDDIE MERCURY

An intimate memoir by the man who knew him best

by

Peter Freestone

with

David Evans

OMNIBUS PRESS
LONDON · NEW YORK · PARIS · SYDNEY

This book is for my late mother, Olga, and my father, Leslie, who always let me get on with my life and yet were always around if I needed them. I couldn't properly grieve for my mother because her death coincided with my growing involvement with deeper care for Freddie and so in some ways this book is my acknowledgment to her.

Introduction

November 28, 1995, and October 10, 1997,

> *"I lived for art, I lived for love*
> *Why does God repay me thus . . .?"*
> – Tosca. Act II. Puccini.

In the *Sunday Times* of September 24, 1995, a league table of artistic achievement, Masters of the Arts, was published. Included in this were two sections, favourite pop performer and greatest pop performer. Amongst the favourite group which included the likes of Elvis Presley, The Beatles and Elton John, the name Freddie Mercury ranked number ten. Amongst the greatest pop performers, which again included Elvis Presley, The Beatles and Elton John, Freddie's name again appeared, ranked at number five, oddly enough above that of Elton John.

During his life, Freddie greatly admired both Elvis Presley and John Lennon, almost regarding them as heroes. He never dreamed that when he died, he would be included in the same league. And in October 1979, when I first had the offer of working with Queen, I never dreamed that I would be involved with a man whom I see as one of the greatest composers of the late twentieth century.

I was involved with Freddie on a day-to-day basis for twelve years, almost to the day, in a multitude of different roles which eventually all came together under the umbrella description of Personal Assistant. I was chief cook and bottle washer, waiter, butler, valet, secretary, amanuensis, cleaner, baby-sitter (the baby being him) and agony aunt. I shopped for him both at supermarkets and art markets, I travelled the world with him, I was with him at the highs and came through the lows with him. I saw the creative juices flow and I also saw the frustration when life wasn't going well. I acted as his bodyguard when needed and in the end, of course, I was one of his nurses.

And I was indubitably one of his friends.

I'm one of a handful of people who were lucky enough to have witnessed the creation of much of his work, from conception to performance. There is so much more to creating music than putting lyrics and notes down on paper. The feelings involved and the reason for them mean so much and Freddie had a bottomless well of feelings.

By undertaking this project, I find I have a responsibility to be as truthful as I can in portraying what Freddie went through both as an artist and as a man. I want to show that there was much more to Freddie than has been written about until now. I also want to dispel some of the grosser imaginings of both press and biographers alike, who, doubtless writing from the best of motives, didn't know the man they were writing about. I realised very early on that the man about whom I am writing was one of the most complex creatures anyone could ever encounter. But, at the same time, in writing about him, I also realised that he was in fact just a human being like the rest of us and I sincerely hope that in reading this, anyone will be able to find elements of themselves contained within this very special person. In my time, I have discovered we are all very special and complex people.

A large percentage of the population of the world have read all about Freddie's comings and goings and doings of this and that but many people have come up and asked me: "What was Freddie *really* like?"

With this book, I hope I can answer some of their questions. I don't believe that any one person can know a hundred per cent about another person and so I would never lay claim to writing anything definitive. What follows is *my* telling of Freddie's life. I want to show both the man and the genius and the results of the collaboration.

Peter Freestone
London 1995–1998

Preface

CAST LIST

I thought it might be helpful to the readers unfamiliar with the cast in this slice of life to have a list of those major players for easy reference as to their place in this tale.

A

HRH The Prince Andrew   *Great fan of ballet dancers.*
Thor Arnold   *Nurse, friend and confidant.*
James Arthurs   *Businessman and longtime friend in New York.*
Debbie Ash   *Actress.*
Jane Asher   *Actress and, later still, cake-maker.*
Gordon Atkinson   *Freddie's General Practitioner.*
Mary Austin   *Former girlfriend. Lifelong Friend.*

B

Roy and Barbara Thomas Baker   *Mr and Mrs Record Producer.*
Tony Bastin   *Lover.*
Jim and Claudia Beach   *Queen's manager and his wife.*
Stephanie Beacham   *Actress.*
Martin Beisly   *Art expert at Christie's auction house.*
Rupert Bevan   *Picture frame gilder and furniture restorer.*
Debbie Bishop   *Actress and singer.*
David Bowie   *Composer, musician. Still a private company.*
Bryn Bridenthal   *Friendly ally at Elektra Records, Los Angeles.*
Dieter Briet   *Physiotherapist.*
Briony Brind   *Prima ballerina.*
John Brough   *Sound engineer and scapegoat.*

Kim Brown   *Wife of Pete Brown, once Queen's day-to-day manager. Cake-maker.*
Michael Brown   *Ballet wardrobe master for the Royal Ballet.*
Jackie Brownell   *Sympathetic contact at Elektra Records, LA.*
Bomi and Jer Bulsara   *His parents.*
Joe Burt   *Guitarist and sometime boyfriend to Mary Austin.*

C

Carlos Caballe   *Artist's manager.*
Montserrat Caballe   *La Superba. Opera diva and friend.*
Montsy Caballe   *Niece and personal assistant to Montserrat.*
Piers Cameron   *Father to Mary's children. Interior Decorator.*
Rupert Cavendish   *Furniture dealer.*
Annie Challis   *Record company executive and friend.*
David Chambers   *Tailor.*
Charles the Canadian   *Lover.*
John Christie   *Actor. Colleague of Dave Clark's. Friend.*
Dave Clark   *Sixties pop star, theatrical producer and friend.*
Trevor Clarke   *Nightclub front man and friend.*
Roger and Kashmira Cooke   *Sister and brother-in-law.*
Carolyn Cowan   *Make-up artist extraordinaire.*

D

Gordon Dalziel   *Chauffeur. Partner to Graham Hamilton.*
Jo Dare   *Singer.*
John Deacon   *Bass guitarist. One quarter of Queen.*
Derek Deane   *Principal dancer at the Royal Ballet.*
Denny   *Hairdresser and friend.*
Jim Devenney   *Sound engineer in charge of on-stage monitors.*
Richard Dick   *Barman and lover.*
Anita Dobson   *Actress and friend. Brian May's partner.*
Rudi Dolezal   *Video producer and director and friend.*

E

Wayne Eagling   *Principal dancer and friend.*
Ken and Dolly East   *EMI Record Company Executive.*
Eduardo the Venezualan   *Lover.*
Gordon Elsbury   *Top of the Pops Television Director.*
Kenny Everett   *DJ extraordinaire, comic genius and friend.*

F

Joe Fanelli   *Chef, lover and friend. Latterly nurse.*
Pam Ferris   *Actress.*
Tony Fields   *American dancer and actor.*
Michael Fish   *Shirt and tie designer. Nightclub front man.*
Leslie Freestone   *My father. Funeral director.*

G

Brian Gazzard   *Consultant physician.*
David Geffen   *Record company executive.*
Bob Geldof   *Singer, composer and event organiser.*
Boy George   *Singer, composer, performer.*
Terry, Sharon and Luke Giddings   *Security, driver and friend.*
Julie Glover   *Jim Beach's deputy at Queen Productions.*
Harvey Goldsmith   *Concert and event promoter.*
Bruce Gowers   *Video film director.*
Richard Gray   *Art director.*

H

Tony Hadley   *Singer, composer and esteemed peer.*
Graham Hamilton   *Chauffeur and friend.*
Gary Hampshire   *Chauffeur.*
Sarah Harrison   *Fashion consultant and friend.*
Stephen Hayter   *Nightclub proprietor.*
Peter Hince (Ratty)   *Member of Queen road crew.*
Jennifer Holliday   *Singer and actress.*
George Hurrell   *Photographer.*
Jim Hutton   *Barber and lover.*
Sally Hyatt   *Administrative assistant at Queen Productions.*

J

Michael Jackson   *Singer, composer and entertainer.*
Elton John   *Singer, composer, performer and friend.*
Peter Jones   *Chauffeur.*

K

Petre von Katze   *One-time friend.*
Trip Khalaf   *PA sound engineer.*

Tony King   *Music business executive and friend.*
Winnie Kirchberger   *Restaurateur and lover.*

L

Debbie Leng   *Actress and Roger Taylor's partner.*
Carl Lewis   *American athlete.*
John Libson   *Accountant.*
Sir Joseph Lockwood   *Record Company Executive, mentor.*

M

Rheinhold Mack, Ingrid and John Frederick   *Record producer and friend.*
David Mallet   *Video director.*
Fred Mandel   *Keyboard player.*
Diego Maradona   *Footballer.*
Brian May   *Guitarist and one quarter of Queen.*
Donald McKenzie   *Household friend.*
Roxy Meade   *Press representative and friend.*
Bhaskar Menon   *Record company executive.*
Robin Moore-Ede   *Interior designer.*
Mike and Linda Moran   *Composer, musician, recording producer and friend.*
Peter Morgan   *Lover.*
Diana Moseley   *Costume designer and friend.*
Graham Moyle   *Case physician at Westminster hospital.*
Russell Mulcahay   *Video director.*
John Murphy   *American Airlines Cabin crew, friend.*
Nina Myskow   *Columnist and friend.*

N

Anna Nicholas   *Actress and friend.*
Lee Nolan   *Waiter and friend.*
Gary Numan   *Musician.*
David Nutter   *Photographer and friend.*

O

Terry O'Neill   *Photographer.*

P

Elaine Page   *Singer and friend.*

Rudi Patterson   *Artist and friend.*
Christopher Payne   *Furniture expert at Sotheby's.*
Yasmin Pettigrew   *Actress and friend.*
Mary Pike   *Cleaner.*
Tony Pike   *Hotelier.*
Paul Prenter   *Personal manager and onetime friend.*
Peter Pugson   *Wine merchant. Friend of Jim Beach.*

R

Kurt Raab (Rebecca)   *Performer.*
Bill Reid   *Lover.*
John Reid   *Manager and friend.*
Tim Rice   *Lyricist and friend.*
Cliff Richard   *Singer, performer.*
Dave Richards   *Recording engineer/ producer.*
Howard Rose   *North American concert promoter.*
Hannes Rossacher   *Video director.*

S

Pino Sagliocco   *Spanish concert promoter.*
Amin Salih   *Accountant.*
Joe Scardilli   *American Airlines cabin crew, friend.*
Jane Seymour   *Actress.*
Wayne Sleep   *Principal dancer and one-time friend.*
Lord Snowdon   *Photographer.*
Gladys Spier   *Cleaner.*
Billy Squier   *Singer, composer, musician and friend.*
Rod Stewart   *Singer and peer.*
Gerry and Sylvia Stickells   *Tour manager and friends.*
Peter Straker   *Singer, actor and friend.*
Phil Symes   *Press representative.*
Barbara Szabo   *Office accountant.*

T

Gail Taphouse   *Soloist at Royal Ballet.*
Mr Tavener   *Builder.*
Chris Taylor (Crystal)   *Member of Queen road crew.*
Dominique Taylor   *Wife to Roger Taylor and friend.*
Elizabeth Taylor   *Great movie star.*

Gavin Taylor   *Video director.*
Roger Taylor   *Drummer and one quarter of Queen.*
Baroness Francesca von Thyssen   *Socialite and friend.*
Douglas Trout   *Hairdresser and one-time friend.*

V

Barbara Valentin   *Actress and friend.*
Vince the Barman   *Barman and lover.*
Paul Vincent   *Guitarist.*

W

Clodagh Wallace   *Artists' manager and friend.*
Misa Watanabe   *Japanese music publishing executive, friend.*
David Wigg   *Journalist and one-time friend.*
Margie Winter   *Cleaner.*
Stefan Wissnet   *Guitarist and recording engineer.*
Carol Woods   *Actress and singer.*

Y

Susannah York   *Actress.*
Richard Young   *Photographer and friend.*

Z

Brian Zellis (Jobby)   *Member of Queen road crew.*

Chapter One

In the beginning, it was 1973.

The very first sighting I ever had of Freddie Mercury was in the Rainbow Room restaurant at the shop called Biba in the old Derry and Toms building on Kensington High Street in London. I remember his very being there was a performance.

The Rainbow Room was originally an art deco ballroom with a wonderful layered plaster ceiling, in which different lighting effects were used, often giving the colours of the spectrum, hence providing the name the Rainbow Room. Freddie was so struck by this ceiling that it influenced the designs of some of the ceilings in his future home. But that was still a long way away.

I'd gone to the Rainbow Room with my then girlfriend, Pamela Curtis. Pam and I had had a hard afternoon's shopping around that wonderful store. Biba was the kind of emporium where you didn't actually have to buy anything but still had to look in every nook and cranny because the stock and its positioning were all changed so often. The displays in every part of the shop were a wonder in themselves. Freddie was there taking afternoon tea with his then girlfriend Mary Austin, who was at this time working at Biba. He still stood out even though at that point I actually had very little knowledge of contemporary music. Queen were not very well-known in 1973 although Freddie, as one of the new rising stars of rock music, was unmistakable.

Freddie's charisma took over the space he occupied. The cream seats of the restaurant were shaped like big seashells and so Freddie, ensconced in his seat with his long black hair and dressed in the short fox fur jacket, really turned heads. Of course, we did not meet then and I was not to meet Freddie properly for the first time until late in 1979. In the intervening years, he would become a household name, touring the far reaches of the world, and I would take up employment full-time in the Royal Ballet wardrobe department, with whom I toured more specific parts of the world: Canada, North America, Mexico and Greece, as well as working in the fabled Royal Opera House in Covent Garden.

Before I go into too much more detail about Freddie, I should fill in a few details about my own life which had brought me to this point. Although I had been born in Carshalton, Surrey, I only spent the first six years of my life in England. My elder brother Leslie and I spent the next five years in a boarding school in southern India at a place called Lushington Hall in Oootacamund, a town set amongst the tea plantations of the Nilgiri Hills. It was one of the often mentioned 'hill-stations' whence the Raj escaped during the summer heat on the plains and the last bastion of the only surviving independent native Indian people, the Todas. Incidentally, it was also in Oootacamund that snooker had been invented many, many years ago. Home was a hotel which was being run by my parents in Calcutta. I call it home although I only spent two months of the year there. Does this already sound familiar? There is an obvious and immediate analogy with Freddie's life, although at least I had the luxury of being able to see my parents for three months of the year because they used to come down and spend the month of May with my brother and I during our Easter holidays.

When I was eleven, we returned to England for what was supposed to be a six month break but in those six months, my father was persuaded by his brother not to return to India. While I regretted this decision at the time and for many years, I suppose that should we have returned, this book would never have been written. I completed my education at Isaac Newton Secondary Modern school in North Kensington and, as most children did then, took up weekend employment first assisting the milkman on his rounds, advancing to working in the bargain basement at Whiteley's in Queensway when what is currently a mall was still a department store and where I was the weekend supervisor.

While still a pupil, I progressed from Whiteley's to Selfridges and it was there that I took up full employment after GCE while deciding what I was going to do with my life. Selfridges created a catering management scheme with me as the first recruit. This was real nine-to-five employment and I was very bored in the evenings after work until a friend of mine from Selfridges suggested that I join him in doing an occasional evening job at the Royal Opera House. On April 22, 1975, I started dressing the men's opera chorus, a situation which brought about another coincidence: the performance of Verdi's *Il Trovatore*, including the aria 'D'Amor Sull'Ali Rosee', featured amongst its great singers Montserrat Caballe, who will figure so much in this story.

In school days at Isaac Newton, my English composition homework was always done to the sound of Wagner overtures from our stereogram, a gramaphone and radio combined which was popular at the time. I didn't have many records but was always drawn to classical rather than pop music, although where my love of classical music had come from I really cannot say. Wagner must have been particularly inspirational, full of drama and excitement and spurred me even to attempt my own version of Enid Blyton's *Famous Five* tales. It was already clear that my life needed that little extra spice.

It wasn't long before the tug of the Opera House overcame my already weakened ambition to be a Selfridges caterer and at the beginning of the new season in 1977, I joined the wardrobe department of the Royal Ballet full time. On Sunday, October 7, Derek Deane and Wayne Eagling of the Royal Ballet were organising an evening charity gala at the London Coliseum in St. Martin's Lane in aid of the City of Westminster Society for Mentally Handicapped Children. Freddie, then at the height of his early career, had been asked by Wayne Eagling if he would be the special guest star at the end of the show. Sir Joseph Lockwood, the chairman of EMI records, Queen's record company, had been the catalyst. Sir Joseph was on the board of directors of the Royal Ballet and had effected Freddie's introduction to Wayne Eagling.

Thus it was that I was first properly introduced to Freddie Mercury in the Royal Ballet's running wardrobe at the Royal Opera House, the department responsible for all costumes that were in use during the performances. Prior to the show, the new costumes would be the responsibility of the Production Wardrobe. My job was to effect the running repairs and the sequences of changes during the performances. Hence, 'running' wardrobe.

Freddie came into our department with Paul Prenter in order that the wardrobe people involved in the gala could see what he would be wearing because his appearance involved a quick change actually on stage. There was no room for error. He had rehearsed with the members of the ballet company with whom he would be performing for some time beforehand at the Royal Ballet school and rehearsal studios at Barons Court but this was the first time he had made an appearance upstairs at the Opera House itself.

Freddie's appearance in the show was not going to be announced until he actually came onto the stage, dressed in his leather biker's cap and jacket to give the first public performance of 'Crazy Little Thing Called Love'. As the song finished, the dancers then masked him from the public and with some assistance from them, he changed into a silver-sequined leotard in which he reappeared before the audience carrying out fairly intricate choreography which included him being man-handled and thrown into the air while singing 'Bohemian Rhapsody'!

This was the first of many times that I was to hear these songs but never again in such a spectacular way because when he performed them live with Queen he was always playing an instrument, either guitar or piano respectively.

Because of my association with the ballet company, I was invited to Legends nightclub for the party afterwards. It was here that I actually spoke to Freddie for the first time, a conversation that lasted no longer than five words. I also got into a longer talk with Paul Prenter who was Freddie's and Queen's personal manager at the time. I must have made some impression.

Paul Prenter was an easygoing Ulsterman, although like many of his compatriots he had a very fierce and quick temper. I well remember a few occasions on which people got on the wrong side of Mr Prenter and came off the worst. However, I only ever personally experienced this wrong side once or twice.

Two weeks later, Paul rang up Michael Brown, the wardrobe master of the Royal Ballet enquiring as to the availability of anyone who could carry out a six-week British tour with Queen and when I offered my services, Paul remembered me and took me on. This was Queen's 'getting back to basics' tour – the Crazy Tour. They wanted to revisit smaller venues, few of which held more than two thousand seats, culminating in their show for relief in war-torn Kampuchea on Boxing Day at the Hammersmith Odeon, as the Labatt's Apollo was then called.

Having made the decision to volunteer and having been accepted, I panicked. I had no idea of even how many musicians were in the band called Queen, never mind what each of them looked like. I knew they had sung 'Seven Seas Of Rye', 'Killer Queen' and 'Bohemian Rhapsody' but that was the extent of my knowledge of their repertoire. I had two weeks before the tour began to find out about my new employers.

On the first day I went to a rehearsal – I was driven there by one of Queen's office staff – Paul Prenter met me and took me into one of the sound stages at Shepperton Film Studios in which Queen was rehearsing. This was one of the few spaces large enough for them to set up their full stage. I was stunned.

Not being an avid Queen fan, I never knew the extremes they went to in putting on their show. The band hadn't arrived yet but just to see the amazing amount of equipment and lights set up on the rehearsal stage was awe-inspiring. The technicians were practising with the 'pizza oven' lights and the effects were staggering. This set-up was so-called because the colors, red, green and orange, brought to mind a Mediterranean flag, I believe, and as it was one massive bank of these colours, it wouldn't have looked out of place in an infra-red bakers' oven. Paul ushered me over to the vast, wheeled wardrobe trunks and told me to sort through them and make sense of them and said he would introduce me to the band when they had all arrived.

You have to realise that in the trunks at this point was an array of Zandra Rhodes originals screwed up carelessly into crumpled balls as nothing had been sorted out since the end of Queen's last tour. There was also an assortment of make-up strewn here, there and everywhere, as well as a special French make-up remover by Rene Guinot, a pink gloop which Freddie used exclusively, cotton wool balls, hairspray, all the things you would expect to find in every gentleman's going-away luggage. There was a special dry shampoo – basically talc-in-a-tube which soaks up grease instead of washing under a shower – for the rock star in a hurry. There was a whole array of boots and shoes, trainers and the special Brian May clogs in various colours. And hairbrushes. Hairbrushes galore!

Someone had thoughtfully opened the trunks before my arrival so most of the mildew smell had evaporated. The trunks had been packed hurriedly at the end of their last show with no thought as to what the state of the unwashed, unlaundered contents would be when next opened. There were also several costumes in both black and white PVC with all sorts of holographic pictures including the Statue of Liberty, The Stars and Stripes and the Empire State Building. These had been designed by an American and Freddie had worn the outfits on the last tour but was rarely, if ever, to wear them again. I think he wore the black jacket once or twice.

I had noticed a large number of people coming and going and bustling about but the only person who actually stood out in all this activity was the figure of – I was soon to learn – Jim Beach, then Queen's business manager, who was walking around wearing a full-length wolf coat, presumably as a protection from the cold. Paul called me over to a small group of people and I was finally introduced to the band who had up until then been indistinguishable amongst the hurly burly. Freddie made me feel immediately at home just by saying, "Well, of course I remember you, dear."

On that first day at Shepperton, Queen soon got down to the real business of the day. In the four or five hours that followed, I was introduced to Queen's music in all its glory. There, for the first time and live, were all those songs that I'd heard over the years and never known who'd sung them. 'You're My Best Friend', 'Somebody To Love', 'We Are The Champions' and many, many more. One thing that remained the same throughout the years I knew Queen was the effort and amount of work that they put into rehearsals. Practice makes perfect, which is what Queen shows were always intended to be.

They started each song and played it until one of them was unhappy with something. Then they would practise and practise until they were all satisfied. They would do this with each of the songs in their set. They might be able to get through five songs in about twenty minutes but then one problem with one song could quite easily take them half-an-hour to correct to their collective satisfaction. At the end of the two-week rehearsal period, they would try to play through the set complete, without stopping, although, even after so much work, this didn't necessarily happen each time.

However, for that, my first day, I merely collected the costumes which needed to be laundered or cleaned and when an available car was going back to London, I was in it with Gerry Stickells, the tour manager. Two days later I went back to the studios laden with clean, ready-to-wear stage clothes and that was the first day each of the band told me what their requirements would be for the coming tour. For John I had to get a pair of black Kickers, size 43, and two white T-shirts with round necks. For Roger, I needed half-a-dozen white wrist sweatbands and assorted black and white socks. Brian's requirements were two T-shirts with a low neckline, one black and one white. He also asked me to look for a western-style shirt in black with white piping which I managed to get.

After having had all his clothes cleaned, Freddie then decided he was going for a new look. I had to buy three pairs of red PVC trousers, a couple of ties in red, one in leather and one in a shiny fabric as well as some thin black ties to act as belts. He also insisted on having skate-boarding knee pads and really lightweight white boots with black stripes, the sort that boxers wear. He'd decided to start the show wearing a leather jacket which he would then take off and perform in a T-shirt until that too came off and he would be left in just his trousers and boots at the end. Unfortunately, I couldn't immediately get hold of the wrestling boots which he specified, although the assorted colours of T-shirts weren't a problem and the braces in white and other colours, I found easily.

After two or three days hunting around the shops of London – Kensington Market and the nearby Slick Willy's were two of them – I was prepared, or so I thought, for the first of the Queen shows which was to be in Cork, Ireland. Unlike the theatre, where all my previous experience had been, I found that Queen did not have a dress rehearsal. In the theatre, during the course of the dress rehearsal, you're able to find the best times and places for changes and I would be able to plan my time during the show. Not knowing the band, I didn't feel I could ask them when the dress rehearsal would be.

I was of course stunned when at the end of the final rehearsal I was told that, "That's it. Next time will be the show!" However, I discovered that there was a general rule of thumb as far as Queen costumes were concerned which was: "If the gig is small, wear black. If it's big, wear white." Having now seen a lot of different shows, this was obviously a general rule with few exceptions.

The tour was to have begun by taking in Cork City Hall and then the Royal Dublin Showground venue at Simmons Court in Ireland. Although, the Cork concert was ultimately cancelled, the one in Dublin went ahead. I think I was dreading this, the first working concert with Queen, having had no trial run. I really hadn't any idea what I should be doing. In the end, everything flowed fairly smoothly.

The routine with which I was to become so familiar ran something like this: I would arrive at the venue with the band for their sound check. While they carried on checking on their various pieces of equipment and the volume in the on-stage monitors, I got started in the dressing room. The band would go back to their hotel after the soundcheck, leaving me to carry on. I had brought with me the list of essentials which were: one powerful hair dryer, one iron, boxes of tissues, cotton wool balls, real sponges, body splash which I seem to remember for some reason was a herbal one by Clairol, dressing gowns, the indispensable electric torches, setting gel for hair.

An hour and a half before the band were due to arrive, I began to sort out what I thought they might want to wear. The crew had put the huge, hanging costume trunks in the band's dressing room and after opening them, I removed an assortment of shirts which could possibly be worn by Brian, Roger and John and quickly gave these an iron so that each Queenie could have a choice from a range of two or three shirts, and I hung these at four points about the dressing room. Although Freddie had been more specific, the T-shirt selection was still in several colours and so I laid all these out for him to choose. Each of them only had one pair of shoes for the shows so the footwear department was easily served.

On a table with a mirror, I laid out the make-up which all of them used in varying amounts, a technique they had developed to suit each one of them over their nine years of performing together. Stage lights bleach colours from just about everything including performers' faces. To accentuate features which would otherwise disappear, you have to highlight them. Freddie especially made use of eye-liner pencil so that the people in the back of the hall could see his eyes. Some people might say that this instinctive use of eye make-up was a throwback to his days in both Zanzibar and India where kohl is used by all women throughout society to accentuate their eyes, the mirror of the soul. The standard list of make-up I always needed was two Max Factor Number 25 pancake, Lancome Maquimat three-and-a-half mascara, Revlon all-weather Ivory number three, Clinique continuous coverage Vital beige . . . Well, call them the Slap Kings of the rock world!

As far as underwear was concerned, the rest of the band took care of their own, although Freddie always required a dry pair to wear after the show and these were my responsibility to provide as part of wardrobe.

I was more often than not in the dressing room when they arrived. The door would open and in they came, generally just to drop their bags before they went off again to the crew catering area to have tea or coffee or just a little snack to keep them going before showtime. Freddie generally remained in the dressing room and had a cup of Earl Grey tea with milk and two sugars or hot lemon and honey depending on how he felt his throat was holding up.

I suppose it was only natural but as soon as the band all returned to the dressing room, they immediately began comparing it to the last. Which feature was better, which one was worse. "There's more seats here than they had in the last one . . ."; "This room's a lot bigger . . ."; "That toilet's disgusting!"

They usually started to get ready about an hour before the show. There were, after all, four of them and so even a five minute burst at the make-up table required twenty clear minutes. Freddie always put on his make-up first, having removed his clothes and applied his eyeliner bare-chested. Each of them had their own robes. Freddie would often, if the room wasn't tropical temperature, wear his in make-up. While the others generally dressed themselves – sorting out shoelaces or ties empirically – Freddie required assistance. Two processes which took time were putting on his boxing boots and lacing them and getting whatever he was wearing on his torso over his head without spoiling the make-up; and back then he would have the hair dryer out making sure that every single hair was exactly in place. Although Paul Prenter, Jim Beach, the band's partners and wives would be allowed access to the dressing room, when the final getting ready began, most of these left to find their seats and to allow the band a short and important time to prepare themselves.

The band would spend the pre-show hour sensibly discussing any failings conceded in the last show or sections which they all or individually thought could have gone better. Post-show discussions of course were the opposite. These were the times for shouting and screaming and acrimonious accusations in the heat of the moment. Pre-show, they might decide on a change in the running order and half-an-hour before the start of the show, the road crew – Ratty, Crystal and Jobby – would come to the dressing room to see if there were to be any such changes. The band would get to talk to the sound people – Trip Khalaf, Jim Devenney – to discuss any last minute requirements like putting the drums up or bringing the vocals down in the monitors. To Trip, the instruction was always, "Make it louder!" I don't know that Queen were happy with the volume of the sound at any of their shows. Always louder, louder, louder . . .

Tour manager Gerry Stickells, who had overall responsibility for the show and would have been in and out of the dressing room, would arrive to lead the band on stage surrounded by their security. Venue security personnel always guarded the door of the empty dressing room which was kept unlocked to cater for the eventuality of Freddie storming off stage and the person with the dressing room key being unavailable.

We would certainly not have been amused.

At the rear of the stage, we were all ushered into the 'dolls' house'. This was a small room made up of scaffolding and thick black fabric material which was positioned always – bar twice – in the same place upstage right at the very back of the stage area. This R and R station was used by every member of the band throughout the show as in it were drinks, anything from hot lemon and honey, through beers to vodka tonics. It was a place for the band to come and sit through Brian's guitar solos and the playing of the 'Bohemian Rhapsody' tape and where I had spare clothes that they could change into if they felt the need. This was also the place, particularly for the first tour I was on, where I would stand with a hairdryer and hairbrush to give Freddie his immaculately coiffed look for the last part of the show after he'd ripped off his sodden T-shirt and any other part of his costume which was uncomfortably soaked in sweat. He would sit down in front of the mirror and I'd give him a blow-dry in two minutes or whatever length of time Brian had chosen for his solo.

There were always five chairs in the dolls' house and always a full-length mirror. I purchased one early on because of the number of times the promoters failed to provide one. The band got really upset at not being able to see themselves as the audience would see them before going on stage. There was always at least one light giving a warm glow and also an electric fan, as whatever the temperature outside, things could get very hot under all those lights on stage.

Going into the dolls' house was where I first noticed the tangible excitement which had developed, hearing the crowd who are almost psychically aware that the band are just about to emerge on stage. The PA system would stop playing the pre-concert tapes and the band's intro tape would start. The crowd roared. This was the point of no return. There *was* no going back.

Jobby would be outside the entrance with Brian's guitar and Brian, Roger and John would then go on stage which was of course smokebound. For some reason, Queen and excess stage smoke seemed to go together. At this point, Freddie's perfect sense of timing came into play. The split second that the tape ends and Brian thrashes out his first chord, Freddie runs on stage and is picked out immediately by the spotlight.

So. Showtime.

This next is the hardest part for me to recount for it is impossible to find sufficiently accurate words to describe the feeling that everyone concerned with the band experienced at this moment when all the work – the lights, sound, all the backstage effort as well as the musicianship – come together. It is indeed the proof of the pudding.

For most of the duration of the show, I would remain on stage. Just in case. Just maybe a seam might rip and I'd have to dash to find another pair of trousers but this never happened once to me. When any of them came off stage for a while – like in the guitar solo – Roger would often change his shirt at the same time Freddie was changing and drying his hair. Brian would change his costume during Roger's drum solo. As soon as these changes had happened, I knew I had to go back to the dressing room to pick up the four different coloured luxury towelling dressing gowns for each of the band to put on at the end of the show. Freddie's was always yellow, although the others had no colour preference and these dressing gowns would be taken home at the end of each tour as new ones were purchased by wardrobe for each Queen outing.

The encores never changed, so stage security always knew when the band were about to leave the stage. As soon as the 'God Save The Queen' tape started, the four of us would take up our positions by the dolls' house ready to throw the dressing gowns around our specific charges. Each of us held torches in one hand and our band member in the other as they came off stage blinded by the lighting rig into what was pitch black.

The dressing room was as close to the stage as was practicable in any of the venues and the only people in the dressing room for at least the first half-hour after the show were the four band members, Paul Prenter and myself. Band security remained outside the door refusing anyone access until permission was given, which was usually by me putting my head round the door and tipping the wink. Paul and I would generally know what to expect of the band's post-show behaviour by the progress of the show itself. Only rarely did matters become so fraught that any of the band members smashed either dressing room mirrors or furniture but I cannot say that it never happened. It was occasionally the only way they could relieve their intense frustration at something not having gone quite right.

While they were 'discussing' their performance, I would be struggling to unlace Freddie's boots as quickly as possible and generally assisting in undressing the band while Paul would be pouring out the champagne and the drinks. If there had been a technical hitch not necessarily within the control of any of the technical crew, Gerry Stickells would come round as soon as possible to explain what had happened. Post mortems were absolutely necessary though not always helpful because the next show would be in a different venue where another, entirely different set of problems would have to be overcome.

Those costumes which could just be hung back in the wardrobe trunk I collected and sorted for delivery to the next venue. Socks and shirts which would have to be laundered I collected and took back to the hotel with me. I had already checked out the hotel facilities to ensure that they could provide the cleaning services in the time I required. I did have enough clothes to keep the band happy should we be scheduled to do three shows back to back where cleaning facilities were unavailable. It was quite a job, although I had been trained well at the Royal Ballet where tights were handwashed after each performance, sometimes having to be dry once again for an evening show.

So. Show over. Back to the hotel.

The hotel where we stayed in Dublin went to great pains to keep Freddie happy. As per usual, the request had been put in for him to have the best suite which on this occasion was on a long-term booking for the celebrated British actor Peter Bowles who was filming a series in the city. He obliged the hotel upon its, presumably, unrefusable request and vacated the suite for the neighbouring one. I believe Mr Bowles was *not* amused.

The other reason that Mr Bowles was not impressed was that we managed to keep him up most of the night with an impromptu party organised by Queen's very Irish everyday manager, Paul Prenter, as Dublin was the nearest he and the band were getting to his home town of Belfast. There was much coming and going and I must admit quite a lot of noise.

The tour returned to the mainland and played the very new NEC in Birmingham, then the Apollo in Manchester and also in Glasgow. It was the first time I'd ever been to Glasgow and I loved the city. I suppose I was prepared for the worst because of the reputation the city had acquired. Remember, it was 1979, still a year or two before it became the European City of Culture. But the feeling of friendliness and warmth in the city was wonderful. On to Newcastle City Hall and then to the famous Empire in Liverpool and the Bristol Hippodrome – where coincidentally I had already worked with the Royal Ballet – before finally getting to Brighton.

A limousine was sent to pick me up at my flat in the Lisson Green Estate for this memorable concert. I didn't know quite what to think as I saw the car pull up. Paul had just told me that a hire car would come to collect me to bring me to a restaurant to meet him and Freddie and take us down to Brighton. The car turned out to be a stretch Mercedes, blue. Back then, it was *the* limousine to have and it drew quite a few surprised glances from neighbours. It took me down to the Meridiana restaurant on the Fulham Road in Chelsea. As I walked in I heard boisterous laughter from one corner and there was Freddie, Paul Prenter and Peter Straker.

Peter had been very close to Freddie since 1975 and for many years to come was one of Freddie's closest friends. That day, his hair had been fashioned by their hairdresser friend Douglas Trout in golden ringlets, as many people will remember. He really did look rather extraordinary. One of the things that has never changed since I have known Peter is his general extrovert joie de vivre which was more than in evidence at the luncheon table. Peter always had the knack of making Freddie laugh when Freddie needed to.

The trip down to Brighton was one long laugh from beginning to end. Between Peter and Paul there was a never-ending stream of banter and even though Freddie had a gig coming up, he appeared very relaxed. It was in Brighton that I acquired my nickname. Following the long theatrical tradition of which I was aware anyway from the opera house, everybody had been given a name by Freddie. If you didn't like it and made it known, that was even more reason for it to stick. It was on the trip back from Brighton that I first heard the name Phoebe. He said that he'd decided that I looked like a Phoebe and it fitted nicely with my surname. I decided not to object. Who knows what I could have been called?

It was on this night of the Crazy Tour in Brighton that Freddie met Tony Bastin. Tony was about five foot eleven with fair hair. Of average build, he had a very winning smile. I have to say that with hindsight, Freddie was not Tony's type at all, although he was to be the first person with whom Freddie had a long-term relationship while I was working for him. They met at one of Brighton's nightspots of which there are many and which constituted the reason for staying down there after the show.

The partying continued back in Freddie's suite at the Grand Hotel on the seafront until the small hours with a group of people rounded up by Paul Prenter. It was hardly anyone's idea of a rock'n'roll party, just a group of about ten people drinking and laughing. It had been an experience for me to see what Freddie went through during the show and how hyped up he became on the exchange of adrenalin with his audience.

As I was to find out, Freddie needed these three or four hours after the show to go out and let himself wind down because while the performance he gave always looked spontaneous and wild, he knew he had to control himself up to a point so that he appeared as fresh at the end of the show as he had been at the beginning. The nights out in the bars and the parties in hotels which were to follow were a necessary part of his life. For me, it was still part of my work. Although I was only free to go to bed after Freddie was in bed, I still had to be up to do mundane organisational things in the morning while he remained asleep, as indeed he had to do in order to be fresh enough to perform again that night.

But at this early stage, I was still working for all four members of the band. The twenty-hour days were still to come and we had as yet not heeded the call of America's wild frontier.

The Crazy Tour ended up with six London gigs, The Lyceum in the Strand, The Rainbow in Finsbury Park, which was where the extra day's booking provided was needed to film the sequence with the dove in the 'Save Me' video and also where the director, David

Mallet, fell backwards off the stage into the orchestra pit, happily not suffering too much damage.

Damage? Heavens above! Inconceivable! It might have even delayed some filming . . .

Then Tiffany's nightclub in Purley. Tiffany's in Purley! I think at this point, the only Tiffany's Freddie knew about was on Fifth Avenue in New York. Due to a slight reduction in size, even from the previous somewhat smaller venues, Queen's lighting rig would not fit. The crew ended by putting up a few lights around the support for the huge gong that Roger was using at this point and, I believe, the mirror ball was also in use. I do remember Freddie had fun on this gig. I think the most difficult thing for him was trying to scale down his own performance for a venue of that size. The little black outfit was worn that night, true to the Queen costume credo.

Then on to the Mayfair in Tottenham, the Odeon, Lewisham and, finally Alexandra Palace in Hornsey, North London, three days before Christmas, where the other bits of live footage used in 'Save Me' were filmed.

And that was it.

Well, not quite. On Boxing Day, December 26, Queen played the Odeon Hammersmith in a benefit concert for Kampuchea which Harvey Goldsmith, the tour's promoter, arranged as an add-on date.

Then that really was it. At the end of the Crazy Tour of England, my six weeks' stint with Queen was up. What was I to do now? Strange, I hadn't thought that far ahead when I'd accepted the work with Queen although I now had a taste of the spice that my life needed. Also, leaving the tour felt quite a wrench, because in those six weeks I had got on with all four of the band very well.

Looking back at this early point in our relationship, I realise that I had learned two essentially important aspects about Freddie. The first was that although he needed the emotional stability to record, it seemed that Freddie needed conflict and confrontation as a vital catalyst to performing. The second revelation was his perfectionism.

Freddie knew in his mind exactly what he wanted and was prepared to throw a tantrum to make sure everything went the way he desired, and this underlying trait of character was to appear throughout my association with him.

Freddie knew the value of the tantrum. To throw one to greatest effect, it had to be done to either the band or business associates.

Freddie realised that if he could make people worried that he was going to walk out on a project, that it probably wouldn't get off the ground. He also knew that the other people involved knew that *he* knew that *he* was indispensable.

He was actually quite modest concerning his knowledge and understanding of many things but people who knew him found that he would never enter into something where he wasn't one hundred per cent sure of the end result. He had this almost uncanny knack of foreseeing events and on many occasions he even went as far as saying, "I told you so". The tantrum was always the signal that the discussion had to stop and it was time for action.

One other marked trait that everybody who knew Freddie observed was his extreme generosity. One of the greatest thrills of his life was to buy a present for someone just to see the look on their face when they opened up the wrapping. He was in a position to buy anything for anyone and it really gave him a great deal of joy. My own first experience of this was my first Christmas present from him. When he had known me for only four weeks, Santa turned up with what was to become, for me, a familiarly wrapped parcel, the scarlet leather trademark box containing, on this occasion, a beautiful desk clock from the Bond Street jeweller, Cartier.

Christmas time in the Mercury house was for all of Freddie's friends who were told that as they had nowhere else to go then they were to come over, make themselves at home and be fed and boozed over the festive season, although I'll save the description of a typical Mercury Christmas for a later part of the story.

It had been quite reasonably explained to me that my first stint with Queen would have a beginning and an end. However, it was also made clear that when future work came up, I would be asked to do it if I was free and also if the band wanted me.

Meanwhile, money still had to be found to pay my bills. I 'signed on' at the Job Centre (Social Security Office) and in those days we had the luxury of earnings-related unemployment benefit which meant you had the basic allowance plus a percentage of what you had earned in your last main job. However, I've never been one to sit around doing nothing even on such comparatively generous terms. And what would I have been waiting for? I had no idea and no guarantee of when Queen would next require my services. If ever.

Thus, a friend of mine who had started work for the GPO telephone service recommended that I also apply. I therefore applied for a job and had an interview and was finally accepted as a telephone operator.

"Operator services. Can I help you?"

As I mentioned earlier, on the night I first saw Freddie at the Coliseum, it was at the party afterwards that I first really spoke to Paul Prenter. He had the ability to get on with anybody, more often than not, total strangers. He was Queen's personal manager, coordinating the day-to-day activities of the band – arranging interviews, transport, being in attendance as the band went about their business. But Paul had a closer affinity to Freddie than the others because they were both gay. I was soon to find out that although they were never lovers, they spent most nights together out in the clubs and the bars. I'd never been a club person as my working hours, often fourteen a day, had precluded this. I had never realised how many bars and clubs there were in the world!

Paul was always the centre of attention in any room, being naturally vivacious and the eternal Clown Prince. I suppose that was part of his job to keep Freddie and his guests entertained and those guests were people like Sarah Harrison from Browns, Peter Straker, Kenny Everett, Annie Challis and her travelling dog and Trevor Clarke.

Paul Prenter remained in touch throughout the time I was answering telephones, be that contact only a call from Paul maybe once or twice a week. I started with the GPO on Monday, May 5, and continued with the telephone operating for six weeks before I received *that* call from Paul, the one I'd been waiting for: "Peter? Would you be able to go on the American tour?"

Would I? No contest.

I had been to America before, twice with the Royal Ballet, but I knew even from my comparatively short experience with the band that this tour would be something else. I jumped at the chance, said, "Yes!"

Only then did I think about handing in my notice to the GPO. I left on Saturday, June 14.

I think for Freddie the United States was his Mount Everest. It was something that he had to climb to the peak of and conquer. By the time I started in late 1979, early 1980, he had just about completed that task. On the British Crazy Tour I had seen Freddie playing to two and three thousand people at a time. I don't think I was really prepared to see 15,000 screaming and cheering fans in the arena venues Queen were playing in America. Only a handful of British bands – the Stones, The Who and Led Zeppelin among them – could play that size of venue in those days with no support act.

Freddie loved the warmth and outgoing personality traits that seemed to be the trademark of most Americans. He felt so much less on show when he was in public in America because in America there are so many stars on the streets of Los Angeles and New York that one more doesn't make that much difference. In those days, London wasn't the cosmopolitan city it has now become. Pubs closed at eleven and clubs at two whereas in America, with a little advance planning, a person could keep themselves entertained twenty-four hours a day and Freddie was always one for entertainment.

America in those days lived up to the old adage, "Everything there is bigger and better" and Freddie genuinely believed that. You only had to look around at the cars, at the buildings, the cities and the vastness of the country itself when compared to Great Britain. He liked the music which was coming out of America at that time. It was the disco–diva variety which he loved and which was so influential in the recording of Queen's *Hot Space* album. He did, after all, spend a great deal of time in discos and bars . . . merely researching the music, of course.

On Sunday, June 22, 1980, we arrived in Los Angeles. The American tour itinerary had begun . . .

June 22–26: Los Angeles

Freddie, Paul Prenter and I were staying at L'Ermitage on Burton Way, just south of Santa Monica Boulevard in Beverly Hills. It was a luxury hotel apartment building with the ubiquitous swimming pool, this time situated on the roof. Freddie had his own duplex suite while I was in a smaller one on a lower floor.

We'd flown first-class from London. The band party in those days always flew first-class while the crew went economy and usually on a different plane – on this occasion directly to Vancouver – not unlike the Royal Family! It had been arranged that the band would all meet up in Los Angeles before flying to Canada, as they were much more familiar with Los Angeles and the nightlife suited them better. It was the first time I'd seen anything of Los Angeles other than the area around the USC campus which is the location of the Shrine

Auditorium where the Royal Ballet had performed. LA is such a huge sprawling metropolis that I had no idea even where Hollywood was, although I obviously knew it existed.

The only place Freddie was ever a classic tourist was Japan. Things Japanese were an all-consuming passion for him, whereas wherever else he stayed in the world was merely a bed for the night. Hence I didn't really get to see any more of LA during that visit. Due to Freddie's nocturnal habits, he tended to get up very late but I still had to be up and about during normal shopping hours to gather in anything he or the others in the band had specifically requested the night before, anything from a pair of jeans which he'd seen someone wearing or to stock his fridge with a drink someone had introduced him to. I have to emphasise once again, that at this point I was still working for Queen as a whole rather than specifically for Freddie. So there were other calls on my time.

Because Freddie had been to LA before, he knew of specific items which were more easily available there and by the time we arrived he had made a list of purchases I was to make. The boots, of the boxing variety, he used to wear on stage and white Levi jeans were just two examples. The jeans available in London tended only to be cream.

Howard Rose was the tour's North American promoter and agent who worked out of Los Angeles. Apart from management, all bands have arrangements with independent agents and promoters such as Howard who negotiate times, dates and schedules with the owners of the individual concert venues. The requirements of such a huge institution like Queen were vast. It wasn't merely a question of the four people standing on stage, it was a logistical problem involving upwards of a hundred personnel: the Queen crew plus the crew hired specifically for the day, the stage builders, the lighting riggers, the electricians. The band's requirements were set out in what was known as a rider, a set of conditions attached to the contract between them and the venue's promoter. Queen's rider included the following: a dressing room with sufficient comfortable seats; a full-length mirror; and at least twenty hand towels.

The food requirements were that before the show a selection of cold meats and salads were to be available and for after the show, a quantity of hot food was to be provided, which generally consisted of savoury finger buffet food to be kept hot by small paraffin heaters beneath the metal serving dishes.

33

The drinks section of the rider included four bottles of champagne, two bottles of vodka, a bottle of Jack Daniels and a couple of other types of spirits, two dozen beers and an assortment of soft drinks, including tonic water and mixer drinks, bottled mineral water and fruit juices – and this list was just for the use of the band.

So, fully victualled, crewed and equipped, the tour was due to kick off in Canada.

June 27–30: Vancouver, The PNE Coliseum

The band rehearsed on 27th, 28th and 29th and did the show on the 30th. Suffice to say that a great deal of very hard work goes into making any successful tour and it was no different with Queen. Work by the crew before and after a show and obviously by the band during the show. As you will see from the following itinerary, there were a lot of back-to-back shows. If you take into account the amount of travelling involved between venues, more often than not journeys which began immediately after a show, the band walking off stage into a limousine and on to the airport, only to be able to change out of their stage clothes on the plane, you can understand how tired everybody was by the time they got to bed in a new hotel, often in a different state. This might also explain why Freddie had no tourist tendencies. There was just no time.

I'm not going to bore you with a fully detailed breakdown of everything that happened over the next five months on this massive tour but there will be points in the itinerary when I'll enlarge on anything which I think will open up further insights into how Freddie worked as a man and also how his mind worked. There are many books detailing the Queen tours. I am not going to attempt to match them although at the end of this personal memoir of this great world tour, I'll fill you in on some of the more pertinent highlights of other tours in so far as they relate to Freddie.

July 1: Seattle, Washington. Show day
    2: Portland, Oregon. Show day
    3–4: Los Angeles, California. Days Off

Whenever you read Day Off, it usually meant that we were for once able to spend the night in the same city in which the band had just played instead of taking the money and running, as Freddie loved to say.

July 5: San Diego, California. Show day
   6: Phoenix, Arizona. Show Day
   7–13: Los Angeles. Two Show Days. The Forum

Freddie hated performing in the big cities of any country because the reception which the crowd accorded Queen was usually so much more blasé and muted than in smaller cities. Every band and entertainer in the world goes to the major cities, thus contributing to a glut of big shows which means audiences are spoiled for choice. Also, it is in cities like LA, New York and London where a band feels they are under even more intense pressure than usual to do a great show because they will also be entertaining their peers, all of whom will have come along basically to check out the competition. As I've already emphasised, one of the maxims Freddie lived by was, "You're only as good as your last performance."

He felt he only had to bungle a high note and rumours started spreading that he was losing his voice and not performing like he used to. Although no one was ever allowed back stage before a show, it was common knowledge who would be out front that night because a star's staff would have booked tickets either, in our case, via GLS Productions (Gerry Stickells, our Tour Manager's company) or through the aegis of the local promoter. Saying this, in all the time I knew Freddie, he always relished a challenge and it was a very rare occasion that he didn't come out on top.

July 14–15: Oakland, California. Two Show Days
   16–20: Los Angeles. Days Off
   21–August 4: Houston, Texas

At this point there was a two-week break in the tour and I went off to visit friends in Houston before flying back to LA when the tour resumed.

Basically the band's set – the sequence of songs to be performed that night – was the same in successive shows. Where the tour played more than one date in a city, then the set would change slightly. If anything, Freddie would give a better show out of the big cities because he was more relaxed. His dialogue with the audience, counting the audience as one party and he as the other, was always spontaneous at every show. Freddie followed no script, unlike some performers such as Michael Jackson or Barbra Streisand. Queen shows were always different. Freddie loved singing 'Love Of My Life' because of the feeling he got when the audience joined in. And seeing the flames from all the waving lighters in the audience during the ballads gave him a huge buzz.

August 5: Memphis, Tennessee. Show Day
*   6: Baton Rouge, Louisiana. Show Day*
*   7: New Orleans, Louisiana. Day Off*

Freddie loved New Orleans. It wasn't only because you could drink twenty-four hours a day, it was a lot to do with the music and overall feeling he got from the city. He always stayed in the same hotel, the Royal Orleans in the middle of the old French quarter, and was thus surrounded by New Orleans jazz all day long. It's a city that truly never sleeps and we loved exploring all-night bars. One thing I learned almost immediately from Paul Prenter was that an essential component of Freddie's touring requisites was the *Spartactus Guide* to places of gay interest. This international publication would list all the bars in all the cities in all the countries in the world. There is a separate guide for the United States and Freddie always set time aside for this essential reading. If truth be known, I think these were the only two books he ever read from cover to cover in all the time I knew him.

August 8: Oklahoma City, Oklahoma. Show Day
*   9: Dallas, Texas. Show Day*
*   10–11: Houston, Texas. Show Days*
*   12: Atlanta, Georgia.*

I really thought I'd lost my job in Atlanta, Georgia. We were there two nights, the day before the show and show day itself. On the first night, as usual, Freddie, Paul and I went with our car and driver out to the bars. Paul got lucky early on in the evening and Freddie waved him and his date off for the evening. For the first time I was left with Freddie as alone on the streets as any two people can be with a limo and a driver in tow! I was quite aware of the responsibility with which I had been implicitly entrusted.

Up until this point, Paul had never gone home leaving Freddie behind. Paul had given me complete instructions of where else there was to go and the telephone number of the hotel if it was absolutely necessary to get in touch with him. Freddie decided that we were going to stay in the bar where Paul had left us and then started drinking with a vengeance. He was the boss so I didn't feel I could tell him to slow down. At about four o'clock in the morning after many spearmint schnapps, Freddie decided it was time to go home. I think it was more in gestures than in words that he communicated, because he couldn't string more than two words together at that point. We got back to the hotel and as we were going up in the lift to Freddie's suite, he almost collapsed in my arms.

I managed to get him into his room and mostly undressed and onto his bed. And this is where the real problem started. He was hallucinating that the room was spinning around him and wanted to be sick. He tried to find the edge of the bed but here was another problem . . . The bed was round so he was trying to find a straight edge over which he could safely vomit but he was going round and round the bed desperately seeking the straight side and leaving little pools of barff all round the circumference.

I couldn't believe what was happening and thought to myself, 'Well, this is it! The first time I've been left to look after Freddie and he ends up like this!' I called Paul to the bedroom and he just laughed.

"Don't worry about him," he said, "he'll sleep it off."

I cleaned up as much as I could and left Freddie to sleep as he was soundly out of it by this time.

Early the next afternoon, I was called to Freddie's suite and I really did think that my end was nigh but as I walked into the room, breakfast had been laid out and instead of my cards, I was given orange juice and toast and we spent breakfast laughing about the previous evening.

We were, thankfully, amused.

August 13: Charlotte, North Carolina
       14: Greensboro, North Carolina

I'm not sure whether it was in Charlotte or Greensboro but it was in one of those cities where we had our first taste of a Howard Johnson.

Howard Johnson was the man who started the chain of motels which now links most of America. This really was the best hotel the city could provide. The band and party were lucky enough to be on the top floor which required a special key in the elevator which separated us from the ordinary business man or woman of the town. One of the first things Freddie did on arriving at a hotel was to order pots of tea. I firmly believe that the hotel really did try to accommodate his wishes but after about half-an-hour, all he had in his room were four tea bags, four waxed paper beakers and an open jug of luke-warm water.

We were definitely not amused.

August 15: Day Off
16: Charleston, South Carolina

It was at one of the gigs around this time that Tony Bastin arrived from England to spend time with Freddie. Whenever Freddie was away from London, every now and then he had an urge to 'call the cats'. He'd get to a hotel, we'd dial through to Stafford Terrace and he really would talk to his cats. Mary would hold Tom and Jerry in turn up to the receiver to listen to Freddie talking. This continued throughout the years with all the succeeding feline occupants of his houses. He would also talk to Tony quite a lot and so therefore although Tony's coming was no surprise to anyone, the news that he was to be almost immediately sent home came as a complete surprise to him.

For some time, Freddie had been aware that Tony had been using him. It had been brought to Freddie's notice by one of those ubiquitous well-wishers that Tony Bastin had been seen out and about with a slim young blond, many years younger than Freddie. Although Tony had been showered with expensive presents, including an amazing camera complete with case and special lenses, he had not really appreciated anything; rather, he had taken all Freddie's generosity for granted. Freddie planned his revenge by ringing Tony up and asking him to fly out to America and meet him. Tony was told that his flight would be paid for and he would be picked up at the airport. Freddie's plan was to meet Tony at the hotel, inform him that the relationship was over and put him on the next plane home, asking Tony to remove his clothes and personal belongings from Stafford Terrace before he, Freddie, got back. The cat called Oscar whom Tony had brought with him into the relationship was, however, the one part of Tony with which Freddie characteristically could not bear to part. Tony was out, Oscar was to stay.

Freddie always accepted that part of being Freddie Mercury was that there would be people around to exploit him. Provided he knew it was going on, he accepted it because he knew he could always turn round and say, "No!" or, "Enough!" What hurt him most was when he was being used behind his back, betrayed and yet he didn't know about it until after the fact. It hurt a lot because the only people who could be so exploitative were those whom he really trusted and who, in their turn, eventually abused that trust.

This was one reason why Freddie always found it so difficult to make new friends. Being thus in Freddie's position, he rather lost friends over his lifetime. And to be seen to have had comparatively fewer very close friends at the end of his life, it explains why particularly in his last year, the press so often stated he was alone and unloved. The truth was, of course, the opposite. Despite the losses, Freddie always had a close-knit group of friends with him until the end. Of these, there were some who were kept at arm's length because, in truth, he did not want to see them having to endure the pain and suffering which he was going through in the last year or eighteen months of his life.

And so another one bit the dust in Carolina. Bye-bye Tony Bastin.

August 17: Indianapolis, Indiana
  18–19th (We stayed in New York)

It was during this stay in New York that Freddie met up with his own personal Viking. Thor Arnold is blond and big and beautiful and we met him in one of our usual haunts, whether The Spike or The Eagle or The Anvil or wherever is immaterial. Thor is a genuine, all-American boy. He lived, then, in Manhattan, near Greenwich Village and spent his day nursing the sick of New York for that was and is still his profession, though now he pursues it in San Diego.

Freddie and Thor had a great night, enjoying each other, but the following day, Freddie accepted it as something that had been and didn't even think to follow the night up with any further dates. Life on the road is like that and try as you might, nobody could possibly keep in touch with all the people you meet and with whom you might wish to explore a friendship further.

August 20: Hartford, Connecticut
    21: Day off in New York
    22: Philadelphia, Pennsylvania

Surprise! As well as an outbreak of Legionnaires' Disease, Freddie and I were lucky enough to discover an outbreak of friendship. Early in the afternoon of the 22nd in Philadelphia, there was a knock on the door of Freddie's hotel suite. I went and opened the door and couldn't believe my eyes when I saw Thor Arnold standing there.

He came in and told Freddie that he wasn't going to let things go just like that. Freddie was stunned because it must have been one of the first times that not only had someone taken it upon themselves to arrive at one of his shows under their own steam but that Thor had also done some research and had discovered where Freddie was staying. The surprise element as much as anything else really won Freddie over. Thor stayed for the show but then had to go straight back to New York.

Thus started what was to be one of the most enduring friendships I have known Freddie to have enjoyed and one which lasted until the end of his life. Thor introduced Freddie to three other friends of his in Manhattan, Lee Nolan, Joe Scardilli and John Murphy and more often than not it was always a crowd of six of us who went out whenever we were in New York. Freddie affectionately used to call the four Manhattan men, 'my New York daughters'.

It was 'The New York Daughters' who were with him in a suite at the Berkshire Place Hotel in 1981 when Freddie's monarchist tendencies surfaced on the occasion of the wedding of Diana Spencer to Charles, Prince of Wales. He insisted everyone stay up, got room service to provide us with a sumptuous breakfast so that we could toast the bride and groom as they walked out of St Paul's. I wouldn't go so far as to say he had tears in his eyes – other than those of laughter due to a multitude of comments being passed about anything from 'the' dress to how dreadful other people's outfits were. I remember it was generally agreed by everyone that the reason why all the royal family disappeared into the vestry was so that they could 'do' lines of cocaine in private. After all, they all came out smiling and chatting to each other in a very animated fashion. More cause for falling on the floor, laughing. I don't know what Charles and Diana's wedding reception was like, if it was half as good as our celebration of their marriage, they'd have been more than happy.

August 23: Baltimore, Maryland
24: Pittsburgh, Pennsylvania
25: Day Off
26: Providence, Rhode Island
27: Portland, Maine

All the above gigs were played from our New York base at the Waldorf Astoria Towers.

August 28: Day Off (Travel Day)
29: Montreal, Quebec
30: Toronto
31–September 9 (Probably spent in New York)

Since Tony Bastin's departure, there had been no permanent man in Freddie's life and as Freddie had new friends to play with he decided to stay in New York. Whereas other married rock men who may have been fathers too might have wanted to return to London and their families for a while, Freddie while on tour was on tour and had little contact with London except the occasional cat-call. There was nothing at that point that tied him to going back to England.

September 10: Milwaukee, Wisconsin
11: Day Off (Travel)
12: Kansas City, Kansas
13: Omaha, Nebraska
14: Minneapolis, Minnesota
15: Day Off (Travel)
16: Ames, Iowa
17: St. Louis, Missouri
18: Day Off (Travel)
19: Chicago, Illinois
20: Detroit, Michigan
21: Cleveland, Ohio

In Cleveland, Freddie was put in the same suite that Bette Midler had occupied fairly recently on her tour of America and where she had uttered the immortal line recorded on her famous live album of the time: "Hello Cleveland!"

The suite itself was done out in shades between pastel and lime green and anywhere that had a flat surface had lace on it. Even the piano had been painted to match. This was tacky with a capital T.

But this time, it was the kind of tacky which raised a smile.

We were *very* amused.

September 22: Day Off (Travel)
23: Newhaven, Connecticut
24: Syracuse, New York
25: Day Off (Travel)
26: Boston, Massachusetts
27: Day Off (Travel)
28–30: New York City, Madison Square Garden.

I don't know whether my memory deceives me or not but I think it was at this set of Madison Square Garden gigs that the backstage entertainment which was always laid on both for the band and their guests was a troupe of female mudwrestlers who performed in what is commonly known in rock'n'roll as the ligging area. Or maybe it was the following visit . . . One ligging area is much like another. The same faces are seen in them all.

It was for big shows such as Madison Square that the band often flew their families out. I always had fun standing at the back of the stage with Chrissie May and Dominique Taylor, singing our hearts out during the choruses to all the songs. Freddie would laugh uproariously when Dominique told him why we all had sore throats and hoarse voices. Freddie was very, very fond of Dominique and their close friendship lasted even after Roger began living with Debbie. Freddie never involved himself in the domestic affairs of the other band members and never judged them. He knew his own personal life couldn't bear too close scrutiny in terms of 'family values' and was therefore never going to throw a stone at someone else's glass house.

October 1: Flew Back To London

And after all this, isn't it amazing that Queen didn't really make a vast amount of money from their tour? Touring, it must be remembered up until the stadium era, was always just an elaborate advertising campaign. Many bands in those days spent their lives in the dark whether it was in the recording studio or out gigging or quite often when talking to their financial advisers – as has been oft brought later into the light.

The whole point of the exercise was to use the shows as giant promotions to sell records; usually in a show any band will perform all the old hits the crowd wants to hear with a liberal sprinkling of tracks from their latest album. Supporting (or opening) acts, of course, buy-in to a tour. They or their record companies pay for their protégés to open the show.

It was Freddie and Queen who were one of the first acts to depart from this philosophy. For example, when Freddie recorded both *Mr. Bad Guy* and *Barcelona*, he never toured as a solo artist to promote either of these albums and following the release of *The Miracle*, Queen never toured either. This didn't prevent the albums going gold and silver all around the world thus indicating, in my view, that it is the quality of the music that eventually sells an album.

The European leg of this, *The Game*, tour started on Monday, November 17, rehearsing in Zurich.

November 23: Zurich, Hallenstadion.

Queen were supported on this part of the tour by the British band Straight Eight. Their manager was a woman who reminded me very much of Francesca von Thyssen although Francesca didn't enter Freddie's life until very much later. The choice of support act had been between Straight Eight and an unknown Birmingham band called Duran Duran also on EMI. Whether Straight Eight was chosen because they wouldn't compete with Queen so much or because they were the better band, I really couldn't comment. History seems to have made the choice.

November 24: Day Off
    25: Paris
    26: Cologne
    27: Leiden, Groenoordhallen.

We didn't stay in Leiden after the show as we had flown from Cologne to Amsterdam on the 27th and we'd already checked in to a hotel there, presumably due to the better quality of the nightlife. We drove to Leiden from Amsterdam and returned after the gig.

November 28: Day Off
    29: Essen
    30: Berlin

To disprove another myth, Freddie certainly never forced anyone to try drugs. I'd been working for Queen for just over a year at this point when I first introduced myself to cocaine in Freddie's corner suite on one of the upper floors of the Hotel Kempinski in Berlin. I think my reaction to it was the same as everyone's on their first try, "What's it supposed to do?" little realising that I was probably talking nineteen to the dozen at the time. But no stars exploded, there was no sudden unaccountable rush of euphoria, just another night on the town. I only tried it once, thinking to myself that it was a waste of someone else's money and saw no need to continue the experiment.

The first rule of travelling abroad is never to cross borders with drugs. As a rule of thumb, if you have to have drugs – which is entirely a personal choice – buy them in the country you're in. Never buy too much because if you do, you have to flush the stuff away or give it away before entering the next country.

The following year, when Queen performed in Berlin, the gig was an outdoor venue in the forest and it was infested with mosquitoes. The dressing room was in an old military bunker and even in its depths there was no protection. I remember having to buy lots of mosquito repellent not only for the band but for the crew as well. I stood at the door of the bunker as the band were on their way to the stage, spraying them all over at the same time as wishing them well.

December 1: Bremen
    2–4: Days Off (Probably back in London)
    5–6: Birmingham, NEC.
    7: Day Off
    8–10: London, Wembley Arena.

The 8th was the day John Lennon was killed at eleven o'clock at night. During the following day, at the soundcheck, it was decided that Queen would perform Lennon's 'Imagine' as a tribute.

44

December 11: Day Off
         12–13: Brussels

During the day, Freddie went shopping because art nouveau and art deco furniture and furnishings were available in very expensive antique shops. He bought a chandelier and a cabinet both reputedly by Majorelle, the latter which he kept and the former he later gave to Jim Hutton.

December 14: Frankfurt
         15–17: Days Off
         18: Munich

Little did Freddie know at this point, how much the city of Munich would figure in his future. He played one show only and left the following day.

December 19: Flew back to London for Christmas.

On returning to England, instead of being laid off as had happened after the Crazy Tour of England, I was asked if I wanted to remain on half salary and to come into the fan club in Queen's premises just off Baker Street in Sussex Place. Barbara Szabo was the band's book-keeper. Although British, she had married a middle-European, hence the surname. Paul Prenter also worked from these rather cramped premises which, of course, included the fan club, which was being run by Amanda and Tony between the stewardship of Pat and Sue Johnson and later Theresa and Fiona Kennedy. At first I helped out packaging fan club merchandise and sending it off: T-shirts, scarves, badges and the like.

In February, the band were due to continue *The Game* Tour and as I had been asked to go with them, it was deemed wise for me to stay on salary. I certainly had no wish whatsoever to return to 'operator services'.

First stop on the next tour was to be Japan and then on to South America where Queen were scheduled to appear in Argentina, Brazil and Venezuela. On the 8th February we flew into Japan for the tour and also for the band to be guests of honour at the Japanese Premiere of *Flash Gordon*. The arrival at the cinema was the usual five car motorcade, the fifth car holding the translation staff. We were met by assorted VIPs but, to Freddie's relief, the friendly and familiar face of Misa Watanabe was amongst them. We were escorted to our seats in the circle and for once Freddie had to undergo the ordeal of sitting all the way through a film without fidgeting. It must have been torture for him.

February 12, 13, 16, 17, 18: Budokan Hall, Tokyo

Gary Numan was at the first three shows and after one of them, we all went out to dinner to one of Tokyo's more exclusive restaurants where Gary proceeded to send one of his minions out to bring in some fast food from MacDonald's for him. Freddie didn't know what to say but I, on the other hand, can quite safely say that we were most decidedly not amused!

At the end of the tour, we were due to leave Narita Airport on February 20 for New York to then fly on to Buenos Aires. There were three of us, Freddie, Paul Prenter and I who boarded the plane for New York. I noticed that the seat configuration in first-class was different to normal but decided to say nothing about it. The three of us took our seats and Freddie finally voiced the puzzlement I could see on his face.

"What sort of plane is this?" he asked.

I had a rough idea but checked the safety instruction card and found that we were on a DC10.

"DC death more like!" was his reply. It was at a time when there had been two accidents in quick succession involving DC10s.

With that, Freddie picked up his belongings and informed the cabin personnel that he would not be flying with them that day. With us in tow, he swept off the aircraft and back into the terminal. The flight was delayed for about an hour while our suitcases were located and retrieved. These were then presented to us back in the lounge. We discovered that the next Boeing 747 was a Pan Am flight fourteen hours later. Due to this, the three of us had to have our cancelled visas voided in order that we should legally remain in the airport. To show the depth of feeling Freddie had for the DC10, he was even prepared to travel tourist class on the later 747 as first and business class were full.

During our sojourn we used the departure lounge as a base for a fourteen hour shopping expedition on which he bought, amongst other things, a beautiful pearl necklace for his mother.

Indeed, we had to travel in economy along with all the crew who were booked on that flight. They couldn't believe their eyes seeing Freddie slumming it with them! We first flew to New York where we changed planes, returning to first-class after a brief stopover and thence, flew south to Buenos Aires in Argentina. Queen's visit was the first of a major international rock band to the countries of South America, playing in gigantic stadia. To meet the band, there was a government official and the band party were ushered through, our passports having been taken from us to ease the passage and were later returned at the hotel. I however had to hang around at the airport to supervise the collection of the luggage. Freddie enjoyed the privileges that he and the band received from government reception parties although he was not fond of meeting the officials in person.

Freddie would sit, accompanied by John Deacon, with a cigarette in his hand, playing with it to disguise his nervousness and to give his expressive hands something to do and allow the less reticent Brian and Roger to do all the chatting, making only occasional interjections. He knew he was expected to involve himself in the talking but did so as little as possible although he always knew that it was important for him to be seen to say something.

Buenos Aires was hot and humid being close to the river. The Sheraton Hotel was right in the middle of the city but it was all very green and reminded us of Paris, lots of grand avenues and very expensive shops. The city of Evita. Freddie had been joined at this time by Peter Morgan, his current beau, one-time Mister UK with whom Freddie had had a tempestuous relationship for some months. Known also as Morgan Winner, Peter had achieved a certain notoriety because of a homo-erotic video he had made – one of the earliest.

The first gig was within the first couple of days of our arrival in the Velez Sarsfield Stadium on February 28. Freddie was very apprehensive because of the size of the venue. Also, the rumours abounded that the crowd would get out of control because finally their dream had been realised – a Northern Hemisphere mega-band was playing in South America.

Hyde Park in 1976 was the largest audience to which the band had played previously and Freddie knew that he had to forge an entirely new performance to embrace the vastness of the next five outdoor dates which were scheduled over the next nine days, five dates which furnished a total audience of four hundred and seventy-nine thousand people.

Freddie also knew that it was imperative for him to pace himself in these performances. But what sort of performance? And what pace? It was completely unknown territory for Queen. The world's press were gathered and although Freddie hated this particular interface, he knew he also had to perform for the cameras again, albeit stills.

The first gig went superbly. Freddie was elated with his perform-ance and was awestruck by the reaction of the fans, the way the huge audience took over the singing of 'Love Of My Life' took his breath away! He wasn't given a chance to 'come down' after the show before his next little adventure began, the journey from the stadium back to the hotel. Such was the apprehension of both the city's authorities and the local police that the only way they considered the band leaving the stadium was in the back of a police van. The four members of the band, Jim Beach, Paul Prenter and some form of security presence were immediately bundled into the back of the van which was then escorted by five police cars and perhaps twenty police motorcycle outriders. The rest of the party followed in cars. The idea was to get the band party out of the immediate vicinity of the madding crowd, a route which took them out onto a nearby motorway. With sirens screaming and the procession hurtling along at eighty miles an hour, we went a circuitous route along the motorway. When the escort was satisfied that no one had followed, the convoy came to a halt and the band got into their separate cars, each having their own limousine. We then made our way back to the hotel.

Freddie accepted that for once he had to rest because he knew he had to pull another cat out of the bag the next day. It took him a while to get over the excitement but it took the next day's audience even longer to get over their excitement at seeing both Freddie and Queen and Argentina's brilliant young football star, Diego Maradona on the same stage. Freddie, not being renowned for his sporting knowledge, knew he had to exchange shirts with this person as per time-honoured football ritual although Freddie did not actually realise who or what Maradona was. He was also quite surprised that footballers came in such small packages.

Mar del Plata. Silver Sea. This is the main resort city of Argentina. I can't remember the name of the hotel but I remember Freddie likening it to a ship; the front of the hotel was like the bridge with huge extensions on the sides. It looked as though it was burgeoning out to sea. Freddie's suite had a very good view of the promenade which for better or worse lead to the ending of his stormy relationship with Peter Morgan.

Freddie knew that at no time in South America would he be able to go on one of his fabled shopping sprees because of the security risk so he had resigned himself to staying in the hotel. After asking Peter to stay and keep him company, Peter replied that he would be going out for a short walk for a few minutes. Having nothing else to do, Freddie was viewing the scene in front of the hotel from his balcony when he saw Peter walking along the croisette next to the beach with a young man whom Freddie didn't know.

From their body language, Freddie could see that Peter's companion was not a complete stranger. When Peter eventually returned, what finally finished it for Freddie was Peter's denying that he had been walking along the beach at all.

We were assuredly NOT amused.

And so . . . Another one bites the dust.

Is it a coincidence that once again at a time of emotional intensity vis-à-vis his creative work, that Freddie also played through the collapse of an emotional relationship with a lover? Were Freddie's creative achievements highlighted or enabled by emotional upset? Over the period of years I knew him, there were many intense emotional moments. It was almost as though Freddie needed these surges of passion to start his creative juices flowing. There were many times that either because of the high-pressure of work he finished relationships or conversely engineered dramatic rows when he needed the extra boost to his energies whether that was touring or writing.

Thus, the conflict engendered seemed to enhance both his abilities and his work. Sometimes it seemed he needed to have a self-administered injection of emotional pain. A fix, almost. Seeing Peter Morgan walking along with another man caused him sufficient anger to carry him through the super-human requirements which the next few days' schedule necessitated. I don't think it helped that Morgan's companion was far younger and prettier than Freddie. In London it was well-known that Morgan was seeing the dancer Philip Broomhead who was also a friend of Freddie's. Complicated stuff. It seemed to be a curse which dogged him, that of his lovers seeming to two-time him with younger and prettier boys. It had been the same with Tony Bastin who, I had discovered after the fact, had been seeing someone I knew, younger and prettier. Although Freddie might have allowed himself to be unfaithful, others were not allowed that privilege.

Whatever. Peter Morgan was on the next flight back to London and thence to resume his job as a bouncer at the Heaven nightclub. I didn't feel too sorry for him. Of all Freddie's lovers in my experience, Peter had had the most lavished upon him in terms of travel. The previous Christmas, because of constant arguments with Freddie, he had been flown in and out of New York on Concorde at least three times. If only he could have been a little more kind. But, having said that, he finally misbehaved at a very convenient time to enable Freddie to erupt creatively on those South American stages.

The way Freddie functioned follows the long trail of genius born from pain. Anger is the furnace which forges genius but it is also one of the fuels which drives the whole process of creativity forward. A prime example being that of Beethoven, who while having written so much amazing music being able to hear, composed some of his best work after going deaf. I'm sure he wasn't pleased. And of course there were the last songs that Freddie wrote . . .

The next city on the Gluttons tour was Rosario, still in Argentina. Not too much to say about Rosario out of the ordinary except that the gig was as extraordinary an event as Buenos Aires had been. Not as large an audience, a mere thirty-five thousand!

We returned for one further show in Buenos Aires before flying down to Rio where Freddie had a much-welcomed break. We were in Rio for eleven days where we stayed at the Sheraton, outside Rio itself to keep a low profile as a gig had been cancelled. The band were not performing due to restrictive legislation concerning the Maracana Stadium, considered football's holiest shrine. So, Freddie didn't do much his first time in Rio, in fact very little at all. It sounds strange now, writing this, that there we were in one of the most exciting cities in the world and yet 'nothing happened'.

In any event, Freddie had to rest up before performing in front of two of the largest crowds ever, at the Morumbi Stadium in Sao Paolo. The audiences on the twentieth and twenty-first of March totalled more than two hundred and fifty thousand. As ever, Freddie always responded to the audience and what an audience! It took hours following the shows for Freddie to come down. But the first leg was over and it had been a triumph.

The second leg was scheduled for later in the year. We returned after the first recordings for *Hot Space* had been completed. This included the track 'Under Pressure' which began life during a twenty-four hour session in Montreux, Switzerland which was the only day David Bowie was available. Then Freddie worked more on it and took the results to New York where he and Bowie completed it in a further session.

On September 15, rehearsals took place in New Orleans for the second leg of the Gluttons For Punishment tour but after arriving in Venezuela on September 21 for concerts in Caracas only three of the five scheduled concerts were completed on September 25, 26 and 27 at the Polyedro de Caracas, due to the inconsiderate demise of that country's President Betancourt. It took a great deal of very quick thinking to get all the passports back so that we could leave before Venezuela closed for a period of national mourning. It had been hoped to return to Brazil for a concert in Rio de Janeiro . . .

It was then on to Mexico where we did a show in Monterey on October 9 at the Estadion Universitano. We returned to the United States on October 11 but were back for two shows at the Estadion Cuahtermoc on October 16 and 17 in the regional city of Pueblo.

It was a nerve-racking time because it was at this show that fans were throwing batteries and various other rubble at the band on stage including a metal bolt which I still have and at which Freddie is pictured pointing rather dolefully in the Queen/Gluttons For Punishment book commemorating the South American experience. I have no memory of the fans being angry. I think the missiles were merely a rather odd expression of their appreciation.

We then went on to Canada to perform three auditorium shows in Montreal which were specifically designed to be filmed for the 'We Will Rock You' concert video as it was less costly to film in Canada than America.

Concert video productions designed for retail was a concept still in its infancy. Music videos were of course being made but mainly for promotional purposes on television. This concert film project was another first for Queen.

This concludes my first and most epic tour with Queen. From here,

I'll try to provide some of the highlights and the lowpoints of the years of the band's performances that remained.

At the Hallenstadion gig in Zurich on April 16 and 17, the band stayed in one hotel, the Dolder Grand, a very ritzy affair on one side of the lake, while the rest of us stayed in another, a much more modest affair nearer the stadium. At this point, Freddie and I weren't sharing the double bedroom suites. This was one of the very few occasions when the band party itself was split up.

While in Brussels on April 22 and 23, we travelled in the hotel lift with the American track athlete star Carl Lewis. Freddie could hardly contain his excitement. By the time he got to his suite, he was squealing after their exchange of grins. I don't think that any of us up to that point realised how great was Freddie's passion for athletics! From my point of view, I think Carl Lewis was actually quite pleased himself to be travelling in the lift with Freddie Mercury. I think the only thing that perhaps Carl envied Freddie was the fact that Freddie had the bigger suite on the higher floor in the hotel and neither of them knew, of course, of their shared interest in collecting fine crystal glassware. On April 24 at Groenoordhalle in Leiden, Freddie had no intention of spending the night in such a sedate town when there was so much more on offer in the nightlife of nearby Amsterdam. We had taken Freddie's 'going out' clothes with us so there was no need to return to the hotel after the show. We went straight out and hit the bars of that liberal city.

In Wurzburg on May 9, we toured this amazing old German town. Freddie happened to want a haircut and he had flown Denny, the fashionable hairdresser from Sweeneys in Beauchamp Place, out from London. Denny ended up staying for about four or five days. One of the more expensive haircuts in the world. Hotels aren't cheap! Freddie was nevertheless very happy with the haircut.

For someone so fussy about his hair, there was never any rhyme or reason behind Freddie's choice of hairdressers. As any paranoid body with a double crown knows, a new hairdresser is made aware in great detail of the presence of the double crown, something which any decent hairdresser would notice immediately. I remember Freddie was once most offended when someone announced: "Oh! You're losing your hair!"

"I'm not!" was the indignant retort. "I have a double crown!" When Freddie's hair was long, he was constantly fighting the naturally curly unruliness. Video shoots were an occasion when he would pay great attention to his hair and take full advantage of whoever happened to be doing hair and make-up on that day. He considered the fashion for short hair a great boon because it meant the end of 'the dreaded curls' and of course when he met Jim Hutton, it was a show of faith in Jim's ability that Freddie – indeed the whole household – would have their hair cut inhouse. It was not the usual case of famous people going to famous hairdressers.

Wurzburg, very close to Hamelin, where the other Pied Piper performed, was a charming town. It was typical of German gothic fairytale magic and Freddie loved it.

In Vienna we stayed in an amazingly grand hotel near the Opera House. I really believe that the best of the Viennese hotels compare easily with the grand old dames of Paris. The performance at the Stadthalle was also filmed in its entirety as were many of the shows on this tour. The presence of film and television crews never phased Freddie either before or during the show. Being filmed never meant that he was conscious he had to give a better performance because all his performances were simply the best he could do on that day anyway.

There's a great difference in having a show filmed by television, however, and the required press photographs which were routinely taken at each concert. One of the strict instructions laid down by the band was that press photographers were allowed close access to them only for the first two songs because Freddie realised that he would have to perform for those cameras ranged at such close quarters to the stage which might have meant the larger audience missing out on some of his more usual elaborate gestures that would not have been capturable at such close range. When the tour moved to England, 'Las Palabras De Amor' came out as a single. It was Brian's acknowledgment of the Spanish speaking countries. The band never played it on stage while I was there and the general enthusiasm displayed to the song's release was at best underwhelming. Why this inoffensive little song never received the full backing of an accompanying video and the usual push is a mystery. Perhaps that old enemy, time, reared its ugly head again?

On June 5, the band were scheduled to play the huge Milton Keynes Bowl. Freddie's lover at that point was a stolid and solid American from New Jersey by the name of Bill Reid. Not the tallest man in the world, Freddie had met him in a bar in New York. In all of Freddie's relationships in the time I knew him, his affair with Bill Reid was by far the most tempestuous and at times frighteningly violent. The day before the show, at home at Stafford Terrace in London, an argument developed from a cause that no one now remembers. While people were used to hearing shouting and screaming from the couple, they were aware that something was going on but raised voices were standard. Someone was around to jump in should it seem that the situation between Freddie and Bill was getting out of control.

This time, before anybody realised what was going on, Bill Reid had bitten Freddie's hand between the thumb and forefinger. Freddie was in absolute agony and blood flowed from the teethmarks of the wound but he refused to have anything done about it. The Milton Keynes show was one of the biggest British shows Queen had ever done and so, in hindsight, I suppose it was only natural that some great emotional eruption would happen. As has been seen, and will be seen again, Freddie needed the catalyst of conflict to bring out his best performance. He had to sing angry. The bigger the concert, the bigger the pain, though not always, thank heavens, physical. Paul Prenter and I did the best we could with the wound, cleaning it with TCP and any other antiseptic we could lay our hands on. I suppose the show was in the back of Freddie's mind all the time but at this point, we were all worried as to whether the show would happen at all.

To get to the venue, we took off in a helicopter from Westland heliport. This was my first trip in a helicopter and this model seated about ten. The party included the four members of the band, Bill Reid, Paul Prenter, myself and some security. The others had gone on ahead by road. The helicopter was used because it was the only way to guarantee the band getting to Milton Keynes at all. They had been informed that traffic problems were enormous and there was no certainty that they would get there at all going by car.

The most noticeable difference between the helicopter and a plane of a similar size is the noise. Everybody's asked to wear ear-mufflers to cut out some of the noise and it wasn't being impolite as hearing people talk is just about impossible.

While in the car on the way to the heliport the frosty silence between Freddie and Bill was apparent, it somehow faded into insignificance during the flight which lasted no longer than half-an-hour, if that. As we flew over the site, it was like looking down on an army of ants and in saying that I'm not being disrespectful to the crowd. You could feel the excitement building in the confined space of the helicopter both because of the journey itself – which, unless you are a helicopter pilot, isn't a regular feature of anyone's life – and also the band seeing all those people below them.

This was another of those 'take-the-money-and-run' shows. Literally, as the band were led off the stage with dressing gowns or towels round their shoulders, they were taken the two hundred or more yards straight into the helicopter which then started its engine and took off, whisking us away from the deafening applause and the blinding lights. There was, beneath us, this island of light in a sea of darkness. It's a memory which has stuck with me.

The shorts'n'suspenders party after the show, back in London at the Embassy Club in Bond Street, was strange in that very few people who had been to the concert were there because of the distance of the show from London and the massive traffic jam which was caused on the M1 and A1 highways by the huge crowd leaving the Bowl at the same time.

We had to land at Heathrow due to a curfew on helicopter flights over London in the dark. This gave us plenty of time for Freddie to go home to Stafford Terrace, get changed into a pair of shorts and prepare himself generally for the party. While Freddie really enjoyed himself at the party, Bill sulked in dark corners. If he wasn't the centre of attention, be it as a satellite moon to Freddie's sun, he tended to be very depressive and morose. Finally, the other on-stage musicians in the support bands arrived. Most party guests got into the spirit and turned up in shorts or suspenders, although I think for some of them it was normal party gear anyway. The Rock'n'America Tour which followed on the heels of the Milton Keynes experience involved Billy Squier as the band's support act. Freddie's first meeting with him was unexceptional but it formed the basis of a friendship that was to last. Billy is one of life's really nice guys. He and Freddie founded a mutual admiration society. Freddie liked Billy's music so much that when Billy asked if Freddie would help out on a current album project, Freddie was more than happy to oblige.

Freddie loved being back in New York for July 27 and 28 but, as was always the way in metropoli, hated doing the shows. The people in large cities anywhere in the world were getting harder and harder to please. On August 9, a few tickets, shall we say, had to be put on hold as the personal allocation of Bill Reid, native of New Jersey, for the band was playing the Brendon Burn Coliseum in Meadowlands. I think probably to counter any possibility of Bill's support group ovewhelming Freddie, Freddie brought all of his friends from New York down, Thor Arnold and the gang, any number upwards of twenty people. He didn't intend to be intimidated by Bill Reid's cronies on their home turf.

In Houston, August 20, Freddie returned to a place he was getting to like. He had learned quite a lot about it from Thor who was a regular visitor and Freddie intended spending a little bit more time there when his schedule allowed. A good time was to be had in Houston and Freddie was always up for a good time.

And talking of good times, on August 25, one of the bands more accommodating fans arrived at the Mid-South Coliseum gig in Memphis, Tennessee. Because the band were not visiting her home patch of Little Rock, Arkansas, this lady arrived in the early part of the concert day with the intention of orally catering to the physical needs of as many people as possible involved in the show. It goes without saying that Freddie had a certain admiration for this woman's perseverance, technique and capacity!

All I remember about the Kemper gig in Kansas City on August 28 is the hotel. There was something about hotels designed in certain eras like ships. The outside of this Kansas example was curved. It was one of the first I'd been in which had glass elevators on the outside of the structure.

If the prospect provided by the local bars wasn't good, Freddie was always happy to have an impromptu party or, if one was already arranged, to attend it. In Kansas City, one such party was arranged in the largest suite of the hotel for band and crew and assorted backstage passholders, particularly those given out during the course of the evening to male and female alike and we all know what qualifications are required for that accolade! And if you can't imagine, get a life!

Poor Billy Squier got trapped by Bill Reid asking him the most mundane, stupid questions that no one in their right mind would ask. It almost looked as though Bill Reid would rather have gone off with Billy than Freddie that night although as anyone knows, it would never even have occurred to Billy Squier who, in his sweet naiveté, would have just assumed that Bill Reid was merely showing interest in his music. Anyway, I remember returning to the main room at one point to find a couple of the road crew had changed clothes with their respective escorts and were dancing up and down on a big table in black mini-dresses and high heels while the ladies were holding up over-large jeans and T-shirts.

All in a day's touring.

By September 4, the band's progress had arrived at the PNE Coliseum in Vancouver, Canada. As a treat, Freddie had flown over four of the posse of his New York Daughters. Perhaps Bill Reid felt left out. I don't know, because Freddie spent all afternoon in the hotel suite's sitting room having afternoon tea. This seemed quite appropriate as Vancouver is quite the most British of all the North American continent's cities. So, it was Earl Grey tea, cucumber sandwiches and Victoria sponge all the way. Admittedly, after the novelty of the tea party wore off, Freddie then ordered half a dozen bottles of champagne and a bottle or two of Stolichnaya vodka from room service.

After the show, we went for a short tour of the city's bars. Even though he had his in-house entertainment,

"You never know what's round the corner," as Freddie said.

We got back to the hotel, Thor and Lee and the others went to their rooms. I went to my bedroom on my side of Freddie's suite and Freddie went to his with Bill. It must have been an hour or two later when I heard thundering crashes and couldn't for the life of me figure out what was going on. Then there was banging on my door and Freddie shouting on the other side, "Let me in! Let me in!"

When I opened the door, Freddie said, "You're just going to have to let me sleep here tonight." I was very curious and asked what was going on. "Don't worry about it. I'll tell you in the morning," he replied. Whereupon, he fell immediately asleep.

The following day, we got up and I was about to walk in to the sitting room without shoes on when Freddie called to me and told me to first put something on my feet and to be very careful; I was then to find out why. As I walked into the sitting room, the whole plaster-board wall to my left was a mess of jagged holes and the floor all around was strewn with broken glass from all the champagne and vodka bottles whether full or empty and most of the glasses which had been used for drinking.

Dangerous broken glass was everywhere. This latest disaster was just another manifestation of Bill Reid's 'love'.

How Freddie had survived without being hit by a flying bottle is anybody's guess. None of the others could believe what they saw when they arrived and they urged Freddie yet again to get rid of the man. But Freddie still persisted in keeping him around. As far as Bill Reid seemed concerned, it was as though nothing whatsoever had happened and, to be fair, Freddie never appeared to bear a grudge over the incident. I think Freddie needed the physical manifestation of someone's love and as far as Reid's was concerned, this debacle appeared to Freddie to be proof of 'love'. It was certainly what Freddie seemed to need.

The tour reached its conclusion at the Forum, Inglewood in Los Angeles on September 14 and 15. Photos show Freddie with Michael Jackson, Olivia Newton-John and Donna Summer amongst other luminaries in the audiences. Between this triumphant end of the tour and September 25, the band flew back to New York as they were scheduled to appear on *Saturday Night Live* singing 'Crazy Little Thing Called Love'. This date marked the end of the continental American tour. The entourage was due to move on. However, *Saturday Night Live* was very important. It was the first time the band had ever played what, at this point, was a very prestigious television show, watched nationwide by many millions of people.

Once again, 'love' reared its violent head.

Once again, the reason for the argument between Freddie and Bill Reid is forgotten in the mists of time but they were screaming at each other non-stop for many hours through the Friday night prior to the show. Were this an ordinary television show, there wouldn't have been a problem as their performance would have been mimed to a backing track. But, as the name of the show describes, Queen's was to be a live performance.

When Freddie awoke on Saturday morning, he found he had simply screamed himself hoarse the night before. We had a run-through of the show that afternoon at which point Freddie just marked, simply going through the motions of a performance. The band played and he merely spoke his way through. I'd gone out earlier in the morning and found some Oil of Olbas. We spent the whole of the afternoon in one of the studio's small bathrooms with the hot tap turned on full and the door shut tight to create as much steam as we could manage and I dripped as many drops of the oil as practicable to infuse the steam with healing efficacy. The electric kettle was boiling constantly to supply hot water for the continual hot honey and lemon drinks that I was making for Freddie. He spent the whole afternoon convinced that he would be unable to perform and felt as though he was letting the rest of the band down badly.

This particular adrenalin boost had gone horribly awry.

Every now and then after the run-through he would try a note and very slowly the voice started to come back. While he actually gave a brave performance, anyone who has seen it will notice that he is not on his best form. The top notes were just not there but ably filled in and augmented by Roger.

Another person Freddie felt he might have been letting down was the then new super-talent of Jennifer Holliday. He had been informed that she was going to be in the audience that evening and he had seen her not long before in the stage show of *Dream Girls*. This came about very simply by me having heard the song 'And I'm Telling You I'm Not Going' on the radio, one day in London. I then found out where the song came from and I proceeded to get a tape copy. I was meeting Freddie that night and knew we would be going out. I took the tape along and lined up the song on the tape deck in his Rolls Royce. We were driving down Kensington Gore when I told him, "You have to listen to this. You'll be stunned."

I told him nothing about the show but merely pressed Play. He was indeed stunned.

It then came about when we were in New York that he found out where the show was playing and managed to get seats. It is one of the few shows that he and I went to together in New York and the only one where the whole audience was on its feet at the end of the first half and all this for a twenty-one-year-old newcomer. He met Jennifer Holliday just after the *Saturday Night Live* performance but couldn't bring himself to stay talking too long because he felt that he hadn't given a praiseworthy performance himself. I think this time Freddie realised that it was he who had bitten off more than he could chew as far as Bill Reid was concerned and somewhere, somehow he decided that enough was enough.

That doesn't mean it was the last we ever saw of Mr Reid.

Freddie had already given him money to buy a car and so Freddie just asked Bill to come around to the apartment building to pick up what few belongings he had and take them away, which Bill did.

A couple of days later, we had got back to Freddie's apartment at the Sovereign Building at 425 East 58th Street from a night out on the town. It was fairly early – maybe four o'clock in the morning – when all of a sudden there was screaming and banging on the apartment door. You must realise that this is very unusual because of the concierge and security in the buildings' foyers. These are not allowed to let anyone in without announcing callers to the tenants. I went to the door and by this time, the glass on the other side of the peephole in the door was smashed and I saw through the aperture that on the landing side was Bill, in a fury. He was screaming, "You'll not get rid of me this easy. You'll never get rid of me!"

I called security who came and removed him. They were obviously extremely apologetic but they weren't to know about the changes in Freddie's domestic arrangements. Up until the time the apartment was sold, I don't think the damage to the metal-faced door was ever properly repaired.

Freddie left the apartment, never to return to it, not long after this incident. I think this was the straw that broke the camel's back and finally put Freddie off New York. The apartment had been purchased because Freddie needed a base in America. He had been spending quite a lot of time there while recording, touring and enjoying himself and the other members of the band had homes in Los Angeles. There was never any doubt that if Freddie had a home in America it would be anywhere other than New York. He didn't like the Los Angeles 'feel'. Everything so laid back you almost fell over, not that Freddie was too averse to falling over.

In New York he had a friend in Gerry Stickells' wife, Sylvia. When he first thought of buying a place, she very kindly offered to have a look round at various properties for him. Up to this point, Freddie had spent all of his time in New York in various hotels, the first one I remember staying in was the Waldorf Astoria Towers. He then took up residence in the Berkshire Place Hotel on East 52nd Street. Another was the Helmsley Palace. After discussions with Jim Beach and John Libson, Freddie decided that he was spending far too much money staying in hotels and he would be a lot better off if he had his own place. It must be remembered that these hotels were costing him a thousand dollars a night and that was just for the beds for him and me.

He lived otherwise on room service and we usually ate out at places like Shezan, the London restaurant in Cheval Place which had opened a New York outpost. Pearls, the Chinese restaurant in the early West Fifties, was another favourite. He said Pearl's served the best Chinese food he had ever eaten. Joanna's down in the East Village was another and was one of the few haunts of the rich and famous he used to frequent. The other favourite place is another one now defunct, Clyde's in the West Village. It was not expensive, the standard American food was very good and Freddie really enjoyed the atmosphere. Clyde's was also very handy for the bars of Christopher Street and its environs.

Sylvia Stickells researched probably a hundred apartments in different areas of the city including Number One Fifth Avenue, an amazing loft in the Soho district and I even looked at spaces in apartment buildings that were yet to be completed. Of Sylvia's hundred, I was dispatched to look at twenty-five and Freddie himself checked out around ten of these. What Freddie was looking at in the building at One Fifth Avenue was in fact two apartments which would have had to have been knocked together to provide the required space. This was on the third or fourth floor which Freddie wasn't too happy with and, added to this, the inconvenience of the construction work deterred him. The Soho loft space sticks in my mind mainly for the circular wood-panelled room with the glass domed ceiling. It was the main feature of the property but none of us could come up with a definite purpose for the room beneath it. The nearest we came was to make it a bedroom but it would have wasted the panelling and the problem of making the room dark in the morning would have been very, very difficult to overcome.

The third place that I remember which Freddie refused to see was on the thirtieth floor of a construction site on the East Side in the Forties. The St. James' Tower. There were literally fifty slabs of concrete supported on pillars. I was taken up the outside in the rattling open cage of an exterior elevator . . . Me! Scared of heights! I spent the time with my eyes shut. On arriving at the thirtieth floor, gales howled around. I made my way to the centre of the concrete floor as soon as I was able. While, the attendant real estate agent was extolling the future glories of the rooms that were going to be built, all I could think of doing was hanging on to something to make sure I wasn't blown away.

Eventually, the agent came up with the Sovereign Building. This huge construction at 425 East 58th Street between First Avenue and Sutton Place. The building is designed in such a way that in certain apartments there were almost unrestricted views of the city. There were forty-eight floors and Freddie's apartment was on the forty-third. Imagine not being able to see the ground because of the cloud.

The apartment was about the same size as Freddie's two-floored flat in Stafford Terrace. There, the sitting room and dining room were knocked through into one huge room. The same could almost be said for the New York apartment. On the north side of the apartment there was a balcony which overlooked the 59th Street Bridge immortalised in the song of the same name by Simon and Garfunkel on their *Parsley, Sage, Rosemary & Thyme* album. Other than the apartment itself, one of the features which impressed Freddie was the building's staff and their organisation. There were doormen, concierges and security staff which alleviated any worries he might have had concerning his own security. Even though New York is known for the violence on its streets, being on the streets never worried Freddie despite the sad demise of peers such as John Lennon.

Not long after Lennon's death, it was made known to Queen that threats had been made to assassinate them during a concert. The only other alert concerning Queen's immediate personal security was in London when the band members were given police protection during the making of a video and two policemen were even stationed in Freddie's Stafford Terrace apartment. The police authorities insisted that the officers remain in Stafford Terrace until Freddie returned home. Freddie was really surprised when he walked in and found them there but it didn't stop him playing up to them, even to the point of teasing them unmercifully.

"Look," he said, "that's my drugs drawer over there!"

They laughed and took it all in good part. It came to us later that Kensington Police Station knew what Freddie was doing and where he was doing it most of the time but happily they left him alone as he was never one to draw undue attention to himself and his activities. It was known exactly, for example, how many times in a week he had been to the Copacabana Club in Earls Court Road. Maybe they kept the same sort of tabs on all the Royal Borough's famous residents?

I don't know exactly what made him decide on the New York apartment he finally chose . . . The views from his bedroom were certainly stunning. On a good day, you could see as far as the suspension bridge across the Verrazzano Narrows, a view which included one of Freddie's favourite buildings, the Chrysler and also the Empire State and the Twin Towers of the World Trade Centre. We were surprised at the continual changes of the lighting set-up on the Empire State Building which reflected the various public holidays i.e. green for St. Patrick's Day, red, white and blue for July 4.

One thing Freddie was very proud of, after he had been told, was that seven bridges could be seen from the apartment. He was really excited during the celebrations for the hundredth anniversary of the Brooklyn Bridge which we watched simultaneously both from the corner window in his bedroom and, once removed, on the television.

The apartment had belonged to a senator or congressman by the name of Gray and Freddie actually purchased the place from his widow. Gray had been his name and indeed grey was the predominant colour in the apartment's decor. Four bedrooms and five bathrooms and a den, particularly the den which was decorated in grey pinstripe men's suiting fabric. There was a mirrored and closeted bedroom at the hub and a dining room with walls covered in silver-grey satin. But Freddie never wanted to nest here. The place remained virtually unchanged from the day he bought it until the day he left and he left it without a backward glance, never to return.

But, conversely, neither did he ever sell it . . .

But back to the marathon world tour which spawned this digression, we left the USA to travel to Japan for six shows. Nobody at this time realised that their most recent New York show would be the last live performance given by Queen in America. But with the combination of future public dismay at the 'I Want To Break Free' video and Freddie's own stage-weariness, it was not a surprise. The band had completed two huge tours in as many years and I think that Freddie thought it would be nice to give America a break.

All Freddie left behind was a cold apartment and a final unhappy memory. Unusually, he had made no firm commitments to return, knowing that he would keep in touch with the true friends he had made and could always fly them to him, wherever he was in the world. Or him to them.

I remember he flew Bill Reid and my friend Patrick Morrisey over on Concorde one Christmas. I think Freddie believed Concorde was the only transatlantic aircraft because it's the only way he ever flew from London to New York and vice versa. I don't know how many times Freddie has been on the plane but I know I've been on it nine. Of course, if I was travelling alone, I would go on a non-Concorde flight. If only he'd had shares in British Airways.

The Japanese tour was an excuse – if excuse was needed – for another shopping expedition. And these dratted shows getting in the way! Freddie loved being in Japan and if having to perform in five different cities meant he could shop in five different cities, so be it. This was an unusual trip in that it did take in all the cities. Generally, any of Freddie's private shopping trips and any length of stay in Japan usually just involved Tokyo. He indulged in his passion for lacquer boxes of which there was an amazing selection available. Each of the cities specialised in different forms of Japanese art and he was able to immerse himself in all things Japanese for a while. There was an ancient Japanese ethic of peace and calm which he perceived as well as the culture's appreciation of beauty which enabled him in turn to find beauty in all things Japanese whether in the lines of the woodblock prints or the serenity of a Japanese garden which was all elemental rocks, pebbles and water.

In February, 1984, the band agreed to appear at the San Remo Song Festival, traditionally a resort which belonged to the blue-rinse and fur stole brigade. This was going to be an easy gig for them as they were only required to mime to backing tracks. This didn't decrease the intensity of the fans' activity and security was still as tight as ever. The invasion of the neon-coloured hairdos of the various rock bands' followers finally eclipsed the blue rinses of the resorts usual clientele.

On the same bill were Culture Club, who were the new band of the era. George and Freddie had met on occasion before and really quite enjoyed each other's company. George then, as now, had a brilliant wit which Freddie greatly appreciated. It seems ironic now considering what was to happen to George, but at that time he was very anti-drugs which made him something of a rarity in the music business.

Freddie had heard through the every-growing grapevine of George's dislike which extended to him forbidding any of his entourage holding stocks of illegal substances. Feeling that this enforced denial was unfair on the others, Freddie arranged a little afternoon tea for George and himself in Freddie's suite while a separate small party was arranged in my adjoining room for the rest of the Culture Club party whose tastes extended to slightly more than tea and cucumber sandwiches. The housekeeping must have thought it strange to see a queue of people outside my room, people coming in and going out in twos and threes, smiling a lot.

This festival is something that the band hadn't done before and was perhaps seen as a warm-up for their second mimed appearance at the Golden Rose pop festival in Montreux later that year in May. It was eventually broadcast to over forty countries around the world. I think the obvious reason for both of these mimed appearances was so that the band could reach the massive audience that these televised broadcasts would attract. At this point, *The Works* had been released and these two festival appearances were the best possible promotion.

We rehearsed for *The Works* European tour in Munich on a Bavarian film studio sound stage just outside the city. Rehearsals were held over two weeks at which everybody appeared to be in a very good mood. One of the crew's ways of relaxing followed the then trend for abseiling which they all took turns at down the outsides of the sound stages. Munich was a city that everybody liked for their own reasons. At that point, Freddie's reasons were Barbara Valentin and Winnie Kirchberger and all those bars. Freddie's partner of the time was expected to trail around after him as relationships never stopped Freddie from going out.

The set for *The Works* was a re-working of a scene from Fritz Lang's *Metropolis* with gigantic wheels rotating at the back of the stage. It was daunting for Freddie with all the different levels and stairs but he loved the challenge. There were more places for him to pose. He seemed to have recovered from the ligament damage in his knee that he had sustained while indulging in some rather silly horseplay with his friends in the New York bar in Munich in April.

This accident had left him in plaster from mid-thigh to his ankle. He had lifted someone up and totally by accident someone else had knocked his knee sideways at which point he collapsed on the floor in agony. He was taken off to hospital where he was X-rayed and it was found the knee wasn't broken. Much to his horror, he was told that his leg would be in plaster but even that impediment still didn't totally stop him from going out in the evenings.

While he was thus plastered, his old friend Elton John was in town performing and insisted on Freddie coming to a show. Because of his obvious disability, Freddie was planted on the side of the stage behind the PA system and, throughout the show, Elton was threatening to drag Freddie out on stage but in the end had to make do with dedicating 'I'm Still Standing' to Freddie, a dedication delivered with a wicked grin. Not long after the plaster had been removed, Freddie actually worked on the video for 'It's A Hard Life' and the only noticeable moment when he favours his damaged leg is in the last shot where he sits himself down on the steps.

The tour started at the indoor Foret Nationale in Brussels. The band were there for one show and used the afternoon before the show to film footage for the 'Hammer To Fall' promo. The show itself was then filmed so that crowd scenes could be included in the video. There followed nine shows in Britain and Eire. The Wembley show was the first time Freddie wore the infamous wig'n'boobs. He had time to put these on as 'I Want To Break Free' was scheduled to be the first encore. The display went down so well that Freddie decided that he would continue using it in all the following shows. It was my job to make sure that prior to the short time it was on stage, the wig looked decent. The second of these Wembley concerts fell on his thirty-eighth birthday and as the next day was a day off, he had a party in Xenon, the nightclub of the moment. There are photographs I'm sure you've all seen of Freddie blowing out the candles on the huge Rolls Royce cake which was presented to him that night.

This was the occasion where the birthday cake was stolen. It was in fact stolen by one of the acts who had been axed from performing at the celebration cabaret because of the large gay content of their show. The act were so pissed off that although they were compensated, they decided to steal the cake on their way home. Sweet revenge!

The tour reverted to the European continent, embracing Germany, Italy, France, Belgium and Holland. One incident that really stands out in my mind took place in the Europehalle, Hannover. As usual, throughout the show, security for each member of the band is positioned around the stage.

I was stationed at the door-flap of the dolls' house talking to Freddie's bodyguard, when we both saw him fall. At first, neither of us could be sure whether it was intentional or not but then we saw him in pain. We both ran on and, between us, picked him up and brought him back to the dolls' house.

As you can imagine, there was total confusion as the band were just

over halfway through the show. Freddie decided immedia
couldn't let the fans down and just leave. So, with rapid
with the rest of the band, the band crew and Gerry Stic
decided there were about three more songs that he could p ..orm
while sitting at the piano. As there were never doctors or first aid
people specifically assigned to the band on duty backstage, Freddie
intuited that it was a repeat of the old Munich ligament injury to his
knee. There was no point in him taking painkillers and so, between
the security man and myself, we carried Freddie back on stage and
placed him on the piano stool. I can only guess at Freddie's feelings at
that point, but I could feel the wave of emotion from the crowd as we
carried him on and he then explained what had happened and what
was to happen. They roared their approval at his courage. The show,
after all, must go on!

After the three songs, Freddie was carried straight into a car and
taken directly to hospital where X-rays showed that the damage
wasn't as bad as Freddie had thought, that he would be able to
continue the tour, very heavily bandaged, provided he didn't put too
much pressure on the joint.

It was from this point on that a newcomer was included in Freddie's
entourage, namely Dieter Briet, a qualified physiotherapist who had
come highly recommended to Freddie in Munich. Dieter was tall and
thin and gangly. He and his family lived on the outskirts of Munich
and the poor man spent much time trying to interest Freddie in the
benefits of actually partaking in sports. In the beginning, he didn't
realise that Freddie's sports were played mainly in the bars and at
home at night and very much in private.

Dieter's love of sports was to be rewarded in the following section
of the tour which took us to Sun City in Bophuthatswana, one of the
South African homelands, now Northern Transvaal. Dieter's main job
was an hour and a half before the show to manipulate Freddie's leg
and, obviously, to be around during the show. Much of Dieter's free
time, however, was spent windsurfing on a massive man-made lake
that was part of the hotel complex, a pastime he very much enjoyed.
He was even trying to encourage Freddie onto a board. He didn't
succeed.

The band went to Sun City because they had secured a record-
breaking run, another notch on Queen's bedpost of achievements. It
was also one of the few places within reach of the boycotted South

Africa where the band knew they could perform to multi-racial audiences. This was the only opportunity that many South Africans – be they Cape Coloured, Indian, Chinese or white as well as the native black population – would have to see Queen or any other of the Western mega-bands in the foreseeable future. Providing, of course, that they could afford it!

Had the band known before how much international fuss would be caused by this visit, they probably would still have gone ahead with the engagement because as far as they were concerned it was a chance to give enjoyment and entertainment to people who, because of the Musicans' Union ban, had been completely ignored. Who, we wondered, gave the Musicians' Union the right to decide what and who the people in South Africa could see? Although he would never have thought of it or mentioned it, it is ironic to remember that Freddie himself had been born and brought up in Zanzibar and partially educated in Africa, like Gandhi. If anything, Freddie could have been said to have been making a statement and taking a stand with his South African fans.

As far as politics was concerned, Freddie had an abhorrence of bands like U2, for example, who used their fame and celebrity status to put over their political views. Freddie was aware that he could say anything and it would be reported round the world and could be construed (or misconstrued) in any way that a particular party or media organ might want. To my knowledge, he never once went to vote at any election be it parliamentary or local even though he was always on the electoral roll. Because Garden Lodge was my home and I was therefore registered to vote in that constituency, I always voted. He was always interested in my voting and in what was happening generally in politics but he himself remained aloof. Had he voted, it would have been for a Conservative government as he had already lived through a period where his income had been taxed at 83% by a Labour administration which had tempted many of his peers to a life abroad as he himself had done for several years. However, he never publicly voiced any of his own political opinions as he regarded political opinions as relevant only to the individual and to tell the truth politics never figured very highly in his thought processes. As far as the annual budget meant, he waited for his accountant John Libson to explain to him what the salient points were regarding his own position.

The band had been booked to do eleven shows in Sun City

although in the end, they performed only seven. This was entirely due to Freddie's vocal chords. He'd always had little nodules on them but while surgery had been mooted at various times, he had never wanted to do anything about the condition for fear of losing what he already had. This time, after the first show, his throat had really tightened up. A doctor was called in and gave Freddie that panacea of all evils – some steroids – and told him he couldn't sing for a few days. Freddie, being Freddie, took the advice but at his own pace and, therefore, performed a show when he shouldn't have done. This necessitated a further break.

The hotel was part of the Sun City complex which consisted of two main areas, one being the hotel and a few one-arm bandit machines and then, a very short drive away, the Superbowl which incorporated the remainder of the gambling facility and also a theatre with shows that would rival the Paris and Las Vegas experiences. Freddie rarely left his hotel room while in Sun City so it really was no more than a luxurious prison. He was worried about his voice and as has been shown earlier he hated the thought of letting down the fans. If there was any chance of performing, he would. Freddie had persuaded Winnie Kirchberger to leave his Munich restaurant for a while and come with him to South Africa and so he wasn't alone. Freddie even persuaded the hotel management to provide a small two-burner gas cooker so that Winnie could rustle up lunch for Freddie. It was really very sweet, seeing Freddie being taken care of by someone who was fond of him and Freddie was delighted. He invited 'guests' for lunch on at least two occasions when 'my husband, the chef' was cooking.

I, who was therefore let out of the luxurious prison, had many a fun adventure in Sin City – sorry, Sun City – but thought it politic not to tell Freddie too much!

Although the band toured a couple of times in Australia, it was not a frequent port of call for them. One of the reasons – it has to be said – was Freddie's aversion to full-strip body searches to which he had been subjected on his first visit to that continent. Although I wasn't actually present, he often told the story of how he got very drunk with Tony Hadley before appearing one night on the tour.

Early in 1985, the band flew back to South America for the Rock in Rio festival. The Copacabana Palace Hotel acted as HQ for this visit. Freddie's personal guests on this occasion were once again Barbara Valentin and Winnie. Barbara had been to Rio earlier, in her capacity as German movie star and gave Freddie many enjoyable hours, regaling him with stories of her past adventures in the art movie houses of the world.

The audiences of between two hundred and fifty and three hundred thousand people were the largest the bands on this bill had ever played to. It seems odd now to reflect that Freddie's need for emotional conflict wasn't evident on these two occasions. Perhaps because he knew he had two shows, he thought the conflict would arise on the second one. The lack of communication due to Winnie's paucity of English and Freddie's unsophisticated German may have been a factor in the relatively unruffled emotional atmosphere. It was sometimes comical to watch the arguments happening with Barbara as the translator for both parties. Both Freddie and Winnie would be screaming at Barbara who had to do her best to try to sort out the jumbled words and jumbled emotions. It was a far cry from her original film performances as the Diana Dors of the German silver screen.

Because we were in Rio for so long, Freddie did actually manage to go out on three or four occasions but it was one of those situations where, when Freddie left the hotel, at least one other car had to accompany him with onboard security. It became such a farce, his attempts to get in and out of nightclubs, that eventually he gave up and had many long-night parties in his suite.

There was a massive party organised by EMI given at the Copacabana Palace but which Freddie refused to attend. There were many occasions where he hated being on show and these sort of industry parties were just such events. Freddie would have been the first to have shown up at a band-organised party but as this was just another excuse for the record company to show off their wares, the band would have to be available to be poked and prodded by the record company's unparticular guest list, all the people who had been promised favours by record company executives. Had this been a purely professional affair, Freddie would have displayed no such disregard. Having never been one himself, Freddie consistently expressed his disdain of those whom he regarded as liggers, a human sub-species which contained two categories – the Professional and the Business liggers. The former he didn't object to as these were mostly his peers. The latter came under the umbrella appellation of 'Record Company' and as such to be reviled.

Freddie was there to perform for the crowds who had paid.

Understandably, he believed he had earned the right to do and behave as he wanted. Put in any position where he was under scrutiny or where he had to be on his 'best behaviour', he felt very uneasy. He was very much an impromptu person. Because of his natural spontaneity, he hated being in the spotlight on unfamiliar territory – for example, when he was asked to meet the President of Argentina. On the other hand, in his own home, he could and would be the perfect host and gentleman. This trait must have been born from his schooling. At a boarding school, life is so regimented. You are under the continual gaze of masters while at school and matrons in the dormitory so much so that you constantly rebel against any perceived authority in later life and this I can attest to as I also attended a boarding school in India very much like Freddie's.

More than anyone, because of his fame, Freddie was forever being scrutinised and he was very sensitive to it. Many's the time I have seen him come in after one of the enforced attendances that he couldn't get out of, throw off the outer layers of his clothes and let rip with the pent-up frustration of the previous few hours and swear and curse about anyone and everyone . . .

"It's the fucking last time I'm going to fucking well go to anything like that for anyone! Fuck 'em!"

At this point in the Queen touring schedule, I bowed out, as Freddie's new house, Garden Lodge, had taken on a life of its own, requiring someone permanently living in to organise the comings and goings of workmen and decorators. I relinquished my touring role to Joe Fanelli. I'd had a ball but being away from home for so long when you consider I'd started in late 1979 and had not spent much more than a matter of months in England since then, I think the time had come to settle down while Freddie continued to bear the royal standard around the world.

However, I was still to be involved with Live Aid.

Although Joe was to take care of Freddie and his needs for Live Aid, I was sent on ahead to Wembley, earlier that afternoon of July 13th 1985, to check the layout of dressing rooms, et cetera. I actually spent a fun couple of hours chatting with other people, both crew and performers, I hadn't seen for a while. The atmosphere was electric. Because of the sheer size of the show – size meaning both the concert length as well as the associated collective ego – many things happened on the spur of the moment.

71

While nothing was left to chance, it couldn't be foreseen when there'd be an electrical or satellite failure or some other such catastrophe. By the time that Freddie and the rest of the band arrived, I knew where everything that they would want was located including the watering hole for both bands and crews and the Hard Rock Cafe's marquee, both of which were being used by everyone, performers and crew alike.

There was a limited amount of space for dressing rooms and, if I remember rightly, there were six that were used in rotation as each band, when they finished its performance, immediately vacated their dressing room to allow the next band to move in like a version of the Royal Variety Show at London's Palladium theatre. I could sense tension with Freddie but I think this was purely because of the enormity of the occasion. It didn't take long for him to be laughing and joking with everybody else backstage whom he knew. Tony Hadley from Spandau Ballet, David Bowie, Elton, the Status Quo entourage . . . It really was a rendezvous for so many old friends, veterans of a lifetime in rock'n'roll. Remembering that so many bands spent so much of their time on the road, very often, friends will only meet when their paths cross on tours.

One thing made Freddie apprehensive about performing this gig and that was that due to timing, the band would have to perform in daylight. He disliked the light because you have to work so much harder for people to see anything. The daylight bleaches the performance, making the spotlights that were working redundant. Even make-up became a useless artifice to communicate the intensity of his personality. Everything would be working as per a normal show but from the audience's point of view, nothing was much apparent on stage as far as subtleties of performance went. Then again, Freddie was never one for subtleties on stage and it showed in his subsequent performance.

This daylight aspect no one else seemed to have quite worked out for they all give good but unenhanced shows. Freddie knew he had to compensate for this bleached-out effect and very soon had everyone in the stadium – not only the crowd but everybody backstage – in the palm of his hand. The available television footage doesn't quite capture the feeling backstage. Even the other performers gladly conceded that Queen had given the best show.

He basically knew he had to channel his usual two-hour show

energy into a performance of a mere twenty minutes. The sight of the packed stadium clapping in time and in unison to 'Radio Ga Ga' was mind-blowing for us backstage and so what it must have been like for Freddie who was controlling it, I have no idea. He must have felt at that point that he could have controlled the world for the whole world, it seemed, was attending upon him that day. He came offstage totally exhilarated and felt he could have done the perform-ance another six times over. Freddie had been under the impression that once he and Queen had done their bit and he and Brian had performed 'Is This The World That We Created?', he would be able to get off home. This was not to be. Just before the finale where everyone was expected to attend and sing, the performers were informed that they should, with respect, all go to the Wembley Conference Centre and remain there for an hour so as to allow traffic to die down. This would make the job of the police much easier. This enforced hiccup also allowed time for Freddie to meet up and chat for a long time – a good half-hour – with George Michael whom he admired. The feeling was definitely mutual. Freddie also chatted to Bowie for a while.

He ended up quite pleased that he had been made to stay on.

We were royally amused.

Almost a year to the day later, on July 11 and 12, 1986, the band returned to Wembley with *A Kind Of Magic* under their belts. Freddie had flown the New York Daughters specifically to see one of these shows. He knew it was going to be something to be proud of. He hired a coach for the show which left Garden Lodge with all his guests including Straker, Mary Austin, Wayne Eagling, Gordon Atkinson, Gordon Dalziel and Graham Hamilton, Barbara Valentin and Trevor Clarke. It was my job to ensure that the coach was laden with goodies for the trip out for the guests and on the trip back when Freddie himself joined in. This was to be the start of one very long party. I don't think there are many stars who would indulge in this kind of behaviour. I don't know that there are that many of his equivalent status who would have that many friends who would come together at one time to celebrate their friend's success. And they certainly wouldn't have travelled on a bus!

Freddie was a master controller but he was a lucky man in that his machinations worked for him as far as his friends were concerned. Freddie was very rarely in a situation which he didn't control or had not organised to be just 'so'. Should such a situation arise, he was quick-minded enough to extricate himself from any possible harm but that day must have been one of the happiest of his life.

On July 12, the second Wembley Show, a party was hosted by Queen and EMI Records at the Roof Gardens which is situated on what was the Derry and Toms building in Kensington High Street. This was the party where a few of the attendant staff wore nothing but body paint designed to look like clothes. There were girl attendants in the gentlemen's lavatory and vice versa. However, once again, to disprove reports which circulated at the time, there were no dwarves with bowls of cocaine. Of course there were drugs around. Drugs went with the territory but the excesses which were noised abroad were never excesses at all. This was the famous occasion when Freddie jumped up on stage with Samantha Fox and they duetted 'A Crazy Little Thing Called Love', as the band played live.

I was there on August 9, 1986, when the band played Kneb-worth Park. This was my second helicopter ride, this time in the wonderfully painted machine which has been seen in photographs so often. I was obviously there should Freddie need anything done that Joe was too busy to do but this show gave me an opportunity to see the band at their best. The show was a huge success except for the record British traffic jams following and in hindsight was perhaps the best last show that the band could have possibly had. Queen showed themselves to be quite simply the best stadium rock band in the world. They didn't expect this to be their last show and I'm sure all of them in their hearts were planning their next tour because this, the Magic Tour had gone so well.

Freddie's Christmas letter to the fan club seems to bear this out:

> *"Hi there!*
>
> *I've finally got a chance to write to you. It's been a pretty fab year – The tour was fun and a great success although I must admit I had to be coaxed into doing it, I'm glad I did it now.*
>
> *Since then I've been to Japan for a three week holiday. I had to get away from everybody and everything to do with business. The result was a fabulous time and I damn well deserved it!*
>
> *The band are now working on the Budapest Live Show to be*

out on video cassette early 1987. I'm also working on a solo project – it's so secretive even I don't know what it's about.

    Anyway, time to buzz off.

    Have a super Xmas everybody.

    Take care. Lots of love . . ."

Chapter Two

It's time I tried to give an insight into the recording processes which characterised the making of Queen's and Freddie's records because without the recordings, there would be nothing to tour, nothing to make a video of, nothing to design an album cover for. I would like this next chapter to show what was put in by the four performer/composers and what the process demanded from them.

Hot Space was the first Queen album I was involved with. It was really exciting because it meant living abroad for an extended length of time as opposed to merely touring abroad when our lives were still based in England. In those days there were still significant tax advantages in spending whole years at one time out of England. Very loosely, for every month you were out of the country, you were allowed back in for one day. So while I wasn't a tax exile, I also reaped the advantages by being paid in England while living on per diem expenses abroad. I therefore managed to save most of my salary.

Hot Space was recorded in both Montreux and Munich. The Mountain Studios in the Casino complex in the lakeside town of Montreux had already been purchased by Queen, both as an investment and as a utility. In the end it was used more as an investment and used by people like David Bowie. For two weeks every year the studio was commandeered for the recording of the internationally famous Montreux Jazz Festival.

On the first day of recording, the instruments and sound equipment would already be set up in the studio. The equipment would have arrived a few days earlier from London with the road crew where it had been in storage in the Queen warehouse in William Road. Rock'n'roll recording isn't a Monday through Friday nine-to-five routine but like most other schedules, to start at the beginning of a week is logical even though weekends often didn't count as week-ends. Recording was done as and when the band members felt like it.

Most bands before going into a recording studio would have some idea of what they wanted to produce. Queen, however, very rarely, if ever, did. They would go in and just see what would come into their heads. The date and timing of the recording of any album would be as the result of a band meeting with Jim Beach. Obviously, the band had to fulfil any contractual obligations to EMI and to the other record distribution companies with whom licensing deals had been signed. In the band's overall schedule, there would be a minimum of six months set aside for recording. This would allow time for exhausted brains to relax and recharge in between the arduous and often tortuous sessions. In those days, Queen recorded beneath the ultimate luxury of the twenty-four hour lock-out umbrella which denied any other band or artist access to the studio for as long as their contract with the studio lasted . . . Six, nine months. Even a year.

I was initially surprised that even at this point in their career seldom would all four members of the band be in the studio at the same time. When they were, it was often for a band meeting. We would joke that Queen must be the only band in the world who would pay a thousand pounds to have a band meeting; the most expensive in the world, maybe? Even though they had a perfectly good office headquarters, the chances of getting all four together around a boardroom table were vastly less than catching them all together in the studio.

Other than for these band meetings, Jim Beach was an infrequent visitor even though he lived and worked in Montreux, although Paul Prenter, then the band's personal manager, would be in attendance all the time. I would be there as well as Freddie's current beau, friends of the other band members and the usual quota of hangers-on. There could be upwards of a dozen people floating around. On creative sessions, there were no standard personnel combinations. It wasn't a Freddie and Roger only or Brian and Freddie next arrange-ment. The daily roll call depended very much on the degree of excess of the activities of the previous night. It was up to the producer/engineer and the tape operator to always be promptly behind the recording desk for a two o'clock start. The presence of the production team was the only certainty as they waited for their charges to arrive. Rheinhold Mack was the producer and engineer on *Hot Space*. Mack, as he was always known, lived in Munich and worked frequently with Giorgio Moroder in Munich's Musicland Studios which Moroder owned.

With Queen, although the recording day generally started about two o'clock in the afternoon, there was an open-ended finishing time to the day's session. In other words it could, and often did, go on all night into the early hours of the following day. Depending on the output, the working week could often last the full seven days. Queen took to recording like a flock of ducks to water although they took to composition as easily as blood being wrung from a stone. For this reason, there is, contrary to a lot of anticipation, not a large treasure haul of previously unheard tracks waiting to be unearthed in some studio vaults.

Because composition came hard and recording was often fraught, the length of sessions was unpredictable. For example, the first of the two sessions for 'Under Pressure' was twenty-four hours and the second, a couple of weeks later and four thousand miles away in New York when Freddie and Bowie finished off the track at the Power Station, was a session which lasted another eighteen hours.

'Under Pressure' came about purely spontaneously. Bowie, who was living in Montreux, heard that Queen were in town and just called round to the studio. Roger and Bowie got on very well anyway, although the lyric and title idea came from Freddie and David's collaboration.

The impromptu jam session soon assumed the twenty-four hour marathon shape I've described. I was overjoyed in New York when Freddie took up my suggestion of the two octave vocal slide which I had noticed being so successfully used on another current chart disco track.

But not all tracks took shape as quickly as 'Under Pressure'. Generally speaking – although with Freddie and Queen as with any band there are always exceptions – a . typical Freddie track came together something like this. As an example, the creative process which marked the emergence of the strangely autobiographical 'Life Is Real' started thirty thousand feet up in the air over the Atlantic.

We were flying back from New York to London on our way to Switzerland, paying no particular attention to anything when Freddie turned round and said, "Where's your paper and pen? I've just come up with some words." I always had to ensure that I carried with me, wherever we were, paper and pen for just such an occasion as this.

"Go ahead," I said.

"Cunt stains on my pillow," he replied *sotto voce* with that naughty grin. I think my face must have given away something because he then turned round and said, "D'you think that's too much?"

He then changed the words to, "Cum stains on my pillow?"

To which I replied, "Next!"

To which he replied with a giggle, "Oh, really! This is *too* much!"

I can see us now, reclining on the first class chairs at the front of the plane. He thought about it for another couple of minutes and finally came up with what is now the classic line, "Guilt stains on my pillow!"

For the next hour or so, Freddie'd come out with phrases, not necessarily sequential but always following the same concept. We therefore disembarked in Montreux with several pages of entirely unconnected lyric lines for a song without a title. Freddie often took the opportunity himself to jot down a couple of lines which had come into his head. On my pad there is a sheet where he has written: "Please feel free, Strain all my love from me . . ."

To the best of my knowledge, this couplet was wisely filed away for future use . . .

When we finally got into the studio from the airport, he sat down at a piano and just started playing. He would let his fingers play over the keys until a tune with which he was happy was finalised. Tape was always rolling in case a gem should get away. Perhaps he might just play chords and then progressions from those chord bases. The rhythm was dictated by the feeling and mood of the lyrics of the song and the time signature and beat dictated by the metre of the dominant lyric lines. Every song had a working title although the final choice would not be made until the end. Everyone would throw ideas for song titles into the arena. Only the fittest survived.

Once Freddie had decided on the tune, he started on what he thought of as 'the hard part' of the song, getting the lyrics into an understandable structure which made sense. Often, when I hadn't heard all that had gone on in the studio that day, Freddie'd come home at five in the morning and he'd say, "Come on. Listen to this!"

He'd then read out the lyrics and he might say, "Look there are just three words that don't fit."

We could then spend a couple of hours trying to find other words that both rhymed and scanned that meant the same things as the words with which he was unhappy. And I mean a couple of hours. At least. It would often be daylight before he'd go to bed satisfied.

What started off as one idea might end up being the starting point of a better and different idea. He was completely pragmatic. Nothing was sacred. Everything was there to be used.

As I've said previously, he was very much the perfectionist. He would spend hours making sure that there was no better way of constructing the song, no better tune to express the feeling that he wanted to put over. His music first and foremost was for himself. It gave him the chance to express his feelings and be himself. Being a musician, he was in a position where other people could enjoy the results of his expression. Of course it mattered what the fans thought, but he wouldn't let anything pass muster that he wasn't a hundred per cent satisfied with himself. Although he was well aware that there were many different ways to say musically what was in his mind and that his end result might not be to the taste of others, it was his perfection he was seeking, not other people's. And after all, it was his music.

Once he'd got the tune sorted out in his mind, he'd put it down, record it, using the piano and then everyone else would listen to it. The rest of the band would then begin, under Freddie's supervision, to put their own contributions to the song down on tape on other tracks. This would start with Roger recording what Freddie called the 'click' track, the backbone of the song which was the basic beat against which Freddie would polish his initial piano track. Freddie always used to say that although drum-machines are *supposed* to be infallible, Roger could be *guaranteed* never to miss even one single beat.

Once this basic structure was sorted out, Freddie would begin the whole process of assembling all the other necessary components to achieve the song. No overall vision of how the song would ultimately sound ever arose before the very basic skeleton had been assembled. So often, the end result would bear little resemblance to the original concept. A prime example of this was 'Radio Ga Ga' which sounded to me when Roger played his initial tape more like the Ave Maria from Verdi's *Otello* – but that's to come. Incidentally, titles of tracks often changed between conception and fledging. 'Radio Ga Ga' on one of the original cassette boxes is called 'Radio Ca Ca'.

Freddie always liked the input from the rest of the band. He never believed his was the only, perfect way. Each Queen track is the result of four people's input even though it might be formally accredited as a composition to only one person. Of course, from *The Miracle* onwards, all tracks were credited to Queen collectively except on *Made In Heaven* but, again, that comes later.

Freddie never knew anyone better at working out harmonies than Brian and always relied on him for the end results where musical harmony was concerned. John was always John. Freddie knew John was like the proverbial rock and could always be relied on. The bass line was put on very close to the beginning after which the guide vocal track was laid down around which the other instrumental colouring and harmonies would be created.

This whole process could take months. Just because the band had started on a track didn't mean that they would carry it through to the end in one fell swoop. There would be times when they'd get fed up with a track and it would be left on the back burner. Anytime a new and exciting idea was brought into the studio, small developments were made to it so that the original thoughts wouldn't be lost and the band would always be in a position to come back to it. If for any reason at all, it was forgotten about, then the original idea couldn't have been much good anyway. Over the years, there were quite a few examples of ideas gathering dust on the shelves. Where these substandard and rejected ideas are now, who knows?

The atmosphere in the studio varied. It was often never the same two days in a row. Sometimes, you could sense the tension and the excitement when those who were there were really thrilled with an idea and other days, it could feel like a dull day at the office. You have to remember all the way through that the studio was their place of work. This was Queen's office.

There would always be at least three members of the road crew there. The three personal roadies (now called Technical Crew, 'Teks' for short), Ratty, Jobby and Crystal. Respectively, Peter Hince looked after John and Freddie's instruments, Brian Zellis was there for Brian May and the ubiquitous Chris Taylor was always there both for Roger and a good laugh! Crystal could always sense when tension was building up and would always be able to defuse most potentially explosive situations with a joke which brought a laugh. He also knew when not to be around, as did the rest of us. One learned very quickly. Of course there were the times when the explosions happened. One such being in Munich when, I forget which album, Brian was being very particular about his guitars and the stereo sound. It was something about not being loud enough because volume seemed to be the root cause of most of the arguments between the band members whether in the studio or on stage. Freddie on this occasion reached a point where he decided he couldn't take Brian's fussiness any more and he exploded. I think he must have seen a *Fawlty Towers* episode in the near past for he exclaimed: "What the fucking hell do you want, hey? A herd of wildebeest charging from one side to the other?" I believe with that, he turned on his heel and walked out. Collecting Freddie's utterances and sayings became a habit in the household and we would write them down, an example on my pad being: ". . . the diva of rock'n'roll and a mouth to gobble the Volga."

I have to emphasise that whoever their personal responsibility might be to, all these three foundation crew members were very fond of Freddie. I remember when the infamous Bill Reid was the boyfriend in attendance for one of the sessions in Montreux. Nobody liked him and nobody less than Crystal, Ratty and Jobby. Reid's very presence put their backs up to the point where they took great enjoyment winding him up. Bill Reid had a penchant for cocaine which was in extremely short supply in Switzerland. It was actually unobtainable. The lads used to make an obvious show of passing little packets to each other when Reid was in their vicinity and in the end he was convinced that they were excluding him from what he perceived was their enjoyment of an illicit drug. Matters then escalated to the point where he could stand being taunted no longer and complained to Freddie about his crew's cruel behaviour towards him.

Freddie, knowing nothing was going on because nothing could go on, was immediately dismissive. "Oh! Don't be so stupid!"

Another wheeze the lads dreamed up was that each time that Bill Reid was anywhere near any of them, they would start singing the Alfred Hitchcock theme. This came about because they thought Bill looked not unlike the cartoon caricature seen at the beginning of the television series *Alfred Hitchcock Presents*.

In Montreux, everyone including the tape-op made teas or coffees or large vodka-tonics as the band members required. The studios themselves were very quiet. For this reason, contradictorily, the band were not comfortable recording there all the time in the early days of their ownership of the place, precisely because of the complete lack of excitement. However, in the latter days, all the band, and especially Freddie, loved recording there precisely because it was so quiet and there were no distractions; no one there to come and ogle, stare and point at him. More often than not, food would be sent out for or they would all go out and have dinner before returning for a late session. In Musicland in Munich there was a fixed kitchen and on more than a few occasions my culinary skills were called upon to rustle up a simple little three course dinner for ten!

In Montreux, we stayed at the Montreux Palace Hotel which was at the opposite end of the town to the studios and it took us a good ten minutes to walk there. This gives you a good idea of both the size of Montreux and how quiet it was. Imagine Freddie walking for ten minutes across the centre of London! He did once try walking from Garden Lodge to Mary's flat in Phillimore Gardens but actually only managed to get part way up the top end of the Earls Court Road before he had to turn back and come home because even in that short distance, people had started to come up and ask him for autographs. He was never allowed to make it.

The band were already part of the Montreux municipal furniture as they were all recognised as being local businessmen and we know how much the Swiss like business.

There was no technical reason why the recording schedule was split between Munich and Montreux. A change of scene was as good a reason as any. In Munich, we were staying at the Munich Hilton where there was the PPP and the HH, the Presidential Poofter Parlour and the Hetero Hangout. Guess who was billeted where? No particular fuss was made over our being there. It was all part of a day's work, both for us and the hotel staff.

As far as the creation of other tracks on *Hot Space* is concerned, 'Staying Power' sticks in my mind and illustrates the degree of international to-ing and fro-ing that can be involved in making an album. One night I was told that the following morning I was booked on the eleven o'clock flight to New York to take a slave/master tape of 'Staying Power' to Arif Mardin in the Atlantic building. I gave Arif the tape about six p.m. He worked overnight so that he could record the brass arrangement he had written in order that I should be able to leave the morning after to return it for further work by the band in Europe.

Passing through the security metal-detector and the hand baggage X-ray on four separate occasions was no fun, trying to get officials to believe that what I was carrying was what it was and could not be exposed to possible electronic damage. "Please! It *must* be taken round the outside!"

Needless to say, I never let the package out of my sight. In existence, there must still be somewhere a version of the track with the alternative words which Freddie composed for 'Staying Power' . . . I think Fucking Power came into it somewhere. Follow the lyrics through and everywhere he sings, "I've got . . .", substitute 'fucking' for 'staying'!

We were still living the itinerant life of tax exiles having toured to promote *Hot Space*. Part of the American leg of that tour involved the band's use of a very special aeroplane. The plane which had been initially booked was found not to be airworthy and so a substitute was rented at very short notice from a very special place. The *Lisa Marie* was furnished by the Elvis Presley Organisation and we used this delightful personalised jet for several weeks. It was the closest Freddie ever got to meeting Elvis. It would have been his dream come true. At a later date, Lisa Marie actually gave Freddie a scarf which had once belonged to her father. It was a treasured possession, one which certainly did not end up in the loft!

In summer 1983 we moved to Los Angeles for an indefinite stay. An initial period of eight weeks had been mooted for the start of the recording of the album which would become known as *The Works*.

Brian, Roger and John, all being family men, had bought houses in Los Angeles to ease the emotional strains of being tax exiles. It was easier for them to be with their wives, partners and children and, obviously, these became the reasons why this next Queen album was being commenced in California. It was also Freddie's gesture of goodwill to the others because previously they had always acquiesced to his choice of recording location.

Our party, Freddie, Paul Prenter and I moved into a rented many-bedroomed mansion at 649 Stone Canyon Road, not far from the Bel-Air Hotel. We had been led to believe that previous occupants of the gigantic bed in the master suite included Elizabeth Taylor which especially thrilled Freddie who was the ultimate movie buff. More recently, George Hamilton had resided there while filming *Zorro The Gay Blade*. Mr Hamilton had apparently learned to crack his whip by the same pool around which we were to be found lounging so often. Coincidentally, by the way, the house was pink.

I was ensconced in the servants' quarters which suited me admirably as basically it was my own little house attached to the big one. Little did I know that it was a foretaste of what would be happening five years later when I was living in the mews house attached to Garden Lodge. We only had a few days to settle in before the first recording session was booked at the Record Plant in Hollywood. All the usual Queen road crew were there to give some familiarity to these new surroundings and Mack was there to lend continuity amongst the American studio personnel.

But a studio is a studio is a studio . . .

As usual there were no songs pre-written. The band knew this had to be a 'good' album because *Hot Space* had been, shall we say, generally less well-received than some of their previous albums. I don't know about any other bands, but with Queen, things followed a cycle. Product, reviews, sales, the reaction of both the public and the industry to their work. *Jazz* had been the first in the latest cycle. Sales had built up from the original Queen album but had dropped off at *Jazz*. They had built up again with *Live Killers* and *The Game*. These figures had continued rising until *Hot Space*, where sales fell off.

Because America is the largest market for any rock band, the performance of an album in that territory is always taken as the touchstone as to whether an album is 'good'. Freddie's maxim was the same whether it was to do with a show or a record and that was, "You're only as good as your last . . ." Whatever. He applied this literally to every one of his activities including the bedtime ones.

The record-buying population on either American coast was always receptive to Queen as this population was comparably more densely packed than the remaining three quarters of the American public who live in the middle of the continent and often in scattered communities. Large mixed communities are more prepared to accept the unusual. It takes a lot more to upset and shock the packed cities. Queen has always been a very radical band. A lot of the Queen phenomenon had, after all, been designed from the outset to be more than slightly shocking. However, as the band were soon to find out, it does not do to cross the people of what is commonly termed The Bible Belt of middle America. It is largely due to this population's rejection of the band – due to the horrified reaction to the video accompanying 'I Want To Break Free' – that Queen never toured America again. While Queen's records were still bought, sales were never quite as big again until the most recent Queen album, *Made In Heaven*.

Freddie's composition 'Keep Passing The Open Windows' was originally created for the film *Hotel New Hampshire*. Anyone who has read the book will remember that the song's title is a phrase of the dialogue which keeps cropping up. The film project had come about when the British film director Tony Richardson heard that the band was in Los Angeles. He approached Freddie and asked him if he would write some tracks for the film. 'Keep Passing' was intended to be the title track of the, as yet unmade, film. After hearing the finished track, although he liked it, Richardson decided that it would be easier – perhaps cheaper? – to use already composed classical music. Cheaper?

We were not amused.

"I'm not going to waste this track. It's going on the album!"

It was during this period that Freddie met up with Michael Jackson. Michael invited Freddie over to his house in Encino on Hayvenhurst Avenue. Freddie just couldn't believe what he saw. It was a brand new Tudor mansion! Security was incredibly tight. There was a tower at the entrance in which a burly guard or two sat menacingly. We had arrived in a hired limo. Just the two of us. Each window casement of the house was framed with a string of fairylights. This house was the predecessor of NeverLand and housed Michael's mini-zoo. He soon took us on a guided tour after he'd met us outside the house.

Michael was accompanied by the man who engineered at the recording studio attached to the house. Michael was very proud of the place and it was really quite fun having him as the tour guide. Although this was at the time when Michael's father was *persona non grata*, we were introduced to Michael's mother and his two sisters, Janet and Latoya. Michael's brothers of course all lived away from home with their own families.

We then had a tour of the house and en route visited the bedroom, where there was an enormous fish-tank which contained a large snake. Freddie, who did not like snakes in the slightest, noticed with great relief that the lid was secured tightly and was also weighed down by numerous bricks. While Michael adored his snake, he obviously preferred to be safe than sorry.

Freddie couldn't help noticing that Michael's bed was only a mattress and was on the floor.

"Why do you sleep on the floor!" Freddie exclaimed. "You can afford a bed, can't you?"

"I prefer to be closer to the earth," Michael replied in his soft, sing-song voice.

"But you're on the first floor!" Freddie retorted in amazement.

One thing that impressed Freddie was the way in which Michael had his triple platinum disc award for the album *Thriller* just leaning up against the wall in the bedroom. Freddie thought it showed great style. As Freddie himself was never one to show off, he used his own gold and platinum awards rather as wall covering as opposed to the trophies which some people's awards become.

Included in the tour was the video library which from what I could see contained just about everything which had ever been released on video including recent music work. There was a room which had a large TV monitor specifically for screening these tapes. There was also a vast room that contained numerous arcade video games. You have to remember that these were the days when *Moonbuggy* was the latest craze. Michael and I played against each other on one of these machines, a primitive version of tennis. There was a black paddle and a white paddle and these were manoeuvred to hit a white spot, the ball, back and forth. Unintentionally, Michael assumed the white paddle and I took the black and he remarked profoundly that we'd done a race reversal. I thought that was very touching.

Passing through the kitchen, Freddie finally plucked up the courage and asked Michael, "Would you mind if I have a cigarette?"

I was surprised that it had taken Freddie so long to ask. At that time, he was smoking something in the region of forty cigarettes a day. I could tell from this that Michael was obviously someone of whom Freddie was in awe because I'd never known him be so reticent before. This only happened once more to my knowledge but all that is to come . . .

"Yeah, sure," Michael said but he looked a little perplexed, the reason being that he did not own an ashtray. Help was at hand in the shape of Michael's mother who produced the lid of an empty preserve jar which Freddie could carry around with him.

One area of the house which Michael was very proud of was the cinema which doubled as a chapel for church on Sunday mornings.

Rather than Michael go to church, church came to Michael. I thought it was commendable that Michael had retained his faith to such an extent. It certainly was a very luxurious church with very comfortable seats set out in auditorium style.

The tour then took us outside into the grounds. Freddie was not prepared for what was to come. It was summer in LA and so Freddie was wearing a pair of clean white jeans. But they weren't to remain clean for long. We were taken through an extremely muddy enclosure where the llamas were kept. Freddie knew to be wary of them spitting at him but while avoiding their heads he couldn't help but walk through the mud. So, the clean white jeans and sparkling boots soon became very brown indeed as he picked his way as daintily as he could on tiptoe, shrieking at the horror of the mudbath. Michael, in plain jeans and T-shirt, was obviously used to it. In another part of this beautifully landscaped garden, swans were swimming in a large pond.

Eventually we got round to the purpose of our visit and ended up in Michael's studio. State-of-the-art everything. Except . . . Given that Freddie and Michael were the only people in the studio, there was a limited amount of musical instruments which could be used. Freddie of course was on piano and for want of another musician, I ended up playing the toilet door!

This came about when Michael wanted to do some work on a track that he had in mind that ultimately became 'Victory'. As there was no drummer around – or drums come to that – and Michael was not happy with the sound that the drum machine gave, he decided that the noise produced by the toilet door slamming was much more suited to his requirements. I therefore spent five minutes slamming this door in the necessary rhythm. I also know for a fact that somewhere in the world, there is a tape of Freddie Mercury peeing in Michael Jackson's toilet. Live! When I wasn't banging studio doors, I went and watched videos with Janet and Latoya. Food was sent out for from a local deli at about two in the afternoon even with all the facilities of that huge kitchen. Cold cuts arrived for Freddie and I while Michael had melon. About ten different varieties of melon which, in America, is always a delicious selection.

They worked on three tracks that afternoon. One, as I said, became 'Victory'. I'm unsure as to the second which I think was called 'State Of Shock' but the third was a track of Freddie's song 'There Must Be

More To Life Than This' which Freddie later included on *Mr. Bad Guy*. Freddie only played the piano on that track while Michael sang, composing his own lyrics as he went along. In essence, they were both trying each other out, dare I say, for size. They worked for about five or six hours that day and we left about six in the evening. Freddie was already committed to a heavy schedule and it was left as a 'Let's get in touch soon' job.

In the car on the way home, the post-mortem began. Can you blame us if we dished a little?

Freddie was impressed with the studio session and Michael's attitude to work but thought his taste in houses left a little to be desired!

"All that money and no taste, dear. What a waste."

So that was our day out in Encino.

As far as our social life was concerned in LA, Freddie preferred going to the bars as opposed to the dancing clubs. We even ventured as far afield as Silverlake where Freddie first espied the man who appeared to have all-over tåttoos. He was fascinated and it took him a while, over the course of a few weeks, to discover the full extent of the tattoos. He eventually found out that they were indeed *all*-over!

He frequented the Spike, The Eagle, The Motherlode and all the usual bars of Boystown, that part of the city of West Hollywood bounded by Doheny and Santa Monica Boulevard. On Sundays, we would go to the tea dances at clubs like Probe and Revolver. It was harder for Freddie to go to these latter places as they played music videos and sooner or later, there'd be mother, in his full glory with his anonymous cover blown to shreds.

One of the few record company people he got on with was the divine red-head Bryn Bridenthal who worked for Elektra Records which was still Queen's record company before they moved to Capitol. Vince, a barman from The Eagle on Santa Monica Boulevard, was Freddie's current beau. Even though it was only a short walk between the bars on this section of the strip, Vince came armed with a piece of equipment which Freddie just couldn't resist and which must have been all of seven hundred and fifty cc! I'm talking motorbikes here.

Freddie couldn't resist a man with a bike. In Dallas, for example, we had gone out to one of the bars in a twenty-five foot stretch limo and Freddie had picked up one such man with a bike. He insisted on returning to the hotel on the back of the bike, while I, in regal splendour, was ensconced in the back of the limo trailing the accelerating bike all the way home.

Freddie and Vince hit it off immediately and got on very well together. Vince was tall, chunky, with dark hair and a beard and I'm pleased to say that Freddie had found a friend. Vince wasn't overtly impressed by Freddie's fame. He wasn't going to make any allowances for Freddie who always had to wait until Vince's shift at the bar was over before they went on somewhere else. Freddie, of course, soon asked Vince to drop the bar work and come away with him on tour but Vince simply said no.

"I'm not prepared to give up my life for what could be six months before you tell me it's over and ship me back. Sorry, Freddie."

We all liked Vince a lot. Freddie never went back to LA to pick up any possibilities which might still have remained untidied. Basically he allowed Vince to get away.

But Vince was certainly around at Freddie's next big party which was the occasion of his thirty-seventh birthday, September 5, 1983, which was celebrated in Los Angeles.

Freddie wanted Joe Fanelli to cook for the party and Joe duly arrived from London. The occasion marked the rapprochement between Freddie and Joe who had been working independently as a chef in several London restaurants including September's in Fulham Road since the break-up of their relationship.

Jacqui Brownell, who worked at Elektra Records and who also looked after Roger's LA house as she was the downstairs tenant, had a female lover who became our cleaner at Stone Canyon Road. The lover had been at one stage of her career in charge of security at a San Francisco annual Gay Pride parade. These really are huge affairs and the responsibility was considerable. She had three or four of her friends become the waitresses for the night at the birthday bash, each dressed in white shirts and black trousers as they all pointblank refused to wear skirts for anyone.

Some of the hundred or so guests included Rod Stewart, Elton John and Queen's former manager John Reid, and Jeff Beck. Freddie was never into 'star' parties. For his personal parties, there was no current 'A' list. He always, always kept to friends.

The house was smothered with Stargazer lilies, those huge trumpet-like pink blooms with red-striped inner petals whose pollen always falls and always indelibly stains anything and anyone touching it. But for all that bother, the aroma is heavenly. No entertainment had been planned. This was a basic eat and drink and be-merry party. The food Joe prepared included Freddie's favourites. Prawn Creole, Coronation Chicken – that British Empire staple favourite – Potato Salad, Rice Salad and a huge array of cold cuts. The party was a welcome high-point partway through the recording schedule and all the band and their wives came.

But time came for the court of Queen to move on and they left LA and flew to Munich. It was during the completion of the recording of *The Works* in the Musicland Studios in Munich that Freddie first met Barbara Valentin who was to become so involved with his life from then on. The band rehearsed for their forthcoming world tour after completing *The Works* and it was also at this time that Freddie's love affair with Munich and all things Bavarian began in earnest.

One thing Bavarian we have already encountered for whom Freddie had fallen was Winfried Kirchberger, a restaurateur whose premises Freddie was to come to frequent nightly. Many a night was started there before continuing on to sample the delights of the multitude of Munich's bars like Pop-As, The Eagle and Mrs. Henderson's which was seen in its full glory in the video of 'Living On My Own'. Winfried, Winnie, fitted the bill in a very timely way. Freddie had just rid himself of that other Bill, the infamous Bill Reid whose exploits have already been briefly catalogued. Winnie was everything Freddie liked, chunky and hunky and a relatively blank slate, someone upon whom Freddie could leave his mark.

All the signs were that *The Works* was indeed, as planned, a 'good' album. Hopes were high. When 'Break Free', with its accompanying video images of Freddie and Roger and Brian and John in various states of character drag – Freddie especially pushing a vacuum cleaner – appeared, those high hopes were immediately dashed as far as America was concerned. Freddie found it very hard to understand how the band having fun and doing no one any harm could cause such an unfriendly backlash. *The Works* wasn't finally released until 1984 and for a couple of years, until Live Aid, it seemed the steam had gone out of the Queen engine after the failure of 'I Want To Break Free' in America. The previous single, 'Radio Ga Ga', had been a huge hit both in America as well as the rest of the world and Queen benefited from this impetus as they set out on the world tour promoting *The Works*.

The disappointment became contagious and the other members of Queen were very depressed. I think there must have been times when they could even have called it a day as far as Queen was concerned. Freddie, fired up anyway to pursue his solo project, thought that this was the right time to call for a Queen sabbatical. He wanted something the others didn't. A more up-beat, disco flavoured future and this direction was one the others weren't keen to follow, given the proven lack of success of the disco-inspired *Hot Space*.

Freddie started the series of recordings which ended up as *Mr. Bad Guy* financing it himself while Jim Beach set about finding the right distribution company with whom to work. Because of the strange nature of this whim of Freddie's – which Freddie never intended to result in a solo career – Jim's job to sign a one-off album deal with anyone must have been difficult. However, when the deal was completed with CBS it was for the highest single advance yet paid for one album. There must have been an option for more work, however, because Freddie ultimately bought himself out of the contract when it came time to consider an outlet for 'Barcelona'.

Over an extended period in Munich – like monntthhssss – Freddie created what he considered some of his best tracks. Produced by Freddie and Mack, the album was recorded at Musicland Studios. His favourite track varied each time he played the album but he was especially proud of 'Mr. Bad Guy' with its integral multi-layered orchestration. Freddie did all the vocals and most of the piano and synthesiser work which American Fred Mandel augmented where the music was most complicated. Fred had been auxiliary keyboard player on a couple of Queen tours and he and Freddie had developed a very friendly rapport. Paul Vincent played some lead guitar and bass guitar was played by Stefan Wissnet whom Freddie had got to know while Stefan had been Musicland's engineer. Joe Burt, one of Mary Austin's boyfriends, played fretless bass on 'Man Made Paradise' . . . It was all very much in-house. As the dedication implies, the rest of Queen stayed tactfully away.

'Love Me Like There's No Tomorrow' was written with Barbara Valentin specifically in mind. Barbara is an actress and one of her more celebrated roles was in a film whose translated title becomes, *Kiss Me Like There's No Tomorrow*. Not all of Freddie's songs were about specific people although like every composer, he had these aberrations from time to time!

We stayed at the Arabellahaus Hotel, a depressing concrete block of a building from the top of which numerous people had both success-fully and unsuccessfully attempted suicide because life there was so bleak. Thinking back on the place, it wasn't the most conducive environment to encourage the flow of creative juices. Freddie loathed it because of the continuous aroma of Arabic cooking. The middle-Eastern residents had taken to cooking on portable stoves in the hallways so that the smells wouldn't permeate their living space. But screw anyone else's sensibilities!

However, the Arabellahaus was convenient, for it was a part of the complex containing the studio, although Freddie's dislike of staying there soon caused him to move in to Winnie's apartment which was in the heart of old Munich, the area containing all the easily walkable gay bars which Freddie loved, including the 'Frisco and the New York.

It was the first time Freddie had ever lived with anyone else under a roof that wasn't his own and even though he expected me to go in everyday and do the laundry and clear up after him, he was happy with Winnie. He took a great delight in living with someone. He always knew in the back of his mind that if the worst came to the worst there was always the hotel or Barbara's apartment to fall back on and so he knew he was safe but it was the only time in his adult life that he knew what it was like to live a relatively ordinary life with another man.

He must have felt safe because it was while living with Winnie that on two occasions Barbara, who had been called first by Winnie, telephoned me to go over to help Freddie who had seemed to have suffered a sort of fit.

He had apparently just blacked out but then had displayed symptoms of severe shaking. We just had to hold him steady and still until the tremors passed whereupon he would regain consciousness. Doctors were obviously called and they diagnosed the results of too much alcohol and use of drugs. Freddie being Freddie merely brushed the episodes aside when we asked him about them and how he was feeling. There was no pattern for these attacks and Freddie displayed no concern. He was quite, quite happy with his life as it was.

Maybe it appeared to take so much longer to record the *Mr. Bad*

Guy album than an average Queen album because there was only the input from one direction. Four people's involvement may indeed be more constructive and productive even though causing a greater degree of friction. Too many cooks can occasionally turn out the perfect broth! When it's down to just one person, there is no one else to point out the weaknesses or errors and supply alternatives and also no one else to blame if the decisions are wrong. When Freddie was working on his own, the results had to be even better than perfect. I have to add that both Mack and Stefan Wissnet, producer and engineers respectively, did fulfil to an extent the function of absent band members as far as supportive creative input was concerned.

That *Mr. Bad Guy* was not patently as successful as any other Queen album did not phase Freddie at all. He was not expecting it.

He knew that when any individual band member breaks away from an established unit, the end result is never as accepted a product by the general public as the band product. The buyers of Freddie's album would in the main be Freddie fans after all and Freddie, as he preferred, was only one quarter of Queen. The disco direction of the material would surely have deterred the heavier rock fans in the massive Queen following. There are the obvious exceptions to this pattern of course, notably Sting and Phil Collins.

During his stay in Munich for *Mr. Bad Guy*, Freddie had been introduced to a petite American singer who I believe was working with Mack at his Musicland Studio. During conversation, she had mentioned that she really admired Freddie and his music and so Mack, as per his métier, engineered a meeting. Freddie met Jo Dare one evening at a city restaurant. He was really taken with her. They shared the same mischievous sense of humour and Freddie readily agreed to do some work on the album she was recording. She was one of the comparatively few people in the music business, other than Billy Squier of course, whose career, in the time I knew Freddie, he kept abreast of. As he did with Billy, Freddie provided Jo with some vocals and helped with a few compositional ideas when she became stuck. He really got a kick out of doing it. Perhaps if his life had been different, production might have been a direction he would have taken when his performing days were over.

A footnote to this period of individual recording comes in the small but perfectly formed person of David Geffen behind whom Freddie and I found ourselves seated on one transAmerican flight. Geffen turned round part way through the flight and very ostentatiously flung open his cheque book.

"I want you to sing on my label," he announced. "Just fill in the amount yourself!"

Freddie didn't. He was, for one of the very few occasions in my knowledge, stuck for words. The reason he didn't take up the pen is one he would never be stuck for and that was his loyalty to the band and the institution of Queen. He knew he could never leave.

Although in the first part of 1985 Queen as individuals seemed to be as musically far apart as they had ever been, there was still the lure of a good offer and the chance of doing another film soundtrack was too good to be missed. The recordings for the film *Highlander* thus became the basis for their next album, *A Kind Of Magic* which more directly came about as a result of the Live Aid concert in July 1985. Part way through the year, at a point where Freddie was distinctly bored, prospects brightened when an invitation arrived through the promoter Harvey Goldsmith to appear at a concert which Harvey, Bob Geldof and Midge Ure were organising to aid famine relief work in Ethiopia.

At first, Freddie didn't think too much of the idea, thinking it was just another of those self-aggrandizing manoeuvres for publicity purposes. After a short period of time when news filtered through of the actual scale and importance of the show vis-à-vis the huge worldwide television coverage involved, the band wholeheartedly agreed to participate. You have to remember that at this point they weren't really into doing anything as Queen.

The band were given a twenty minute slot just like everybody else. Then the hard part came trying to decide what to perform to give the very best of Queen in twenty minutes when one of their shows which obviously showed the band at its very best normally took anything up to two hours. They decided on the content and running order of the set and stuck to that throughout rehearsals even though, as we all know, Brian and Freddie came on again later in an auxiliary spot to sing 'Is This The World That We Created?'

I think the reason that Queen came off best from that concert on the day was due to their professionalism and their instinctive realisation that even for a twenty minute set, extensive rehearsals are a hundred per cent necessary. It would never have occurred to them not to rehearse.

The band hired the Shaw Theatre on Euston Road and rehearsed solidly for a week. It was a mini-tour atmosphere which was created, their appearance having brought back so many of the tour crew like Gerry Stickells from America as well as Trip Khalaf and Jim Devenney, taking care of the outfront sound and stage monitors respectively as well as the sound and lighting crew the band already knew.

The resulting publicity from the Live Aid appearance made the band aware that they were still wanted and brought about a change in their thinking regarding their future as Queen. So, while it wasn't exactly as reported in the press that the band thought they would 'cash in' on their renaissance, it certainly became the platform for a new adventure and got their creative juices flowing.

'One Vision' was the first track, which was subsequently used on the film *Iron Eagle*. I imagine the inspiration came from the Live Aid experience because ultimately, Freddie's original opinion on the gig was worn away and he actually appreciated what the whole project was about. Freddie was always of the opinion that there were at least two motives for anything; he was a cynic in the true sense of the word. The band really loved getting back to work as Queen, instead of just fulfilling their solo ambitions.

'One Vision' was begun in Munich at Musicland Studios and the association with the cinema was continued when 'Who Wants To Live Forever', 'Gimme The Prize', 'Don't Lose Your Head' and 'Princes Of The Universe' were used in the hugely popular film *Highlander* starring Christopher Lambert and Sean Connery.

This album also furnished another of the band's crowd-pleasing anthems, namely 'Friends Will Be Friends'. The co-composition credit on this track and on 'Pain Is So Close To Pleasure' was merely because John Deacon insisted that Freddie's contribution be recognised and acknowledged. John's honesty and integrity would not have allowed him to do otherwise.

It appears that all bands travel the recording road with one producer for a while until the ideas from their collaboration have been exhausted and so after five albums, Dave Richards took over the role of nanny, which is basically what the co-producer on any of the Queen albums had to do for the band.

After *A Kind Of Magic* and the tour promoting that album, once again Queen as a collective went their separate ways to pursue their individual projects.

I really don't know when Freddie and Dave Clark first met but word came to Freddie that Dave Clark would like to have Freddie involved in a project that he had initiated. His show, *Time*, was already a hit in London's West End at The Dominion Theatre, starring Cliff Richard. Dave wanted an album made of the songs but had decided not to make it one of the routine 'cast albums' because these were usually made on a Sunday, the cast's day off and the quality tended to suffer a little.

Dave hit upon the idea of having guest singers of celebrity status to participate in the recording of the show's songs. Freddie was approached and performed three songs one of which was pronounced so good that it was released as a single, entitled 'Time' on the EMI label. It wasn't the first time Freddie had contributed a couple of songs to the soundtrack of a show. A couple of years earlier in 1984, Freddie had been approached by Giorgio Moroder, Mack's partner who successfully persuaded him to sing two tracks on his new musical reworking of Fritz Lang's classic film *Metropolis* which was re-released to cinemas in its newly colourised state. Although there was an album released of the *Metropolis* soundtrack, Freddie's contributions, one of which was called 'Love Kills' were never included by him anywhere else. Freddie was not usually one to show interest in singing other people's songs. He had to have a personal involvement as well.

It was during these *Time* sessions with Dave Clark that Freddie started what was to become his close musical partnership with Mike Moran. Other than being associated with Lynsey de Paul and the Eurovision Song Contest, Mike was celebrated for having originally been associated with Blue Mink, the famous Seventies band of top session musicians which included Messrs Greenaway and Cook and Madeleine Bell. Mike is one of the music world's gentlemen. He is also an amazing technician, can play keyboards like you wouldn't believe and has his feet planted firmly on the ground. He has been professionally involved with just about all of the luminaries of the London musical stage and has created a lot of music for use on television and, when Freddie met him, was playing keyboards for the *Time* sessions at the Abbey Road Studios of EMI.

For all Freddie's talents and ability, he found working entirely on his own very difficult. He had to have a sounding board. Perhaps it was that he didn't have enough self-confidence in his own abilities? All the songs he had created before now had always been the result of collaboration with the rest of Queen, except of course for his own album, *Mr. Bad Guy*. That was the way they worked. He wasn't a hundred per cent sure of his own judgements. But, as has been shown, given the right set of circumstances, the most amazing work could be produced. It's like Freddie was the firework that needed to be lit but which once up in the sky explodes into all those glorious colours. You know the one, always the biggest one at the climax of the display.

In the relationship with Mike Moran, there was outwardly no boss. I think that both parties admired each other for different talents and abilities. Freddie, amongst the rest of the world, found it difficult to believe what Mike Moran could do with his fingers. For those who have not been fortunate enough to be a witness in my position, I can only confirm that given any keyboard, Mike Moran can play up a masterpiece. For one of Freddie's birthdays, Mike gave him a cassette on which was written simply, 'Happy Birthday'. However, on the tape he had taken the familiar 'Happy Birthday' theme and then created half-a-dozen variations in the styles of different composers. Quite superb. Freddie just threw up his arms in joy as he listened to it. I think Freddie really enjoyed this collaboration because the end results were achieved without confrontation whereas so much of Queen's work, although superb, was coloured with the memories of confrontation and conflict. It was because of the prospect of argument and disharmony that on occasion Freddie would refuse to go to the studio.

Freddie and Mike had been in the music business for approximately the same amount of time and they were equals. While Freddie had the more meteoric rise, Mike Moran had been a mainstay and continual presence behind more famous artists than himself. Mike was also quite content to allow Freddie to do the shining in public.

So, it should not come as any great surprise that the next product of this burgeoning partnership was one of Freddie's great joys, 'The Great Pretender'. This was recorded in early 1987 in Mike's studio in his old house in Radlett in Hertfordshire. Freddie went off with Peter Straker late one morning with Terry driving them without really letting us at the house in on 'the secret'.

Much later that night, he came back, obviously thrilled, pissed out of his brain, clutching a copy of his day's work and played us the rough mix of 'The Great Pretender'. I don't know that the original plan was ever to release it as a single, but over a short period it became apparent from the comments from everyone who heard it that this version of the song had prospects. Perhaps one of the main reasons it was released was because Freddie already had his idea of what was to happen in the video and so, obviously, the only way to make a video practical was to release a single. Even Freddie, while having enough money to do it, wasn't silly enough to spend a huge amount of money to make a video just to make a video. That vain he wasn't! By March 'The Great Pretender' had reached number five in the national charts.

In the context of studio recording, I have to mention Scrabble. Whenever boredom threatened to raise its ugly head, the Scrabble board was brought out and anybody available was press-ganged into playing. Freddie didn't care how many people played just as long as the game was in progress. Quite often there would be four teams with two or three people on each team. He insisted no one was left out from tape-op to other superstars. I suppose it must have been the boarding school upbringing again but he was quite ruthless when playing and also, if truth be known, wasn't the most gracious of losers. Dictionaries were only ever used, however, after the fact. Just to check. Having said all this, Freddie wasn't on the losing team very often. He had a very good mind, not only for the words themselves but also for their most advantageous placing. We started to take Travel Scrabble with us at one point but the flights weren't really long enough – especially Concorde ones – for him to get bored.

Whenever he caught me playing solitaire or patience in the studio, he regarded it as a waste of time and that other things should be being done with that time. He himself was entirely uninterested in card games. Any games. Anything where memory was a requirement. With Scrabble, everything was in front of him, not unlike the elements and intricacies of a studio's sound desk and the contents and whereabouts of all the tracks. It was, after all, only a matter, like Scrabble, of configuring your assets to greatest advantage.

We now progress to what I believe was the pinnacle of his solo work. It is in recounting the recording of his *Barcelona* album that I can go into greatest detail about Freddie and the way he worked because it is unalloyed by any overall Queen consideration or involvement. This album above all others was something he and only he wanted to do. He didn't do this album to rake in a fortune. It was done purely for his own delectation and where it led, he didn't care. As you will see, it was an entirely different recording process to any he had previously encountered. It was almost as though he was growing up. If Queen were his childhood playmates, *Mr. Bad Guy* and 'The Great Pretender' were his rebellious teenage, then *Barcelona* was the final flowering of the grown man and it's the grown man who then went on to record *The Miracle* and *Innuendo*.

It must also be borne in mind that although nobody else knew, perhaps Freddie was getting an inkling that all was not well with his health. In hindsight, he often said that he had thought that *Barcelona* might be his last work and so of course he was thrilled when he made it through *The Miracle*. He never even dreamed that he would see *Innuendo* completed.

Barcelona was his essence. Because it was a record he desperately wanted to make, he was determined that it was to contain the best of Freddie Mercury he could offer. After all, it could have been his memorial.

Although a great deal of Freddie's work had been considered as operatic, he in fact knew very little about opera and even less about opera singers although by the time *Barcelona* came about, I could recognise many similar traits between the diva of the opera stage and the diva of rock'n'roll.

For the following recording I am prepared to accept either the blame or the praise. Up until early 1981, Freddie had a passion for the voices of operatic tenors, mainly Luciano Pavarotti. He was always taken aback at the control that tenors maintained over their voices, the only operatic vocal range in which at that point he had any interest. He realised that this was the culmination of years of training for most of them and was fully appreciative of the result, particularly the way some could produce high notes extremely softly. Now, that was control as far as he was concerned.

Until January 1981, he had only heard Pavarotti's voice on disc or tape or perhaps, occasionally, on television and so as I became aware of Pavarotti's appearance at the Royal Opera House in Covent Garden that month, I persuaded Freddie to put his money where his mouth was and Freddie subsequently bought some tickets for the opera.

As we took our seats all dressed to the nines in evening clothes, I gave him a rough outline of the plot of *Un Ballo In Maschera* by Giuseppe Verdi. He was excited at the prospect of hearing his hero live. Freddie was used to recording and then going out on tour to reproduce the recordings live. With Queen in particular, they tried to ensure that the live version was easily recognisable and comparable with the studio version. Freddie now wanted to see if that was the same in opera. The lights went down and in this particular opera, the tenor has his first big aria in the first scene. Freddie really enjoyed it. During the scene change, I explained to him the action moves to a Gypsy Fortune Teller's camp where the heroine makes a brief appearance trying to find some herbs to make her fall out of love.

"Well I *certainly* don't need any of *those*, do I?" piped up the voice beside me. The scene began and the soprano made her unheralded entrance. While the piece that she sings is only a small trio, this soprano certainly made her presence felt. Freddie watched and listened spellbound. The soprano sailed and soared through the trio which exploited much of her talent and range and power. At the end when the heroine slips away, Freddie's jaw had dropped and he applauded wildly. Once the applause stopped, he broke all opera house tradition and started talking, asking me, "Who *is* this woman . . . What's her name? . . . Tell me . . ." His words almost tumbled out, so excited had he been. I looked in the programme just to double-check. It was indeed, as I had thought, Montserrat Caballe.

It was Montserrat who had been a major contributor to my own love of opera as on April 22, 1975, my first night of work at the Royal Opera House, she was singing the role of Leonora in *Il Trovatore*. It was a coincidence that Freddie's favourite aria in opera was to be 'D'Amor Sull'Ali Rosee' as sung by Montserrat on one of her early opera aria discs. Having fallen in love with her voice, Freddie took great pleasure in taking the disc into the studio with him, putting it on a turntable, plugging it into the main speakers and turning it up full volume. It amused him to hear the orchestra members' seats making a noise and the pages of the score being turned.

"My god, this is real! You couldn't fake those noises."

He learned a lot about her voice this way as prior to our night at the opera he had shown little interest in female voices. His love for Montserrat's voice never diminished but it wasn't until 1986 when he was on tour in Spain that he made his admiration public on Spanish Radio. When asked by the interviewer whose voice he most admired, I believe the expected answer was to have been Aretha Franklin, Michael Jackson or Prince. He surprised everybody by saying that it was Montserrat's. He accentuated the fact that he was not being patronising just because she was Catalan and he was being interviewed in Barcelona.

Freddie thought nothing more of it until Jim Beach came to him saying that he had been approached by Carlos Caballe, Montserrat's brother and manager and Pino Sagliocco who was Queen's concert promoter in Spain and who had first been inspired to approach Carlos Caballe.

The idea was, what did Freddie think of the idea of writing an anthem for the Barcelona Olympic Games for Montserrat to sing? At first Freddie was very unsure, even a little scared. This was asking him to do something for someone he had admired for so long. It was also a new direction for him, specifically writing with someone else in mind, particularly someone with whom he had never worked before.

Eventually, with all the powers of persuasion applied to him on one side by Jim Beach and the nagging voice of me on the other, he succumbed and the project was agreed. The original idea was to produce a single which would be entitled 'Barcelona', that could be used as a theme for the Olympic Games, to be sung at their opening. Even so, that didn't prevent Freddie coming up with ideas above and beyond the call of duty.

A meeting was arranged at which Freddie could meet and present some ideas to Montserrat. He knew her capabilities well by now, having listened to so many of her recordings and after the idea had been finalised, Montserrat had kindly picked a selection of her performances and sent him some video copies that were not available to the general public and, in his turn, Freddie had sent her a full collection of his work including his latest work, his recreation of the classic rock song, 'The Great Pretender'.

Freddie knew within himself how much he wanted to make Montserrat do. He wanted to push her to her limits but in the best possible way. He had a few weeks to get the germs of some ideas down on tape to take with us to Barcelona where the meeting had been arranged. Much the same as now, everything had to be organised around Montserrat in that she was hardly ever at home. If you want to get in touch with Montserrat, try anywhere around the world where she is so much in demand. As you will see in the recounting of the recording, Montserrat is a workaholic, one of the things which she has in common with Freddie.

Mike Moran was the first to be taken on board. Because of the relationship which had developed between the two, Freddie found it easy to collaborate with this genial gentleman. By doing so, the responsibility of some of the difficult intricacies of orchestration was removed from Freddie's shoulders. This initial collaboration with Mike produced a cassette of three very rough tracks. One of these became 'Exercises In Free Love' which then became 'Ensueno' on the *Barcelona* album. The other two were the basic format of 'The Fallen Priest' and, similarly, 'Guide Me Home' which Mike had put together with Freddie using a falsetto voice to approximate to Montserrat's part.

Mike Moran, Freddie, myself, Jim Beach and Terry flew into Barcelona the day before that auspicious meeting in March 1987 and stayed at the Ritz hotel. As you might imagine, the talk over dinner that night was of little else but Montserrat.

"What's she doing now."

Probably eating, Freddie.

"No, but is she watching television as well?"

Probably, Freddie.

What Freddie didn't know was that very night Montserrat was in fact giving a recital in a town just outside Barcelona.

The hotel arranged for a very basic, hi-fi, speaker system to be placed in the Garden Room of the hotel where there was a grand piano in the corner.

After a very restless night, we all gathered in Freddie's room. I don't think I have seen Freddie more nervous than he was that morning. As we went to the lift to go downstairs for lunch, he looked like the condemned man being led from his cell. At one point – and I really don't know even now whether or not he was serious – he even said, "Come on. I can't go on with this. Let's go home!"

The lunch had been arranged for one o'clock. We walked into the room perhaps five minutes early. There to greet us was a vast circular table with a huge centrepiece which blocked the vision of anyone sitting opposite. That was soon removed. Freddie picked his seat and wouldn't move. I had ensured that he had two packets of cigarettes with him as he was smoking rather a lot at this point. He wasn't necessarily inhaling very much but he found cigarettes were the easiest things to use to keep his hands occupied. I was not permitted to sit down as every two or three minutes I was asked to go to the door to see if she was coming yet. I only had to go to the door three times and on the third visit, a wonderful sight presented itself. Without being disrespectful to Montserrat, the scene that I saw reminded me of the lyrics of an old song often sung by Joyce Grenfell which began, "Stately as a galleon, she sailed across the floor . . ."

As Montserrat's procession advanced, the pathway opened before her. People stood back. You must appreciate that particularly in Catalonia, Montserrat is more than a queen. She is the supreme symbol of Catalan culture. She was dressed in a knee-length frock in colours and design entirely reminiscent of a Spanish spring. With Montserrat were her manager Carlos, Pino Sagliocco whose idea the project had been and her niece, Montsy, who was my counterpart both in the court of Montserrat and also that day at lunch, when, that is, I was finally permitted to sit down.

Freddie didn't know what to do.

He could meet Michael Jackson whom he respected. That was fine. But although Freddie was a huge, huge star himself, I don't think he ever got over an inherent shyness which had been with him all his life. I know that nothing at boarding school takes into account anybody's fear of being themselves in social situations. Shyness can be crippling and Freddie felt it acutely. I can understand his feeling because while I have played video games and met some of the greatest names in rock music, someone finally arranged for me to meet a not-particularly-famous English opera singer whose career I had followed for many years. When I was led into her presence, I became a gibbering wreck. All I could mumble was, "Oh, it was brilliant."

Freddie was now meeting *his* idol. It was an incomparable moment, one for which nothing could have possibly prepared him.

She swept into the room through double doors. Freddie jumped up from his seat and after shaking hands, he ushered her to her seat next to him. He said simply, "Hello, I'm Freddie Mercury and that's it. We've started!" and then sat down.

While Jim Beach and Carlos had met prior to the lunch and were able to carry on a conversation, it took Freddie and Montserrat a few minutes to gauge each other but once the ice had properly been broken, there was no stopping them especially after a glass of Louis Roederer Cristal champagne. After discovering her love of this champagne to which he had introduced her, Freddie delighted in sending Montserrat a full case on her next birthday.

Once the initial awkwardness had been overcome, it took Freddie and Montserrat about five minutes flat to discover that they shared a wicked sense of humour and the pair started talking nineteen to the dozen. There was much giggling and talking with their hands to make up what they couldn't manage to say due to their babbling torrent of words. They were each trying to communicate in three hours what they'd have liked to have been saying for three months. Montserrat had been kind enough to let Freddie know that she really did only have three hours to spare before her prior commitments to a rehearsal called her away.

I was instructed to start the tape ten minutes later and the tape was played and rewound, played and rewound several times. The tracks were listened to in silence the first time. On second playing, comments were passed about specific parts that they liked and then other people chimed in with their opinions. Finally they were ready for the food to be brought in at about two-thirty. Strict instructions had been given that no dining staff could be present until called for.

These musical ideas were there so that the best of them could be taken for a record which, to Freddie's mind at that time, would consist of the A and B sides of a single, the 'Barcelona' track and another, although at that point 'Barcelona' as such did not exist. It could have been, for example, that the music for what was to become 'The Fallen Priest' could have ended up as 'Barcelona'. Everything at that point was up in the air. It was when lunch was being eaten that talk turned to how long it took Freddie to record an album . . . An album?

It was at this point when Montserrat enquired, "An album? What do you mean by an album?"

Freddie said, "Oh, you know! You've done them. Eight or nine tracks on one disc. That's an album."

Montserrat said, "Fine. That is what we will do. An album."

So, in the space of two hours, Freddie's pet project quadrupled in size and once more he wasn't sure whether he wanted to do it or not. He wasn't certain that he could come up with enough ideas.

Straight after eating, Mike Moran and Montserrat went to the piano because she wanted to try out the *vocalise*, 'Exercises In Free Love'. She only had a short time to spare before her rehearsal and in that time, she decided that she would come back to the hotel after the rehearsal was over. Mike Moran was given four hours to completely transcribe the song from tape onto manuscript paper. She duly returned with Montsy to spend the ensuing few hours trying out 'Exercises In Free Love' to see how well it suited her voice. When she had exhausted Mike Moran, she left, taking the manuscript with her. He hadn't even photocopied it.

Freddie's party flew back to London, exhausted but elated. He couldn't wait to get to work. Freddie went into the Townhouse Studio and started work straightaway.

At the end of the week, Montserrat flew into town because she was giving a recital at Covent Garden which she naturally insisted Freddie attend. This time there were about six of us in the party including Mike Moran. Jim Hutton and Joe were there, as well as myself. The arrangement was that in return for Freddie attending upon her at her recital, she would attend upon Freddie for a post-performance supper at his home, Garden Lodge in Kensington.

To Freddie's surprise, towards the end of Montserrat's show, Mike Moran made his excuses and left his seat, saying, "Sorry. Gotta go to the loo."

Well into her encores, Montserrat stopped and announced, "Now, we have a change of pianist. I am now going to perform a song for the first time in public. It has been composed by someone whose name you might know but not from inside this opera house and who just happens to be sitting over . . . there!" She pointed at Freddie and at the same moment Mike Moran walked on stage and Freddie wished that the ground could have been opened up. You have to realise that in opera houses, during recitals, lights are never dimmed totally and Freddie was fully visible, dressed as he was in a pale blue suit.

Montserrat made him stand up and take a bow, which he very reluctantly did and then tried to hide in his seat. She then proceeded to sing 'Exercises In Free Love' which, unknown to Freddie, she had been rehearsing intensely the whole of the previous week. While the audience reaction couldn't be described as ecstatic, it showed many people there a fact that few realised. Music is very difficult to categorise. Freddie least of all ever dreamed that something that he wrote would ever be performed in such an august hall. To me, that night just went to show that music is music, whoever composes it.

The arrangement on departure was that Freddie would go straight off home to get the supper ready! I was to accompany Montserrat. She said she was going to execute her version of Freddie's "Take the money and run" scenario after the concert which meant in her world that she would not as per normal stand at the stage door signing autographs. For some reason, though, some two hundred people found their way to her dressing room so she took the money and ran about an hour and a half later!

The Opera House had tried to facilitate her exit by arranging for her car to be parked outside the back door but this all had to change when, ten minutes later, Montserrat, Montsy and I were scrambling over scaffolding and holes in the ground as the Opera House staff had forgotten to mention that some reconstruction had begun.

We eventually got to Garden Lodge with much laughter en route in the car about midnight. I heard later that Freddie had been pacing the kitchen wondering whether he'd been stood up.

After dinner, Freddie fully expected Montserrat to take up her wrap and go. Instead she asked where the cigarettes were and wanted to know what work he had done in the week since she had seen him. He was actually very honest and admitted that not a lot had come out of his week's work but because Mike Moran was there he would be happy if Mike wanted to play the ideas on his piano, the same piano incidentally that Freddie had used to write 'Bohemian Rhapsody'.

Little did Freddie know it but this was to be the start of a mammoth session even by his own standards.

On my tape of the evening, there are snatches of various melodies, some of which were to be later used on the album *Barcelona* including the title track which had emerged in the last week at the Townhouse Studio in London's Goldhawk Road. Freddie was constantly asking Montserrat if she was okay and shouldn't she be going home because she had a flight to catch at eight-thirty and she would reply by asking for another cigarette at which Freddie would burst out laughing. Afterwards, Freddie told me that it was one of his most enjoyable times because he had got to know his idol and they spent five hours having fun. If you were able to hear the tape, you would be caught up with the infectious laughter and the good time that was had by us all.

Because of Montserrat's work schedule, Freddie's work on the album was almost dictated for him. He knew the first track had to be 'Barcelona' as it had to be ready for the submission of all the prospective anthems to the city because the selected anthem would have to be finished for the arrival of the Olympic Flag in Barcelona in 1988, four years before the actual games.

In some ways, recording for this album was a lot less strenuous than with most Queen albums both because of Freddie's inspiration from Montserrat personally and also his dedication to and passion for the project as a whole. A lot of the material can and must be looked at as autobiographical as this album mirrored exactly the real Freddie Mercury.

Freddie knew that he would only ever be able to have Montserrat for perhaps two days every other month. Montserrat knew her commitments as with all opera stars had been organised on a schedule of anything up to five years ahead. Therefore, Freddie's method was going to have to change drastically.

The way he went about this was to record a complete track minus Montserrat's vocal. He would then, with his vocal track already completed, use his falsetto voice to put a guide vocal track in for her. He would do this for maybe two songs and then with the voice part on manuscript, send these off to Montserrat in time for her to look over them before her arrival in London. It was actually during the recording that their relationship changed a little. After the first session, where Montserrat put her vocals down on 'Barcelona', Freddie clapped his hands with joy and exclaimed, "This is it! I've got it. I have *her* voice on *my* tape. I now have *her* voice!" You could see in his face what that really meant to him after all the years of admiring her, he now had trapped that fabulous voice. He listened to the tape over and over again and was once again awestruck with what Montserrat was capable of doing. It seems strange but from then on, he found it more and more difficult to talk to her and a lot of what he wanted her to know, he would tell me and then I would tell her. It was like the awe had overtaken him and he felt he wasn't able to talk freely to her again. This by no means diminished their working relationship and with each track which she completed for him, he grew more and more ecstatic.

I think it was more through pressure of time than his inability to write all the words that he used others to assist him with some lyrics. Tim Rice, of course, he had met while working with Elaine Paige on her album of Queen songs. Because he had offered 'Ensueno' to Montserrat as a present those months before in Barcelona, he asked her to provide the words for that song which is the one track out of the seven on the album where they were both at the microphone at the same time. To many this might sound incredible but with modern recording techniques, believe me *anything* is possible.

It was on this track that Montserrat made Freddie sing in his natural voice which, as you can hear, is a baritone rather than the forced tenor which he naturally used because it delivered what was expected of a pop/rock'n'roll vocal performance. Again, it was a time when he found out the benefits of having had singing lessons for many, many years. One of the main things teachers impart to their pupils is the ability to control which Freddie, never having had a singing lesson in his life, wasn't able to master. So, at the point where the voices get quieter and quieter, while Montserrat stood still at the microphone, Freddie had to take steps further and further away from the mike so that the voice faded through distance rather than control as he exhaled. As Tim Rice said, "Freddie had an amazing set of pipes", but while never really showing off, Freddie knew he had an amazing voice which he realised came to him naturally. Although he wasn't around to hear it, I think even he would have been astounded at how almost all the vocalists in the Aids Awareness concert following his death had to drop the pitch several tones in order to perform his songs.

The song 'Barcelona' basically describes his admiration of Montserrat whom he saw as the embodiment of not only her native city but the spirit of a people. 'La Japonaise' expresses his love for all things Japanese, his own 'living treasure' on earth. Freddie found a Japanese translator in England who not only translated his lyrics into Japanese but also wrote them out phonetically for him and Montserrat to sing. 'The Fallen Priest' was most theatrical due to Tim Rice's input but it does mirror his love of the operatic and the theatrical. It was Freddie's contribution to grand opera other than 'Bohemian Rhapsody'. The upbeat side of 'The Golden Boy', 'Guide Me Home' and 'How Can I Go On?' showed his appreciation of gospel and the deeply personal aspects of writing and composing.

There were a couple of other ideas which Freddie would like to have attempted with Montserrat at this time, one of which was a recording of 'La Barcarole' from Offenbach's *The Tales Of Hoffman* but due to Montserrat's restricted time availability, this was put on the back burner, possibly for a later date. Montserrat, for her part, adored the upbeat side of the album and wanted to attempt more in this direction as it was so new and strange and wonderful to her. The whole project excited her. There is a point in 'Barcelona' when he made her 'trill' in harmony with her own track, layer upon layer upon layer and she was thrilled with this, having never had occasion to do it before.

Montserrat became very emotional at the first playback of 'How Can I Go On?' because of the sentiment and the sound of Freddie's voice talking the lines that she sings after her. Tears flowed down her cheeks and almost brought tears to Freddie's eyes as he saw the depth of her emotion. Perhaps he too was actually listening to the words for the first time rather than living inside them.

While *Barcelona* took a lot out of him, it showed him how much music there was still inside him and Queen therefore once again embarked on the recording of another album. *The Miracle* was made over a period in 1988 and 1989. The band were eager to record and from the results, five singles were issued, of which four were top twenty hits. It was indeed a miracle.

I'm not sure whether Freddie was a hundred per cent over the moon about this album. He was very pleased with the result but perhaps he found it a little strange to be working in partnership with the other three members again after having to please only one other person for the past two-and-a-half years. This was the first album where all the tracks were suddenly credited to the band as a whole as opposed to each separate member. Maybe this stopped some arguments and made the accountants' lives easier but in the studio things were just as fractious. As anybody in a long-term marriage knows, which is basically what the Queen partnership was, tantrums and walkouts have to happen so that people can make up, get back together again and let life be good once more.

However, for the record, I can assert that 'Khashoggi's Ship' is Freddie's. 'Party' was, of course, Roger's. 'The Miracle' itself was a true studio collaborative creation. 'I Want It All' is down to Brian. 'Rain Must Fall' is Freddie ... The guitar is the giveaway where Brian's tracks are concerned. The guitar work on them is unrestrained although he was very happy to contribute what was wanted of him on all the other tracks. The band didn't change their time-honoured way of working just because the accreditation had been changed.

It must be remembered that at this time it was patently obvious to us all that something was wrong with Freddie's health, but exactly what it was he refused to talk about. I suppose for that reason, we in his house were thinking more about him than what he was producing. Like, was he wearing himself out? In those days, it was obvious to suspect that what he was suffering from was HIV infection but no one knew. People only really knew for sure and certain on November 23, 1991, when Freddie chose to release his statement acknowledging that he had Aids. However, that he was sick with something we were absolutely certain and we were very, very worried although he himself made no allowances for his invalid state in his recording schedule.

Freddie continued his association with Townhouse and the Olympic complex in London as well as working in Montreux. Freddie had decided that if he was going to 'the office', then it might as well be on his doorstep. By this time, on his visits to Montreux, Freddie was no longer staying at the Montreux Palace Hotel but rented what became known within the group as Duck House. There were ducks of the feathered and the carved wooden variety absolutely everywhere. The owner obviously had a passion for them. It was a beautiful villa in a setting on the edge of Lake Geneva in Montreux.

It was during these visits that he grew to appreciate the peace and quiet that this alpine town had to offer whereas as we know in the past he had found it somewhat dull. He surprised us all one day by announcing that he would like to buy a permanent place somewhere in Montreux. Jim Beach had already made his home there and so the wheels were put in motion to look for a suitable property. I believe approaches were made to the owner of Duck House who at that time was not in a selling mood. No specific details were given to Jim Beach, just a general 'home' idea.

1990 brought the ideas for *Innuendo* to the fore. Freddie must have realised by now that time was really short. He must have known deep inside that this would be the last album that he would be involved in. I'm not even sure that he was thinking in terms that went as far as 'an album'. He was going from track to track which was basically what he did until the end of his life. While he had a voice, he would continue recording.

Once again, the work was recorded between London and Switzerland. This time, though, the London studio was Metropolis in Chiswick. Mountain Studios was not Freddie's idea of a perfect studio set-up. I think the reason was that the studio itself was on a different level to the control room and there was no quick walking through a couple of doors to hear something being played back. Everything in Montreux was communicated from the control room to the studio and vice versa via both audio and visual monitors. This, I think, is a fairly rare configuration because in both Townhouse and in Metropolis Studios in London, it was a matter of feet between the studio and the control room. Freddie felt that because he could see the producer through two sheets of plate glass, it made the recording easier. The same applied to the Musicland set-up.

Freddie really loved the *Innuendo* album. Listening to it, you hear some of the more flamboyant aspects coming back into the arrangements. Whereas *The Miracle* had been a bit straight and basic, *Innuendo* had all the flair and magic of Freddie's fingerprint. It was like he was putting his stamp on what would be his swansong because I obviously cannot count *Made In Heaven* as his, although I am sure he would be very happy with the results of John, Brian and Roger's very hard work.

Again, five singles were released from this album. Each time, he brought a cassette of the day's work home, he was incredibly excited. Even if some of us might have been asleep, he would wake everyone up and make us listen. He was giving it his all. He didn't care that he would fall into bed totally exhausted. If we were still worried that all this hard work was shortening his life, he made it very clear that he didn't care. Once he had started work on this album, there was nothing, absolutely nothing, going to stop him from completing what I believe he considered some of his best work. He always considered his best work as that which he did with Queen. Freddie and Mike Moran still remained very close and Freddie thought Mike would bring out the best on the keyboards on 'All God's People'. Freddie after all had only ever got to Grade Three or Four on the Royal Academy of Music's piano exams and Freddie only ever wanted the very best on this album. The four tracks whose words and musical outline were Freddie's are obviously 'All God's People' and 'Slightly Mad', as well as 'Delilah', which, as all Freddie-lovers know was written about his favourite cat. On first listening, everybody was shocked because they couldn't understand writing a song about a girl who pees on his Chippendale suite. It is not until after this part of the song, that it is revealed that he is indeed writing about the cat. I think some people may have even been offended. But, did that worry Freddie? This time, we *were* amused.

And then, of course, there was 'Bijou', the fourth. For those of you who remember BBC Radio's *Round The Home*, the title perfectly describes Freddie's 'little trifle' that he insisted on going on the album and which of course afforded such a wonderful showcase for Brian May. Who else but Freddie could come up with a title like 'Bijou'?

The whole world thought that Freddie was being prophetic in 'The Show Must Go On' although he never wrote the lyrics for this song. The whole album is of course prophetic because Freddie knew it would be his last but it is not the final goodbye from Freddie which is how the world has come to see it. While he knew his music would always be played, he didn't see himself as the 'great composer' and therefore the idea of consciously writing his own epitaph would never have occurred. Events force a meaning especially on lyrics and words where none was originally intended. For example, songs like 'The Show Must Go On', given different circumstances, is actually a very triumphant, 'up' song.

One of the tracks that sticks in my brain is 'Going Slightly Mad' when I distinctly remember Freddie coming home and having great difficulty with the lyrics. This again was one of those occasions where he came in and we were searching for about three hours for the elusive words. And with 'All God's People', he was having his last blast at gospel which he loved.

Looking back after *Innuendo* was finished, it had been two decades since the members of Queen had started to work together. Their recording story had changed so much over these years. From having the lion's share of the hits on the earlier albums, Freddie saw the other members' share of the tracks increasing. He always said, "Brian writes more songs, but I have more hits." He wasn't bragging or boasting in the slightest, he was merely stating a fact. It is absolutely true that on the earlier albums Brian is credited with several more compositions.

Over these years, Freddie never closed his eyes to change. He never let Queen follow fashion except for the one lapse into disco in *Hot Space*. He was always innovative with his music. As far as I know, the ability to create music is something you're born with. It's not something you can learn in school. He was one of the lucky ones to have been born with a surfeit of this talent which he never wasted. At the time of his death, there was still so much music left in him. It was his one regret. Apart from the obvious . . . Oh! That as well!

A studio is a place of work and while the locations for these places of work might sound so wonderfully exotic, once inside the studio and control room, you could be anywhere in the world. The desks look the same, the baffles look the same, the people *are* the same. It seems hard to believe now that there was a time that I had never dreamed that I would see the inside of a studio. To actually create masterpieces in this environment, it could surely take a lot out of a person. In the end it did . . .

Chapter Three

Remembering that the video medium itself was in its infancy, Queen's 'Bohemian Rhapsody' is now accepted as the first of rock music's videos to stand on its own as an integral production as well as a tool to promote the product it was designed to support. Queen, and therefore Freddie, always felt themselves under scrutiny as far as this visual part of their work was concerned. Each video production thereafter had to be more innovative or at least remarkable enough to maintain their position as leaders of the pack.

As can be seen from the call sheet for 'It's A Hard Life', keeping the band sweet for a video shoot was an operation which required great delicacy and diplomacy. For a start, they were always called last for make-up and wardrobe and this call was always left as late as possible. This still didn't prevent them from having to sit around for an hour or two before the first shot but it did stop them from having to be there by six o'clock in the morning which, had that been the case, could have easily meant that by eight o'clock the shoot would have been cancelled as by then they would have stormed off the set and gone home.

When a band hires a film or television studio, what is provided often varies. Some come with plush dressing rooms with all mod cons and either a refectory or canteen and others sport one caravan for wardrobe, one caravan for make-up and one caravan to relax in and many other variations in between including luxury mobile homes and Winnebagos. Whatever was provided by the studio, if the shoot was in England, Freddie would always take his own catering with him. He learned fast.

I had very little to do on 'Save Me', the first of the videos in which I was involved. I was mainly around with a drink and a hairbrush and I can say nothing about the conception of it. Animation was used as well as the live footage from the concerts at the Rainbow, Finsbury Park (now closed as a concert venue) – where the filming of the sequence took place where the dove is never quite caught – and then at Alexandra Palace.

'Play The Game' was filmed while I was doing the wardrobe for the whole band and the video production company used their own specifically contracted wardrobe department and thus I wasn't required on set.

'Another One Bites The Dust' was filmed during the American Tour while the stage set was erected but shooting took place before the actual show. Basically, the director just filmed the band performing the song half-a-dozen times. It started off as an accident when Freddie put on a different cap for one of the takes whereupon Freddie decided that he liked the idea and started changing both caps and vests which accounts for the apparently strange costume continuity of the final cut. The trendy baseball caps adorned with various additions like bull horns et cetera caught Freddie's fancy.

'Flash Gordon' I wasn't involved with as the filming had substantially been completed before I was employed. It takes a hell of a lot longer to finish a film than it does a music video.

'Under Pressure' was a combination of Bowie and Queen and it was obvious that getting them all together for a video would be difficult and so the work was made up of stock filmed footage from libraries of various social pressure situations. The egos and schedules of all the participants pre-empted any joint creativity and so it was left to the director.

'Las Palabras De Amor' was performed live at *Top Of The Pops* in London. There never was a proper video for this single and all visual evidence of its performance subsists in the *TOTP* recording. The song only ever reached seventeen in the British charts. The band had it easy for this show because, generally, performing at *TOTP* requires attendance at the studio all day. Queen were allowed to turn up at about five in the afternoon which gave them a short time to rehearse but the advantage that they only had to sit around for an hour or so before they actually performed. Gordon Elsbury was the show's director in the studio with whom Freddie got on very well.

'Calling All Girls' from 1982 featured the band each dressed in white. It was filmed in studios near Wandsworth Bridge and seemed to me to be a piece dedicated to George Orwell and *1984*, which in real life was still a date two years into the future. Big brother is watching. It's about a rebel in a computer society. Many robot policemen appear to capture and abuse Freddie. Sounds like one of his dreams come true? I can remember seeing the band running down a corridor. There was also a cage, with Freddie trapped inside, all wire mesh and bars, until the rest of the band appear to cause a computer malfunction and Freddie escapes. All very weird and all very much of its time. Perhaps, along with 'Radio Ga Ga', the most derivative of the band's video catalogue.

'Body Language' as many people know was originally banned. This video, shot in April 1982, was the first time I realised that so much of the end product was the result of Freddie's input. It was definitely a case of the full Freddie, the ideas being mostly his which the director put into effect. Because by this time I had become solely employed by Freddie and was personally on hand, I had never fully appreciated before how extensive his involvement was.

The original concept of the posed and choreographed male and female bodies, sexily clothed but sufficient to ensure coverage of all the rude bits, was spoiled by the decision to put out the video with more of the red 'censored' arrows over so much of it. This was done to comply with the censorial attitudes of the time. Only twenty-four years ago and yet, now . . .? Freddie's concept, intended to come over as intensely sexual, was tame compared with what is commonplace nowadays.

He was involved from the very first and certainly with the casting of the various characters including the large black ladies doing the sexy dance routines in the showers on the sauna set and especially the lady in green satin and sequins who falls into the cake, the last shot of a twenty-four hour marathon filming session. The shot could only be done once as there was only one cake. Freddie also insisted on having the LA-based dancer Tony Fields who at that point was part of the famed show *Solid Gold*, which was the American version of Britain's *Top Of The Pops* and makes the *Solid Gold* dancers the equivalent of Pan's People. Except they were very much better!

The shoot was done in Toronto even though the casting and the major crew had been recruited in Los Angeles. It was cheaper to fly everyone to Toronto for the two day schedule. The kerchief on Freddie's wrist which he occasionally used on stage in addition to his sweatband was one of a large collection which we bought at various Los Angeles sport clothes stores like the Sports Locker on Santa Monica Boulevard which was run by my good friend Gary Jeske.

Then came 'Backchat', also taken from *Hot Space*. It's a sort of non-video. There is a huge piston-pumping performance from Freddie in a partially flooded factory. It only took a day as it was a 'performance' video and I'm afraid it shows. Freddie was in a white track suit from his own wardrobe, cavorting around the piston poles and pipes like he was Felipe Rose on the bar at The Anvil. The others are placed bemusedly around him and just let Freddie get on with it. I really think they had no idea of what Freddie was driving at and it appears on tape that their minds are elsewhere on more important things. None of them apart from Freddie were dancers or movers of any description and this was the main reason why they had no appreciation of the basic disco idea behind *Hot Space*. As usual they took their lead from Freddie. Why on earth did Freddie pick up the wrench (spanner in English)? He certainly wouldn't have known either what it was for or what to do with it. No wonder he throws it away so quickly like a hot coal.

The 'Radio Ga Ga' video was an excuse to have access to the footage of legendary German director Fritz Lang's *Metropolis*, licence for which permission had already been negotiated so that Freddie could appear on Giorgio Moroder's soundtrack for his musical re-working of this classic silent movie. Watching the video again having not seen it for many years, I realise what an incredible piece of filming it is. The inter-cutting of original *Metropolis* scenes updating it to the Second World War, especially the superimposition of Freddie's features on the robot's and then the sequence featuring the band in the flying car in the futuristic scenes, works very well.

The band's involvement was filmed over two days, one day at the Carlton TV Studios in St. John's Wood and the other at the Shepperton Studios where fan club members were recruited to be part of the crowd of workers and worshippers. The day at Carlton was directed by David Mallet with whom Freddie had a great working relationship. David knew instinctively where Freddie was coming from artistically and he loved working on Queen videos because he knew that even if it was the simplest concept he would be up against a challenge which would also stretch him artistically.

The sequence involved the band dressing up in leather trousers and red crepe bandages, a wardrobe overseen by Diana Mosely who had been introduced by David Mallet as costume designer. The band spent most of the day in dressing rooms and when they were actually on set in the car, they were just sitting in it against the technical blue background as the actual 'flight' process of the car seeming to fly down the avenue of buildings would be added later by means of a special effects department.

This video was also, I believe, the first occasion on which old footage of the band's previous videos was used interspersed with the current filming showing their very substantial past, their present and pointing the way, therefore, to the possibilities of the future. Little did they know that the results of the next day's filming at Shepperton would stay with them forever. The handclapping sequence has now become the stuff of the Queen legend. In fact, while making the video, when the band persisted in getting the sequence wrong, the crowd was so knowing and well-rehearsed that they were able to put the band right. Some years later, I'll never forget Freddie's amazement when the band started the chorus of 'Radio Ga Ga' in the Live Aid Concert and the whole stadium began the entire clapping sequence independently of Freddie with no prompting from the stage at all. Probably many of those present for the video were also at Wembley.

'I Want To Break Free' was another David Mallet epic which was filmed at Limehouse Studios over the course of three days. The first day was the *Coronation Street* segment. Freddie was never a huge fan of any soap but if he was at home at the right time, he would sit and watch *Coro*. Freddie's character was therefore loosely based around that of Bet Lynch. But before everybody says, "But Bet Lynch was blonde . . .," Freddie knew he would have looked silly in a blonde wig. So, instead he looked silly in a dark one. This video proved a lot of things to Freddie. The first was that he couldn't walk in very high heels. An assortment of sizes of high-heels were provided ranging from a five-and-a-half inch heel to the two-inch variety which is what Freddie ended up wearing.

Prior to this trial by heel, he had always thought that he had a good sense of balance but when he put his feet into any shoe with a heel over two inches, he discovered that he was wobbling everywhere. Brian May's character was modelled, again, very loosely on Hilda Ogden, the lady with the permanent rollers permanently in place. Roger was the typical St. Trinians sixth former while John's persona leaned heavily on 'Grandma' from the popular Giles' cartoons which appeared in the *Express* newspapers.

The band all had a great deal of fun doing this segment. I believe it was the first time that any of them had ever worn women's clothes in their lives. How naturally it all came to them, however!

While Freddie occasionally enjoyed a drag act in a pub or on stage, it wasn't something that he would have made a point of going to see. Men in women's clothing had never really attracted him at all. It was a surprise to me to hear when we were told the ideas for the video that Freddie had actually agreed to wearing women's clothes. This sort of dressing-up was work. It was something that Freddie would never have dreamed of doing in his own home. Any fancy dress parties he threw featured him wearing nothing more outlandish than his stage outfits. The nearest he ever got to wearing women's clothes at home was when occasionally he would enthusiastically urge his guests to try on his large collection of beautiful antique kimonos which spent all their time in delicate wrapping in a wardrobe. It was their yearly airing to check for moths, I suppose!

I think it was his almost total disinterest in drag which was the reason why the now famous hat party in 1986 for his fortieth birthday remained in fact just that. People were dressed just as they wanted but in outrageously flamboyant hats. Obviously, it never stopped Freddie camping around when the mood took him as do a large proportion of British men in party mood but he never entertained the remotest thought of wanting to be a man pretending to be a woman.

Day two of the schedule brought on the miners with the pit lamps on their heads and this cast was once again composed of willing fan club conscripts, both male and female. Generally, the fans, clad in their androgynous boilersuits, could not have conducted themselves more professionally. Considering they were in the presence of their heroes, they helped as much as possible with the filming by always being in the right place at the right time. There were surprisingly few who plucked up courage to come and ask the band for autographs but when they did, the band gave them freely.

As per many of the David Mallet/Queen productions, this was the video equivalent of the Hollywood epic, with casts of hundreds as opposed to thousands. Considering the number of videos he made, Freddie never considered himself an actor. The making of videos was just an extension of the making of records. Although Freddie would certainly never have wanted to be Cleopatra, the idea of being the star in a biblical epic of Cecil B de Mille proportions appealed to him enormously. Perhaps that's why the videos were always as they were. Even as a schoolboy in Panchgani for those long eleven months a year, apart from his family so far away, it must be remembered that Freddie was brought up on a diet of Hollywood films which were as readily available in India as they were in Indiana. Hollywood movies and Church of England pomp and ceremony was patently a heady combination in the heat of an Indian boarding school.

In the mining sequence, we see yet another scene of a bare-chested Freddie. Anytime he's seen with a bare chest in a video, it can be guaranteed that there would be Joe or myself very, very close by waiting for the word "Cut!" when we would run on and cover him up. Any space the size of a film studio always felt cold to Freddie, summer or winter. Freddie was not a cold person. He always liked his warmth.

The third section featured principals, soloists and members of the Royal Ballet company. It was also the section which was to cause almost as much legal trouble as the drag sequence caused public furore and outrage in the United States. It was this video which effectively killed off Queen in America. The general American public as well as quite a few industry movers and shakers in those days just couldn't accept four grown men dressed up in women's clothes.

The ballet sequence featured Briony Brind, the current prima ballerina sensation at Covent Garden and Freddie's friend Wayne Eagling who specially choreographed and participated in this section. The inspiration came from many sources including *L'apres Midi D'un Faun* from which was taken the idea for Freddie's Spock-like ears and the pan pipes which we see at the opening of the ballet sequence. It is Briony whom Freddie up-ends and turns and with whom he disappears into the mists at the end of the sequence. Gail Taphouse, the soloist, was the owner of the hair and the hand at the beginning of the sequence.

The whole exercise proved once and for all to Freddie that, while he thought himself reasonably balletic, real dancing was a very different kettle of fish. The dancers unintentionally made him feel as though he had two left feet. Nevertheless, he very much enjoyed filming this sequence. It gave him the feeling of being involved in the real thing.

The legal trouble caused was not because of the *L'apres Midi D'un*

Faun section which was choreographed by Nijinsky but from the celebrated choreographer Sir Kenneth Macmillan who noticed that some of Wayne's choreography and costumes were very similar, if not identical, to his own as included in his ballet *The Rite Of Spring*. Choreology can prove many things now and subsequently Queen Productions donated an undisclosed sum to one of Sir Kenneth's elected charities, the Institute of Choreology.

'Hard Life' was directed by Tim Pope who had made his name by releasing a single entitled 'I Want To Be A Tree' and this was to be his only collaboration with Queen. He was certainly qualified to reproduce Freddie's outlandish vision of the end product. It was filmed in the Arri film studios in the centre of Munich. Freddie had damaged ligaments in his knee inside the New York Bar in Munich in this year, 1984, as was widely reported in the international press.

The whole point of this production from the *Pagliacci* opening onwards was to create a surreal fantasy. From the eyes sewn onto his costume to the feathers on his back, Freddie achieves the look of that of a giant prawn in a palace of excess. The voluptuous images were often more akin to nightmare. Many of Freddie's Munich friends were involved, Barbara Valentin as the seductive temptress and Mack's wife Ingrid feature heavily as does a transvestite ballerina, Kurt Raab whom we also knew by the name of Rebecca.

The rest of the band were obviously somewhat bewildered which is maybe why it is so easy to play 'Spot the Deliberate Mistake'. At one point, Roger is to be seen walking across the set in his trainers whereas in fact he should only have been in his tights. This incident indicates that not all the band were always in on the editing process. Had Roger been involved in this one, the mistake would probably never have been let through.

Towards the end of the video, on the scarlet staircase, Freddie visibly favours his damaged right knee as he inevitably sits down on the stair and the whole manner in which he lowers himself indicates the pain he was in. We were in the studio on that day until very, very late, after a couple of bottles of vodka and champagne were brought in. Only Freddie's immediate coterie stayed on to drink as everyone else was completely exhausted.

Live performance film footage was used for the 'Hammer To Fall' video which was filmed just before the first show in Brussels on *The Works* tour in August 1984. It was directed by David Mallet.

'Love Kills' was Freddie's contribution to the *Metropolis* project. It only utilised footage from the film itself but got to number ten in the UK charts.

All the following taken from Freddie's own *Mr. Bad Guy* album were filmed in Munich and thus, it was Joe Fanelli who was 'on duty' for these schedules. 'I Was Born To Love You', 'Made In Heaven' and 'Living On My Own'. This latter video used footage of Freddie's black and white birthday party held in Munich. There was a camera set up on a rig on the ceiling and it continually revolved filming the crowd for the whole evening. Filming was also done two days later, returning to the Mrs. Henderson bar where Freddie could include specific set pieces, again involving friends from Munich who had once again to don the same costumes and make-up. It could have been a nightmare of continuity but because the whole concept was a party, if there were any mistakes they went unnoticed.

The occasion of Fashion Aid at London's Albert Hall provided wonderful footage which shows Freddie dressed in a military-style tunic with solid silver chains and epaulettes, with a sashed pair of dark trousers all designed by David and Elizabeth Emanuel, who came to fame after designing Lady Diana Spencer's wedding dress. Freddie portrayed the dashing bare-foot bridegroom opposite Jane Seymour's stunning bride as the finale of the Bob Geldof/Harvey Goldsmith inspired Fashion Aid Show for Africa. Anyone who has not seen the footage has missed out. Freddie was totally relaxed and was having a marvellous time and, as usual, he put on a quite magnificent show.

Dancers of the Royal Ballet danced in the Emanuel costumes designed for the Wayne Eagling ballet entitled *Frankenstein, The Modern Prometheus.* We had a sort of rehearsal in the afternoon at the Park Lane Hotel where Freddie met up with quite a few of his co-models on that evening's bill. The Marchioness of Douro, his friend Francesca Thyssen, Fiona Fullerton, Selina Scott, Anthony Andrews, Michael and Shakira Caine and Richard Branson. Arlene Phillips had worked with Freddie on 'Crazy Little Thing Called Love' before and they had known each other from the Seventies.

It is noticeable that Michael Caine was unamused as he watched Freddie's outrageous antics, throwing the remnants of the bride's bouquet to the assembled audience. It might have been outrageous but it was exactly the touch that the audience needed. It was a tricky manoeuvre guiding Freddie and Jane halfway round and a floor below the oval Albert Hall for their final entrance. I had no idea where we were going. I had a barefooted Freddie on one hand and the petite Jane Seymour on the other, her huge wedding train thrown over my arm beneath which even six-foot-two of me almost disappeared. It was a case of the blind leading the blind as we hadn't rehearsed this move before.

'One Vision' was filmed over an extended period of time at Musicland Recording Studios in Munich. There was minor criticism alleging that the band were climbing on the Live Aid bandwagon as this single was made and released very soon after they had made their conquering appearance on the televised charity marathon. Whether or not this is true I don't think is relevant because if they hadn't done a single we would never have had the subsequent albums *A Kind Of Magic*, *The Miracle* or *Innuendo* which by anybody's standards must contain some of Queen's best music. Never forget, 'One Vision' reaffirmed the faith of the band in themselves.

'A Kind Of Magic' filmed in the Playhouse Theatre in Northumberland Avenue in London, once the home of many a BBC radio programme, was directed by Russell Mulcahy. Russell came over to the house and it was he who had the idea of the venue. Freddie and he then talked through the idea for hours and came up with the inspiration from the location. Because the Arches at Charing Cross was and is home to many of London's homeless and people who sleep rough in the streets, that brought about the idea of Freddie being a magician who changes the reality for three down-and-outs (Brian, Roger and John) bringing them into the magic of the old abandoned theatre where he, Freddie, was once the star.

Magically, Freddie just appears and disappears with his retinue of cartoon backing singers. Only halfway through do the transformed tramps realise something might be wrong when Roger turns quizzically to the camera. Joe Fanelli accompanied Freddie on this shoot as we had started to take video duty almost in turns depending on our other work and commitments. While it might seem to be an exciting part of the job, let me tell you that there are many long and boring hours involved and it wasn't unheard of to be on call for twenty-four hours on the trot. What sticks in my mind most were Freddie's comments about how, ". . . fucking cold it was!" He didn't realise it could be so cold inside a building but the Playhouse Theatre hadn't been in use for many months and had had no central heating.

Considering the shoot was in March, the place had had a long winter in the freezing cold.

After doing the shoot on the *Time* set, Freddie had had a drink or two and stayed while the audience came in and he started giving the ice creams away from an usherette's tray. The schedule was short. The video had to be shot in the morning and afternoon of one day before an evening performance at the Dominion Theatre in London's Tottenham Court Road. Freddie enjoyed resting in the star dressing room that had been specifically renovated and tented in cream silks and satins for Cliff Richard. Certainly a dressing room appropriate for rock'n'roll royalty.

We were particularly amused!

I have to mention, purely as an aside, Freddie's penchant for nicknaming people also involved Cliff who, because of his huge collection of silver discs amassed over such a long career, was immediately dubbed Sylvia Disc. Neil Sedaka suffered the same fate and was called Golda Disc.

'Friends Will Be Friends' was filmed in a Wembley studio with huge audience participation. Once again, a Joe day. I stayed at home. There were eight hundred and fifty ecstatic Queen fans who found themselves cast as the audience. As a fee, they were all given a T-Shirt proclaiming the legend: I AM A QUEEN FRIEND. A T-shirt!!?!!

'Who Wants To Live Forever' was filmed with Christopher Lambert to give continuity to the *Highlander* movie, in which he starred. This is another Mallet B. de Mille affair. The vast National Philharmonic and the forty unidentified choirboys give the authorship away. This was another of Joe's video duty days. It was filmed in a warehouse at Tobacco Dock.

There are two versions of 'The Great Pretender' video, one to accompany the single and the second, the twelve-inch version. They were both generally available at one point but as to their current availability, I know not.

This shoot lasted three days and was filmed at two different studios. Straker was playing Cassius in Julius Caesar at the Bristol Old Vic at the time and Freddie, Joe and I had driven down with Terry Giddings to see him. Debbie Ash was cast by the production company to play the real female interest and Roger . . . Well, Roger was just one of the girls. Denny was the hairdresser, Carolyn Cowan did the make-up and Diana Moseley supervised the complicated wardrobe. Terry Giddings acting as

Sweeney Todd shaved various parts of the cast's anatomies – i.e. chests and armpits!

Very few people knew the real Freddie. To show he was indeed a pretender, in the video he used many of the personae portrayed in Queen and solo videos. By assembling them all together, it showed that he spent much of his work life pretending . . . It was quite a difficult task assembling the various costumes, stored in several places including Freddie's and Diana Moseley's lofts, which he had worn in the past as he had to wear them all again for this shoot.

The twelve-inch version shows that while a five-minute promo takes three days to create, a lot of hard work goes into it but as is obvious from this footage, a great deal of fun can also be had. I suppose it's the only way to keep the participants sane. Many people, including fans who have helped out by appearing in Queen videos, know that the majority of the time is spent sitting around getting exasperated. There is ten minutes of filming followed by four hours of rearranging the lights for the next shot. Is it all worth it? Answer, yes! Of course!

The pink suit was designed and made by David Chambers who also made quite a few of Freddie's suits including the dark blue tux seen in the video of 'Barcelona'. The pink-suited Freddie was turned into a hundred cloned cardboard cut-outs for extra emphasis which appear, ranked either side on the grand staircase, at the end of the promo. David Mallet, the director, had originally wanted these standing on top of the white cliffs at Dover while a helicopter shot pulled away from Freddie standing amongst them. This idea was turned down by Freddie on two counts: first, the cost as the shot would have added thousands of pounds to the budget; and second, Freddie didn't relish the thought of standing at the edge of the cliffs in the freezing cold!

'Barcelona' was filmed at least three times, twice in performance. The first was directed by Gavin Taylor at the KU nightclub on Ibiza, now renamed Privilege, the largest venue on the island. On this occasion, staged to commemorate the five hundredth anniversary of Columbus' discovery of America, it was to be the first public performance of the song. There was no real rehearsal. Freddie stayed at Pikes Hotel and Montserrat stayed at a five star hotel in Ibiza town. Pino Sagliocco organised the show which included Duran Duran amongst others. Jim Beach was one of the executive producers along with Dominic Anciano and Ray Burdis. Freddie was very nervous and I was sent on ahead to make sure the dressing room was okay and to be there when Montserrat arrived. She wore a blue dress originally designed for her role as the diva Ariadne in Richard Strauss's opera *Ariadne Auf Naxos*.

I think because the KU appearance was Montserrat's first exposure to this sort of gig, Freddie wanted to make sure that there was a familiar face around for her. It was strange that during the course of the evening I spent more time with Montserrat and her family – who were all there to support her – than I did with Freddie. But Freddie wasn't alone by any means as he had the two Jims – Beach and Hutton – and Barbara Valentin with him as well as Mike Moran.

The second filmed performance was at La Nit in Barcelona on the occasion of the delivery of the Olympic flag to that city in 1988. He and Montserrat were backed on stage on this occasion by Peter Straker and their friends Debbie Bishop and Madeleine Bell, both of whom were backing vocalists on the recording. Mike Moran, as always, supervised the musical arrangements performed by a local orchestra. On the same bill was Jose Carreras, his first performance after battling with leukaemia, Dionne Warwick, Eddy Grant, Rudolf Nureyev, Spandau Ballet *und viel andere*.

It was a huge occasion, the dressing rooms being mere partitioned spaces in a vast hangar-like building. Everything that anyone said echoed around so all the participants tended to be very quiet. When Freddie and Montserrat appeared, she was obviously glowing in the adoration of her home Catalan crowd. It was her show after all. She had performed with Carreras and sung a song on her own with the orchestra. She sang an arrangement of an aria written for a tenor by Giuseppe Verdi called 'Hymn Of The Nations' in which, if you listen, you hear at least three or four different national anthems.

Freddie's nerves had only just quietened down from his meeting a scant hour or so before with the King and Queen of Spain and the royal family. Although his nervousness is apparent, Montserrat had the knack of responding to what is essentially a solo Freddie performance for, as you will understand, he had spent his stage life working only on his own or at best interacting with the other three members of Queen. If you watch this show, you see Montserrat's instinctive reaction to Freddie's movements and the whole duet works successfully. For those carpers who have invented so many reasons for the show not being sung live, including Freddie's health, there was never any intention of this song being sung live. To produce any of Freddie's live performances, a lot of intensive rehearsal took place. Time was a commodity then that neither of the artistes involved had much of.

'Barcelona' in its third incarnation was filmed at Shepperton or Pinewood. Freddie wore his dark blue evening suit and performed on a stage with hundreds of candles and once again a cast of thousands, drawn from the ever-eager fan club. 'Golden Boy' also used footage filmed during La Nit in Barcelona on the same occasion as the video for 'Barcelona'. Montserrat is in the same blue dress but with a vast red evening coat with a long train. The drama on this occasion was that the backing track was out of time. It was being played slower than it should have been which made the making of the video extremely difficult as Freddie and Montserrat's lip-synching was out of sequence with the recorded track which was used. A passable video was cobbled together but it wasn't much seen.

When Freddie came off stage, it was almost like the cartoons where you see steam coming out of people's ears. He was absolutely furious as there was no chance to be able to re-take. He blamed any and everybody. The person nearest to hand to bear the brunt was sound engineer John Brough. There were a few present who wondered what was the matter with Freddie because the sound wasn't noticeably slower except to an expert. Freddie knew it was slow because it was his track through and through and he realised the implications for the video.

'I Want It All', a rather nondescript video from 1989, was filmed at Elstree Film Studios and it was Joe's turn that day. Watching it now I get the impression that Freddie didn't really want to be there. He looks the archetypal angry young man and I don't know how much of that was acting. The excessive use of lighting – sixteen supertrooper followspots, the ones made famous by ABBA, and twelve fifty-foot Dino football pitch lights – succeeds in bleaching out most of the footage. I think perhaps time was at a premium because, generally, when Queen didn't have time, performance videos were the norm and they hadn't performed in concert for two years. They needed to broadcast confirmation that they were still capable of performing as a band.

'The Miracle', directed by Rudi Dolezal and Hannes Rossacher, was filmed at Elstree Studios once again. Many children were auditioned to find the four lookalikes. The time spent was well

Freddie Mercury, John Murphy and Joe Scardilli, in Vancouver.

Lee Nolan, Freddie, John Murphy, Jim from New York
and Jim Cruz in Vancouver.

Thor Arnold, John Murphy, Freddie and friend in the hot tub
649 Stone Canyon Road, Los Angeles.

Freddie and Thor Arnold in Los Angeles.

Freddie blowing out the candles on his birthday cake, Los Angeles.

Freddie with Vince The Barman, in LA.

Freddie with Rod Stewart in Los Angeles.

Bryn Brydenthal, Freddie and Jaqui Brownell in LA.

Roger Taylor, Rod Stewart and Freddie, Los Angeles.

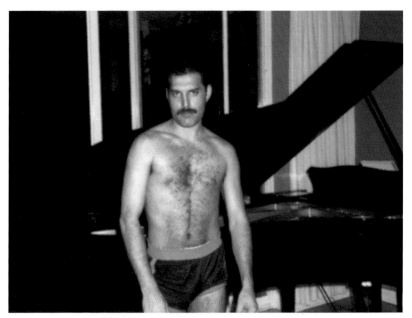

Freddie at 649 Stone Canyon Road, LA.

Freddie at 649 Stone Canyon Rd, and below with Jaqui Brownell.

Fred Mandell, Rheinhold Mack, Freddie, Lee Nolan and Joe Scardilli,
at the Record Plant in Los Angeles.

Freddie at the grand piano.

Freddie and friends, including author Peter Freestone (third from left) at the New York apartment at 425 East 58th Street.

Freddie with Tony King.

Thor Arnold, Peter Freestone, John Murphy, Patrick, Freddie
and Lee Nolan in New York.

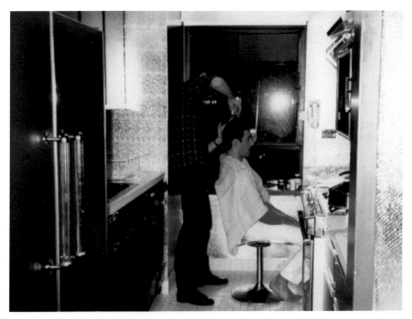

Freddie gets a haircut at the 425 East 58th Street, NYC apartment.

The Famous Hats, as modelled by Freddie and friends in New York; clockwise from bottom left: John Murphy, Joe Scardilli, Lee Nolan, Peter Freestone, Thor Arnold, Paul Prenter and Freddie.

Freddie and Peter Freestone.

Freddie in Munich.

FM with Lee Nolan.

FM at the Berkshire Place Hotel, New York.

FM with Charles 'The Canadian' at the Berkshire Place Hotel.

FM on a video shoot, 1983.

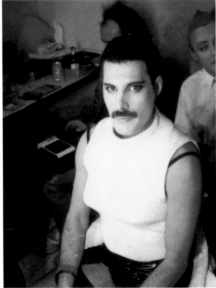

This page and over: Freddie filming the notorious video
for 'I Want To Break Free'.

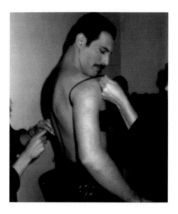

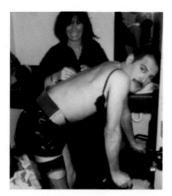

Freddie with Peter Freestone.

Freddie with Mary Austin.

Freddie with Winnie Kirchberger.

Peter Freestone, Paul Prenter, Freddie, Kurt Raab
and Barbara Valentin.

Freddie with Trip Khalef

Freddie in bed with his cats at Garden Lodge in the autumn of 1981.

worthwhile as the end result produced four very good doppel-gangers.

Watching 'The Miracle' for the first time in maybe five years had me in tears. I can't explain why but perhaps juxtaposing Freddie, who in hindsight we now know had only a limited life left, with the young child who had his whole life ahead of him was why I found it so affecting. The band didn't have a great deal to do in this shoot and only had to act as they normally performed on stage. The real stars are the kids and I defy anybody not to find their performances any different from Queen's. The boys watched many videos over and over again to perfect their technique. The band were given an impromptu performance by the boys at one point during the filming and the four men gave the kids a standing ovation. I don't think anybody on set could believe how good the young boys were. Certainly not Queen.

The video for 'Breakthru' was shot during an incredibly hot two summer days and I remember vividly Freddie complaining on the morning of the second day how he had had very little sleep the previous night in the stiflingly hot hotel rooms which, in the midst of the English countryside, of course had no air-conditioning.

The video was filmed on a steam train on the Nene Valley private railway in Cambridgeshire, which provided Freddie with all the cool air he required. However, although the train appears to be hurtling along the tracks, it reached only a maximum of some thirty miles an hour. Debbie Leng, Roger's partner, who opens the video, was Freddie's choice for the enigmatic masked beauty. He thought she fitted the bill perfectly.

The one part of the video that neither Freddie nor Rudi nor Hannes were ever happy with was the opening sequence where the wall bursts open. Because of the onrushing train and the air press-ure building up in the tunnel, the polystyrene block wall collapses moments before the train breaks through which detracts from the initial shock of the explosion. Freddie thoroughly enjoyed making this video, even spontaneously effecting the dangerous unrehearsed pull-up stunt over the side of the moving train.

In the 'Invisible Man' video, directed by Rudi and Hannes, the band are characters from a young boy's computer game which come to life. This was another of Joe's days on duty and suited him down to the ground due to his affinity and expertise in computing. Perhaps he was the reason behind the idea. The job of the person left behind in the house – whether it was Joe or me – was to have a hot meal ready for the workers when they arrived home whatever time of day or night that might be.

'Scandal' did not turn out to be a huge hit and the band weren't very impressed with the video, having had limited time to get it together.

'Innuendo' involved no filmed reality of any members of the band. Characters were drawn in various artistic styles using as models previous filmed footage of the band. These characters therefore did all the acting that was needed. Freddie was always very impressed whenever he watched this video for he acknowledged the amount of work which had gone into making it.

Departing from tradition, this video was the work of Jerry Hibbert and Rudi Dolezal and I think the only Queen input was that it used ideas from the Grandville cartoon on the *Innuendo* album cover. The juggler is projected on the walls of the Metropolis Studios in Chiswick and the idea for the doll's house and the *commedia del arte* characters came from the video creators.

'Headlong' which was the second single from *Innuendo*, was filmed in Metropolis Recording Studios in London where the band were completing this, their last proper album. The initial sequence is projected on the outside wall of the studio as was the last, the same site as the video of the title track of *Innuendo* which preceded this. It was filmed in the same year as all the last videos and it seems strange to see it now as Freddie really looks quite well. The performance footage was the first part of the filming and then a day was spent in the control room and in the relaxation suite. You can see by Freddie's face that he was really enjoying himself. Come to think of it, on the whole he thought that making videos was the fun part of his job. It was his escape from his real world. While the band as a whole accepted by now that they would never tour again, they wanted to maintain the perception that they were still a performing unit.

At the time of the filming of 'I'm Going Slightly Mad', Freddie knew he was ill and knew he looked ill. While talking various ideas through with Rudi Dolezal he knew he had to come up with a way of disguising his appearance. He used the black and white film and excessive make-up and wig to create the right over-the-top effect. It worked to a point but nothing could really cover the gaunt appearance of his face.

For a change in a Queen video, the visuals followed virtually word-for-word the song's lyrics. This production was very much an implementation of Freddie's ideas by Rudi and Hannes Rossacher. The character was inspired by silent movies and mime artists and the surrealism came from making visual that which was literal. The screw, the daffodils, the banana tree . . . Freddie wearing his slippers for the majority of the shoot was the only outward sign of the pain he was in making this film, as he was finding it difficult to wear tight shoes although when he does wear shoes, the clownishly pointed pair were a fashion statement that we had picked up on our last holiday on Ibiza.

The most observant of viewers will notice that the gardenia which he wore in his buttonhole actually changes over the period of the video. Filming was to take one day as Freddie knew that his physical resources would limit him to that. Gardeners amongst you know that once the gardenia flower has been picked it takes only a fairly short time for it to start turning cream and then yellow. Though the video was being filmed in black and white, the colour change would have been obvious so rather than noticing this difference, they decided it would be less noticeable to replace the flowers. We used three during the course of the filming and there were a further two on stand-by.

The band knew by now of Freddie's illness and were full of admiration for his perseverance in completing the video. Even at this stage he was not about to let things get on top of him. Freddie fully expected this to be the last video he would make. In fact he was to make two more. The making of 'Slightly Mad' really did take a lot out of him.

'Show Must Go On', another compilation movie, was a promotion for the *Greatest Hits II*, *Flix II* and *Pix II*. It contains footage from *Princes Of The Universe*, the fuller length video made with Christopher Lambert for the *Highlander* project at which Joe Fanelli was in attendance, not me. However, there is one small scene from the 'Calling All Girls' video which was never available due to the lack of interest in the record. There are clips also from 'Scandal', a video with which Freddie was very disappointed. He always thought it was just plain boring. It was the one video where he wasn't around from the onset of the creative process and I have to say, his absence of input showed.

'Days Of Our Lives' was the final video in which Freddie ever appeared and I wasn't on set. Seeing the end result, I sometimes think it should perhaps never have been made. If you play that after even something like 'Headlong' you can see how frail and ill he looks. On the other hand, I think it was good for Freddie to do because it proved to him that he was still able. He loved the waistcoat which he wore for this shoot. It was a present from Joe's friend Donald McKenzie who with the help of Joe had managed to get hold of photos of all Freddie's cats and had given them to a friend of his who had painted them onto the silk body of the waistcoat.

Another way you can tell that Freddie wasn't well other than his mere appearance was the fact that he didn't move. Any performance video of the band has the cameraman in trouble as he tries to figure out where Freddie is going to move next. In this, Freddie just stands there. At this point, it was sheer agony for him to be walking because of the huge lesion on the ball of his right foot. A scab had formed and the edges had hardened and were digging into his flesh each time he put any weight on the foot. In fact, Jim Beach had organised for an animated video to be made to side-step the possibility that Freddie wouldn't have been well enough to appear on set and this video, beautifully created, was not shown or available in Britain for quite a while. In the end of course it was far from a thrownaway investment.

Freddie's awareness of this safety-net video persuaded him to actually perform in front of the cameras one last time. He hated the idea of being remembered as what he regarded as a pencil drawing, a mere cartoon.

Chapter Four

I suppose, because of Freddie's background in art – he gained a diploma in graphic design from Ealing Technical College as it was called in those days – it was only natural that he was very closely involved with the artwork and set design of anything to do with Queen. I have to emphasise his qualification was in graphic design. He wouldn't class himself as an artist, as in the paintbrush and palette variety. He knew he was an artist in as far as his singing, his performance, his composition and his design ability were concerned. They all started with an image in his mind. He saw it as his job to make these mental images a reality. However, there are some quite creditable examples of his graphic artwork around but none available to the public as far as I know. Except one: Freddie really could draw.

The story behind one of his sketches was really rather funny. Freddie was browsing through an art auction catalogue and saw some drawings by Matisse, the famous French impressionist. He looked down and the estimated price was between ten and twelve thousand pounds. He exclaimed, "This is ridiculous! I could draw something like this but it wouldn't be worth a fraction of that! Here. Give me some paper."

And then, in twenty seconds, he virtually did a copy of what he saw in front of him. And so here it is, in the photo section. His purchases of paintings were always eclectic. He bought a wonderful abstract in Brazil which he hung in the kitchen for several years above the bench seat at the kitchen table. It was a long time before this was replaced by a print by the Catalan Joan Miro which took his fancy. But never fear. The Brazilian artwork was not disposed of, it was merely moved elsewhere or found a home where many of Freddie's and our possessions ended up which was hidden away in the loft! He had more

Japanese prints than he could hang in the house at any one time and so beneath the stairs which led up to his suite, he had built a storage area in which artwork could be slid in and stored upright in purpose-made compartments until such time as he felt the need to re-hang it. The frames housing the Japanese prints were also made so that they could receive another print with ease. He was very fond of a Goya woodcut which hung in the upstairs landing at Garden Lodge.

He must have known when he came to England in his teens that an artistic direction was the one he was bound to take. If he was going to go to college, at least by doing graphic design he would be doing something he enjoyed. The artist becomes an artist because of one thing only. Perception. A banker, walking along a street looking at cracked paving stones, would figure out the cost of repairing and replacing the broken slabs. Someone of an artistic mind, following in exactly the same footsteps, would see amazing designs and beautiful patterns.

Strangely, you need to be both a banker and an artist to create. Freddie never let cost interfere with what he saw as a complete design. If it meant paying a little extra to get as near to perfection as humanly possible, then he was happy to spend it. He was one of the lucky few to be in a position to be the total artist. You'd only have to see Garden Lodge to know what I mean. I could be wrong but I believe that Freddie never had an ambition to be the most famous rock star or the biggest or the best in comparison to anything or anyone else. Freddie never set any specific ambitions. His ambitions were to complete the next project, whatever he set his mind to, whether it was an album or a video or a tour. Perhaps any ultimate ambition was never set in stone because he never wanted to have the disappointment of not having achieved it. Each achieved ambition became a stepping stone to the next. The feeling of having completed a project to the satisfaction of not only himself but the others in the band, spurred him on to the next goal.

He was a great believer that the work, anyone's work, should speak for itself. That's why he regarded album covers as being of such importance because the punters saw the album cover even before they had heard all the music on the album. Pretend an album is like a Christmas present. When you look under the tree, don't you go for the best-wrapped one first?

The whole band obviously had to okay anything that was representative of the four of them but Freddie relished getting his teeth into everything artistic. The band very much liked Freddie to initiate the process of design because it gave them something to work from. Occasionally one of the others might come up with an idea which Freddie would then develop but they all trusted his eye and judgement. So often, particularly in the later videos – the master videos – there was a certain amount of trepidation as the time for filming drew near as they were wondering what they would be dressed up in and what he would make them do.

The first album cover that I was really around for was *Hot Space*. Because of the title of the album, Freddie thought of the word 'hot' and worked on that. That really was the reason why the colours came up. They were bright, vibrant and could hardly be missed among the many other albums on display on a store shelf. The designs were made in those days to fit the twelve inch by twelve inch frame of the old vinyl album covers. Although compact discs had started to appear and were gaining in popularity, Freddie loved working with space and therefore preferred the old vinyl albums. With the new CDs, everything was small and small was not in Freddie's nature. However, he was more than aware that anything he designed for the twelve inch square would have to be transformed down into cassette format and therefore the jump to CD was not that huge. This also gives an idea why the covers that Freddie had anything to do with are so striking.

He started working on the *Hot Space* cover in his suite in L'Ermitage in Los Angeles. Because of its title, he wanted hot colours. Also, the members of the band had to feature individually so that even if people couldn't read the writing from a distance, they would know who the album was by. A meeting was set up with Freddie and Norm Ung, John Barr and Steve Miller who had been brought in by Elektra Records as art directors. Freddie knew which colours he wanted – the red, blue, green and yellow. At that point, he wasn't quite sure how each band member would feature or which colour would represent each person except that red of course was a favourite personal colour of his. Not that he was averse to yellow either! He was never, however, a blue person. The red and the yellow were obvious choices of colour for the Freddie Mercury Rose which has since been developed.

Freddie had decided that he didn't want to use photographs on the front of *Hot Space* because he thought it would be difficult to compete with and follow-up the cover for *The Game* which had been so monotone. A few ideas were kicked around and then the idea of the four cartoons was put forward. What Freddie wanted was striking features, something for the fans to recognise in each of the four likenesses. He came up with the idea of the hair being the most distinctive feature and this was duly incorporated by the design team. At that time, short hair and moustache was Freddie's trademark.

At the subsequent meeting when the draft cartoons were shown to the other three band members, I don't remember them being particularly impressed although the idea soon grew on them.

You wouldn't believe the amount of time that has been spent on each album, just on the letter Q. The style had to be acceptable to everybody; also, the size. There could be huge arguments over a fraction of an inch. Notice, how the Q changes on each subsequent album cover. Never in my life have I ever known one letter to have caused so much fuss. But that's perfectionism for you. Frequently, up to ten different sizes of letter were produced on transparent overlays and yet only one of those was going to be acceptable to all four and even then only after each had changed their minds over their first choices.

For those of you who might be planning an album, do remember to set aside a month or two for decisions on artwork. Each Queen band member had to be given a duplicate of all written copy including lyrics and acknowledgments in case someone had been left out or a stray comma had been omitted. Try coordinating that operation while each person is six thousand miles apart. An album is the end product of many people's input and work, from the tape-op to the printer of the cover.

Another thing that has to be taken into account which only comes with practice is visualising what the end product should look like. Colours on the mock-up sent out for approval are very often a few shades darker than that which will end up in the shops on the finished product. Here again, in order to achieve the required perfectionism, a wealth of experience comes into play. What the band sees is not necessarily what the album buyer gets. It is therefore a huge part of the art director's responsibility to advise the band accurately what will happen to a colour during the commercial printing process. Strong colours are notoriously fickle when it comes to reproduction.

The cover for *The Works* was once again done in Los Angeles. Freddie jumped at the opportunity to be photographed by George

Hurrell. Hurrell had become famous for his use of shadow in his photography. The man was a legend in Hollywood having created masterpieces with Marlene Dietrich, Joan Crawford and of course Garbo. George Hurrell must have been seventy-five when he photographed Queen and he was still working every day.

It wasn't the first time that the band had been photographed by a maestro. Lord Snowdon had turned his lens on them for the *Greatest Hits* cover but because of Freddie's knowledge and love of the stars of the Thirties, Forties and Fifties, to be photographed by this master I think helped fulfil a dream. Freddie was being photographed by someone who had walked and talked with his heroes and heroines, the film stars of Hollywood's heyday whom he had seen on the silver screen as he grew up. Freddie and his good friend Tony King started up what was to become an international game known to more than a few of his friends. The 'B' Moviestar game started in a bar in New York where we each had to name an actress who while being a known name had never made the 'A' list. The likes of Viviane Ventura, Laya Raki, Britt Ekland, Tania Elg, Viveka Lindfors – sorry, girls – but you were at the top of Freddie's list. Even Joan Collins who has since become a household name due to her wonderful work on television.

The design team for *The Works* cover was changed and reduced in number to just one, Bill Smith. He came to the Pink House. Freddie must have got on with him. If he hadn't, Mr Smith wouldn't have had his name on the album cover. In any event, it was Bill Smith's idea to use George Hurrell because on this occasion, Freddie's starting point had been the idea of a photograph.

Freddie learned a lot about the fine art of the photographer's brush, used to paint away any imperfections on the plate. Hurrell still used what appeared to be amazingly old cameras because he found that the results they gave him were still the best and they were achieved in his own studio in Hollywood. Many shots were taken to try out different effects with the band in different tableau arrangements. Perhaps only one or two shots were taken of each tableau which was re-set like they were shooting an old-fashioned movie or an up-to-date video. It was all to do with lighting and was, obviously, a completely different experience for each of the band from the usual click-click-click of less exalted photo sessions.

The session took place one morning. Hurrell wore cord trousers, shirt and waistcoat and Freddie behaved quite reverentially towards his hero. For a change, Freddie was prepared to be led by Hurrell every step of the way. Everyone has their idols whom they look up to and admire from afar. Being able to meet one and work with one brought about a very different Freddie whom I observed that day although he did contribute several ideas. He was not for once in total control and yet was pleased to be so. It was very much like being a child again and sitting for a family portrait in the studio of the local professional photographer. Freddie was on his best behaviour.

The Works was the last but one album to be toured and it was the responsibility of tour manager Gerry Stickells to commission the design for the touring set. I think the only brief a designer would have been given for any Queen tour would have been '. . . something spectacular and memorable' which is what all Queen shows were.

An initial design was submitted for the band's approval and if that was forthcoming, a model was made and also submitted. Changes always arose between model and final product and these, if problematic, were always ironed out with the help of Gerry's silver-tongued diplomacy. These submissions were supposed to be made in committee but if one or the other of the band wasn't available for joint consultation, a majority decision of approval was made with the verbal consent of the missing party. The first time the band would see the end product would be in the space where they were rehearsing. On this occasion, for *The Works*, the space was the film studios in Bavaria.

A Kind Of Magic returned to the concept of an illustration on the cover which took the form of a caricature of the band. The art director was Richard Gray who was to remain with the band in this capacity until the end. Richard Gray worked freelance and commissioned Roger Chiasson. The characters Chiasson came up with were utilised in both the video for 'A Kind Of Magic' and also on the tour, when huge inflatable balloon versions of the caricatures were tethered on either side of the stage.

For the cover of his own album *Barcelona*, he used the fashion and portrait photographer Terry O'Neill whom he had met several years earlier when the band were managed by John Reid. The shoot was at Terry's studio and lasted all morning. Freddie and Montserrat arrived, had a quick discussion with Terry to discover what it was he was attempting and then the hard part for the pair began. "What should I wear?" I'd brought an assortment of clothes from Garden Lodge, everything from a full evening dress suit to various less formal clothes.

Several bow ties had been thrown in. Montserrat and her niece Montsy had brought half-a-dozen different outfits and there was at least one change of clothes as can be seen in the accompanying CD booklet. During the 'hard work' that Freddie and Montserrat went through deciding what to wear, Terry's two assistants were put into various poses for at least an hour so that when the stars came out after hair and make-up had been put on by Terry's crew, they simply adopted the positions already decided.

The Miracle heralded a sea change in the band's idea of itself. All the tracks were credited as being written by the band as a whole which I think might have led on to the idea of creating the one face on the front of the album. Morphing as such was a very new concept and this computer generation once again ensured Queen were in the forefront of graphic design in the music industry.

In the last couple of years of Freddie's life, Jim Hutton bought him a water colour paints set and Freddie did use them a couple of times. However, he was so ill that he didn't want to start anything that he wouldn't be able to finish. The cover design for *Innuendo* was therefore Roger's discovery which he found along with others of Grandville's work in a magazine. The ideas contained in the collection were extended and used in the videos and again on the live album recorded on the *Magic* tour. The surreal content of Grandville's work appealed to Freddie's sense of the bizarre. Grandville must have been rather *avant garde* for his time, surrealism being, in the early nineteenth century, completely unidentified as an artistic genre.

Freddie's own taste in art was eclectic. His tastes varied and in the time I knew him, they ranged from Japanese woodcut prints through Erte and Dali to his last passion which was Victorian artists' work, ending with the pre-Raphaelite painters. This was the context in which he met Rupert Bevan, the frame restorer whose expertise was often called upon to refurbish the frames of pictures Freddie bought at auction. Rupert's expert touch was also used in renovating gilded and jesso-ed French furniture which had to have care lavished on it to restore it to its former glory. Very, very public school, Rupert and Freddie got on very well and Freddie enjoyed his friendship enormously. Freddie had great respect for people who had been through the British public school system, who spoke authoritatively. He saw that system as a perfect grounding for whatever expertise the person later developed.

Freddie's artistic endeavours weren't solely to do with his recording and touring work but embraced his whole life. He spent his life collecting, whether it was people or pieces of art. Each had a place in his grand design. The culmination of a great deal of dedication was Garden Lodge. It was not only a home. It was a canvas upon which he painted his life and surrounded himself with his image of beauty. He put in a huge amount of work to the design aspect of the house to bring it back to its former glory.

Once the house had been completed to his satisfaction, he then had to fill it with splendid objects and furnishings to complement the decorative scheme. His attention to detail was exhaustive and demanding on those who had to execute, for example, the mahogany and maple woodwork on the gallery overlooking the drawing room which was exquisite. This spirit of perfection was maintained throughout the house which was a masterwork. In a way, his masterpiece.

Although Freddie bought Garden Lodge in 1980, it was a long-time in its transformation. When he first saw the house, it was in a sorry state, having been split in two in order to be occupied by separate households. It was his aim to restore it to one grand house, making his personal alterations along the way. I shall try and give as good an account as I can remember of how Garden Lodge looked in its heyday although I'm sure that it must be very different now.

Garden Lodge started life as a two storey, eight-bedroomed property. There was a large room upstairs which the original owner's wife – a sculptress – used as her studio. This, and two other rooms, Freddie transformed into his suite of bedroom, mahogany panelled and mirrored dressing room and twin bathrooms en suite. Into the dressing room and one of the bathrooms, Freddie incorporated his version of the ceiling in the Rainbow Room at Biba in the old Derry and Toms building, where I had first seen him. The rainbow effect was created by three hidden switches which when turned on operated concealed strip-lighting covered with various coloured film gels. The intensity of colour was varied by twiddling the knobs.

This lavishly appointed suite was accessed from the raised landing via the dressing room through a normal-sized door. From the outside, no one would have had a clue what was to come. It could have just been a door to a cupboard. Once inside, with the door closed behind, the dressing room displayed a series of mahogany panels, each of which was a door to either the bathrooms, closets or mere shelves. In the centre of the room there was an octagonal ottoman upholstered in a cream moiré satin. It was impossible to know which of the panelled doors led to the bedroom except that opposite the entrance were the two largest panels and when slid back, the entrance to the bedroom was revealed. This room, with its balcony directly above the sitting room, overlooked the rose garden at the front of the house and the wisteria-covered pergola.

Freddie had two bathrooms adjoining the dressing room, the smaller of which he used most. It was finished in the same wooden panelling as the dressing room and was the only room in the house which had no outside window. He used some Japanese tiles that he had found on one of his numerous visits to Japan which were randomly placed in the tiling around the bath. The walls were covered in a sage-green steamproof wallpaper.

The second bathroom, opposite, was the larger which was finished in cream marble. This room contained the Jacuzzi which was recessed in a pillared alcove to which access was gained by a raised step. This bathroom also housed one of Freddie's ill-fated showers as well as two oval hand basins set into a specially made vanity surface. Brass taps and fittings set the seal on the style. Gold taps didn't figure too highly on Freddie's scale of taste. Had it ever worked, the shower would have been a splendid affair. It was built into the corner of the rectangular room. The walls were of cream marble although the base was, strangely, a fibreglass tray. There was a large central brass shower rose and there were three brass pipes running vertically on the walls through which water jets also sprayed. Talk about sensurround! The sensation was truly Brut-al: "Splash it on all over!"

The bathrooms were, like the rest of the house, crammed with objets d'art which Freddie had accumulated over the years from all corners of the earth. Bits from Japan, bits of France, bits of Germany as well as Tiffany artefacts from New York and souvenirs from South America. Scattered around were various bottles of cologne, eau de toilette and soaps. Among his favourites were Armani for men, Monsieur de Givenchy and the one he wore most in the last two or three years was L'Eau Dynamisant by Clarins. By reason of all its properties, this latter was his favourite.

Also, one perfume which secured a permanent position in whichever bathroom around the world he used was L'Interdit by

Givenchy. Apparently this was created for Audrey Hepburn and Freddie adored the perfume from the first time he smelt it. He didn't care that it was originally designed for ladies. He just liked the smell. As far as shampoos were concerned, he was quite prepared to use any one that we bought from a supermarket. In the end he did quite like Johnson & Johnson baby shampoo which appeared not to irritate his sensitive scalp.

He liked the soaps made by Roger et Gallet, again in their various perfumes but in the end he used Simple for his own purposes more often than not, keeping the Roger et Gallet for display. He loved going into the perfume departments of stores and occasionally would select a basketful to give as presents to friends. His wicked sense of humour came into play once in New York when from Bloomingdales he bought a bottle of Joy by Patou to give to Tony King (nickname Joy) and for his photographer friend David Nutter (nickname Dawn) he bought a plastic bottle of the washing-up liquid of the same name!

We were much amused!

Freddie loved towels and bathroom linen of all description; the bigger the towel the more he liked it. He found a great source in Munich. Barbara Valentin of course knew the best places to shop and Freddie found a large array of exotically patterned bath sheets, huge, almost the size of bedsheets. In the same place he also discovered some amazing blankets which he used to wrap around himself while watching television rather than putting them on the bed. He might not even have been cold but he just loved the blankets which were of a fluffy man-made fibre representing angora, patterned in circles, stripes and triangles of bright primary colours on a white background.

I often think that had he not been a musician, he would have made his fortune in interior design. He had an amazing eye for structure and shape and I think this is also the reason why he bought the occasional property – like the Mews for example – just so that he could decorate it. He bought Garden Lodge at the beginning of the Eighties at a time when he was rarely in the country. I think it was part of the reason why it took so long to complete, because he insisted on being a part of all stages of the house's decoration.

He employed Robin Moore-Ede as his interior designer but Robin's job was more to tell Freddie what he couldn't do rather than do any constructive designing himself. This is not of course to deny that Robin came up with many original ideas which Freddie

142

developed but Freddie would be more likely to say, "I want this, this, this and this . . ." and then Robin would consider and then say which of the wishes were feasible. It's a good way of working if it can be achieved. Robin, of course, introduced Freddie to his builders, Messrs. Taveners, Mr Tavener being the father of contemporary classical composer John Tavener, one of whose works featured in the funeral service of Diana, Princess of Wales. At least Mr Tavener the Elder knew what he was in for regarding artistic temperament when he first took on what was going to be a very long job.

Freddie's bedroom incorporated not only his bed which was on the left of the entrance but also a sitting-room area on the right. The room was much more a boudoir, such as the room in *Der Rosenkavalier* where the Marchelin receives her callers. He had an assortment of furniture. There was an Edwardian *chaise longue*, a Louis XIV *fauteuil* and a modern two-seater sofa. It was a place where he could feel comfortable and still receive friends and visitors without people continually walking in and out. It was a room where one received. In those days, when Freddie lived in Garden Lodge, he accumulated a large collection of prints by Louis Icart and twenty-two of these decorated the walls which were covered in the same cream moiré satin which was used in all the drapes and soft furnishings.

The bed's headboard was built into the wall and continued the same wood-pattern as in the dressing room. On either side of the bed, he had had made two commodes, large bedside chests of drawers, whose veneers ran with the mahogany theme.

There were five-foot high French display cabinets, bow-fronted on short legs from the mid-nineteenth century against the walls, containing various small pieces of porcelain, crystal and objets d'art, Lalique boxes and Japanese lacquer boxes. I often think that as far as these lacquer boxes are concerned, the smaller they were the more expensively they were priced.

As with the rest of the house, where there was carpeting, it had been woven specifically to fit the room according to Freddie's cream colour scheme. One of Freddie's bedspreads will have been seen by anyone who watched the 'Slightly Mad' video. Made up of countless thousands of dyed multi-coloured ostrich feathers, Freddie wanted ". . . something colourful" for the video and found exactly what he was after lying on his own bed. It wasn't actually in use overlong on his bed as the cats took a liking to it and showed their affection by trying to destroy it. I don't know if this was because of the colours or the feathers.

Access to Freddie's suite via the raised landing was due to the extra height inbuilt into the north-facing drawing room below which was originally built by the sculptress's husband as an artist's studio. In fact, Garden Lodge was no more than a stone's throw from the artists' colony of houses begun by Lord Leighton at Leighton House and the various Norman Shaw-designed houses in Melbury Road.

On the walls of the landing was the one common denominator between Freddie's New York apartment, Garden Lodge and Stafford Terrace. He used up some of his supply of gold and platinum discs to form a wall-covering. We spent quite a few hours with tape measure, hammer and nails to ensure that none of the original wall-covering showed beneath the massed framed records. It can be quite frustrating taking into account that the frames were of different sizes and the hanging wires at the back of different lengths. The tape measure was in constant use. The master of course supervised and measured with the best of us.

Off the main landing, there were several rooms. One was the library at the foot of the stairs leading to Freddie's bedroom, decorated in wallpaper which Freddie had bought in Japan many years before. It was a room which Freddie made a library because Jim Hutton's carpentry phase had been given full rein by Freddie, thus allowing Jim to build shelves in this room which Freddie ultimately intended to be used for books. Although Freddie was no reader, the shelves contained catalogues from auction houses and the standard books which all households contain, dictionaries, atlases, encyclopaedia as well as the coffee table books of cats, art and design which he would recycle as he was given or acquired new ones. From the window of the library, there was a view directly down the garden path to the front gate of the house in Logan Place.

The next door along was a little door to a closet which, because it backed on to the hot water tanks, was used as the linen store.

Next door to that was the entrance to the main guest suite which consisted of a large square bedroom and a connecting dressing room and bathroom which was furnished with beautiful pink marble. Freddie obviously had a fascination for moiré as the walls in the guest suite were covered in a dusty salmon pink version of this fabric. The suite had a series of Dali prints of surreal subjects on the theme of

Hades on the walls. This room was later to contain some Biedermeyer and Empire pieces of furniture and some that were made specifically for the room. Freddie spent a lot of time in Rupert Cavendish's shop on the Kings Road in Chelsea. Whenever Freddie arrived at this shop, it didn't matter how many were in his entourage, Rupert always made all of us very welcome and was very happy to talk about his latest acquisitions.

I think I should say at this point that one thing Freddie was always very unlucky with was showers. The shower in his own bathroom and the one in this guest bathroom caused huge damage to different parts of the building, the Japanese Room below the guest suite and the Gallery above the drawing room respectively. Eventually, the shower in the guest bathroom accommodated some hastily made shelves and he abandoned the shower in his own bathroom in disgust. He couldn't believe that even the best builders in Britain couldn't build him a shower that worked. Unlike America, where every household, however small, had a bathroom *and* a shower room that was operational without apparent complication.

The last thing to be said about the guest suite was that it had the best views from the house. As it was on a corner at the front of the house, it overlooked both the fishpond and the lawn with its magnolias in front and towards the conservatory on the other. Because of the position of the house in the grounds, the view from Joe's and my bedrooms were very similar and were of other people's windows. It's amazing what you could see some evenings without even trying! There was very little land at the rear of the house before the high boundary wall of the adjoining properties.

Turning back on the landing, there were two doorways, the first on the left leading to a bathroom which was actually en suite with Joe's bedroom. To get to Joe's room from the main landing, there was a door separating the upstairs from the downstairs. This separation was made even more obvious at this threshold where the plush Prussian-blue carpet of the landing finished and a workaday grey stair carpet began, leading past Joe's and my bedroom to the stairs descending to the kitchen.

Joe's bedroom was the first doorway on the left and was decorated in a pleasant Messel-green emulsion. My room was next and was resplendently pale-yellow. My room was diagonally opposite the main guest suite so that my view was concomitantly diametrically opposite to the guest suite's. I occasionally had an intimate view of other people's lives. But that's other people's fault for doing it without closing the curtains or turning the lights off.

At the head of the kitchen stairs, almost opposite my bedroom door, there was a doorway which led to the modern-day minstrel's gallery which was, once again, back into the kingdom of the blue carpet. This enclave above the sitting room was crammed full of the most up-to-date, state-of-the-art sound equipment. Also up here Freddie stored a vast collection of videos and albums and had had built a drinks bar and various items of bar furniture like stools, seating and a table, again following the same design principle of the mahogany and maple wood pattern used throughout the house. On the wall behind the bar hung a massive painting, ceiling to floor and twelve feet long, of a jungle scene that Freddie commissioned from his friend, the Jamaican artist Rudi Patterson. At the other end of the gallery, stairs led down into a big sitting room made to look even larger with its sixteen foot high ceiling and its polished parquet floor.

Some twenty-five by thirty feet, this room was dominated by huge windows which almost formed the entire north wall. As Freddie had no intention of painting, this former painter's studio was turned into his sitting room. In fact, it consisted of three separate sitting areas. The first beneath the windows on a dais, where he had had constructed a banquette window seat to fill the entire bay. Opposite this dais and beneath the overhanging gallery was the area he most used at home in front of the big marble fireplace. He wanted to have an open-fire but without the mess that a coal or woodfire would have involved. He compromised by installing a gas log fire which produced the right visual effect and also he got the warmth from it which he always craved.

To one side was a twenty-eight inch television set which served a seating area comprising a large squashy four-seat sofa and two comfortable chairs with a low Japanese table in front of them on which was placed a silver wild cat bought for him by Billy Squier and various coffee table books and porcelain ashtrays courtesy of Limoges via Hermes in Bond Street. Two lamps sat on tables at either end of this main sofa.

Backed on to this sofa but facing the centre of the room was an Empire period drawing room suite consisting of sofa and four chairs, purportedly made for the brother of the Emperor Napoleon

Bonaparte, upholstered in pale green and gold with a bumble bee imperial motif. The piano on which 'Bohemian Rhapsody' was composed was in the corner of the room by the window and covering the top of it was arranged a crowded gallery of silver and polished wood-framed photographs of friends and cats.

There were two large pieces of furniture. In the corner facing the piano was a plain mahogany display cabinet, some eight feet high, filled with a priceless Meissen porcelain dinner service, decorated with various hand-painted still-lifes of fruit on a white ground. Freddie needed such a massive display cabinet so that it wasn't dwarfed by the room. After much searching in antique shops all over London, we came across this cabinet in Chelsea. It had been used in a huge shop so wasn't specifically designed for anyone's front room but it was exactly what was required. Terry Giddings and I took the polaroid camera and photographed the cabinet from all angles. These photos we rushed back to Freddie for his approval. He immediately said that he wanted the cabinet but only after it had been renovated to an acceptable condition. The shop upholstered the interior and checked and reinforced the internal, separate metal framework which was to support the plate glass shelves on which the priceless Meissen was to sit. The cabinet was ultimately delivered in two parts by four stout men and the toughest part of its journey from van to sitting room was its entry through the garden gate which was only achieved after the removal of the eighteen inch high drawer section of the cabinet's base. Freddie of course nervously supervised every inch of the cabinet's arrival.

"Up a bit . . . Oooh! Careful of the floor . . . Down a bit!"

The other piece of furniture in the drawing room was supposedly made at the Majorelle workshop at the turn of the century. It was a blind walnut cabinet with glorious, in-built buttresses appearing to hold it up, curving from the wider base to the narrower top.

There were rugs on the floor although the dais was carpeted in the kingdom of blue.

Dotted around the walls, wherever there was space, were many French sidetables, Victorian copies of eighteenth century originals, all of which bore some expensive vase or ornament. Pride of place was given to a Tiffany lamp in the design of five lily blooms which stood on a commode which housed his collection of photographs. Large vases made by René Lalique and the Daum factory were ranged on the window ledge so that the light streamed through them from outside showing their colours to best advantage, everything from a flaming orange with gold leaf somehow applied to the moulded surfaces to vases of sea-deep blues and greens to others of plain, lead-crystal colours.

On the rag-rolled walls, antiqued with two layers of tea-coloured yellow and a topcoat of dark varnish, hung a variety of paintings. He had another series of Dali prints, this time of various Greek mythological characters. Did he have, unknowingly, an affinity to Catalans? So many of his favourite artists came from Catalonia – Gaudi, Picasso, Dali, Miro and Montserrat. Interspersed with these were large Victorian oil paintings. He liked pictures of people as opposed to landscapes and still lifes. Above the fireplace hung a Chagall print and in one corner of the room Freddie had fulfilled another of his ambitions by hanging a lovely portrait of a woman by the pre-Raphaelite artist Tissot.

Freddie loathed overhead lighting and so arranged around the room were many table lamps which could be operated individually and which were made by the likes of Tiffany and Galle and which Freddie could illuminate at will depending on which areas of the room were in use.

Walking in through the main entrance to the sitting room, no eye could fail to miss hanging on the wall opposite, by the window, a full-size, full-length, framed woman's dress. It was the costume worn by Montserrat Caballe when she first became an international star singing the role of Lucrezia Borgia. Montserrat gave this to Freddie and although he gave it to me upon his death, the dress is now once again the property of Montserrat herself. Full dress circle!

The sitting room was thus at the same time both the grandest room in the house and yet it was very personal and where Freddie spent most of his time. The one thing he always complained of was how he still felt it looked like a museum with displays at all levels around the walls, with the furniture and artwork using up all available space. Like all square rooms, the middle is often empty and it was certainly the case at Garden Lodge. Had he lived, I have no doubt that it would have been a problem which he would have solved.

A set of double doors opened from the sitting room into the entrance hall of the house. Surprisingly, considering the size and period of the house, the hallway and main staircase were disproportionately small. The hall's floor was, as all rooms on the ground floor, laid to parquet woodblock tiles. There was a beautiful *pietra dura* (inlaid marble) centre table which Freddie had bought at auction which stood in the middle of the hall under the porcelain chandelier and opposite it a writing desk with a green leathered top which he had brought with him from Stafford Terrace.

Another set of double doors led in direct line with the sitting room to the withdrawing room, commonly called the Japanese room.

This room got its name because it was where Freddie's fascination for anything oriental was displayed. Here he brought together his love of things Japanese – prints, lacquerware and netsukes – much of it displayed in a Chinoiserie display cabinet in a style much used in the furnishing of the Brighton Pavilion. The cabinet was part of a large suite of furniture which Freddie had bought many years previously from Harrods and which consisted of armchairs and sofas and tables as well as the cabinet. The walls were painted a very pale lemon which provided a suitably neutral background which did not distract from the multi-coloured Japanese prints from the studios of such artists as Utamaro. Also displayed in this room on what looked like a mediaeval pillory was one of his large collection of kimonos. He bought this antique kimono display stand on his last visit to Japan and it allowed the exquisite and intricate design worked on an unfolded kimono to be appreciated in its entirety.

A set of French windows led into the garden where, across the lawn, another set of doors led into the conservatory and then into the Mews house itself, which formed the last section of a full through-view from one side of his property to the other.

There were two other doorways in the hall, the first leading to the small downstairs cloakroom and its matching pair opening into the dining room. This was the room where Freddie had allowed his imagination to run riot. The walls were painted in a strong saffron yellow gloss. The woodwork was picked out in a rich, dark racing green, again gloss. The ceiling's plaster centre rose was then painted a multitude of colours – lilac, red, purple and green amongst them to create a totally exotic, tropical effect. Gold leaf was used on many of the doors to pick out various beadings and panel borders. The rear wall of the room was floor to ceiling windows outside which, on the boundary wall of the property he had had put up a *trompe l'oeil* in trellis work to give the impression of an extensive pergola for in fact there was little room, only three or four feet, between the dining room windows and the property's boundary wall.

The windows were dressed with dark green curtains matching the woodwork, made in thick, dark, heavy satin with very full hems which draped on the parquet floor and which, incidentally, provided a useful toilet facility for the cats who could never be weaned out of this disgusting habit.

All the furniture bar one cabinet was hand-crafted for the room. He had a sideboard specially made as well as a breakfront cabinet. It was in this cabinet that he had a 'secret' drawer created and of course immediately blew the secret because he just couldn't resist showing people the whereabouts of the drawer. Ultimately, the drawer always contained absolutely nothing at all!

Because the dining room wasn't huge, Freddie couldn't have a full-sized dining room table and although the table could seat ten comfortably, it wasn't really wide enough to put a multitude of platters along the centre length. He used tablecloths, some plain white Irish linen used on high days and holidays and others delicately embroidered in small floral motifs bought in both Ibiza and Germany. There were sets of table mats to dress the table, one set being in silver which he bought at Thomas Goode and Co. in South Audley Street. The silver Christofle flatware was kept in specially made drawers in the sideboard along with Lalique, Tiffany and Waterford table crystal as well as the St. Louis glasses, blue glass with stars cut out of the blue, which to my certain knowledge he bought for two hundred pounds each and which were kept in a matching armoire.

There was a French Empire display cabinet which Freddie had bought from Rupert Cavendish on one wall which contained a large dinner service of Noritake ware amongst other treasures. The Royal Doulton dinner services were kept in the kitchen and Freddie left it to us to make everyday decisions about what to use for lunches and dinners. For special occasions, Freddie of course made all such decisions himself, including the one as to which cutlery to use. Although the main service was the Fleur de Lys pattern by Christofle, there was an equally splendid alternative which was an Art Nouveau set which Freddie had found in Belgium along with other pieces he treasured. In Garden Lodge, he had made special cutlery drawers for this almost antique service. He sent away one piece of each part of the service to the cabinet makers so that compartments were literally made to measure. The Fleur de Lys service was housed in a Japanese chiffonier in the kitchen in six very shallow drawers lined with green baize.

From Rudi Patterson, Freddie had bought several paintings, two of which he had specifically commissioned to hang in the dining room. He had been collecting works of art by Rudi for many years and by looking round the walls the various artistic directions which Rudi had explored were obvious. Rudi loves colours. He went through a phase where there were many bright colours in abstract forms and the theme of the tropical landscape features heavily especially those in the countryside scenes from his native Jamaica, including one of the two specifically commissioned for the dining room. This painting showed a house set in amongst the trees which we figured out must have been in the process of being blown over in a huge storm because the house was slightly crooked.

One of the four doors led into the most-used room in the house. The kitchen. The floor in here was black-and-white square ceramic tiles with a border in dark green. The green was followed through in the doors of the huge Amana refrigerators, the larder one in the American style with double doors and the other which housed the ice-making and drinks-chilling facility. The kitchen's cabinets were in oxblood red and made by Boffi. Freddie got the idea for these from the time he spent in New York staying in the penthouse suite of the Berkshire Place Hotel. He certainly had a 'thing' for the colour oxblood; even his car in New York was of the same colour.

Robin Moore-Ede persuaded Freddie to use what was then a new work surface called Corian which, believe me, is all that it was advertised to be. Namely, indestructible. If you accidentally cut into a Corian surface with a bread knife, the incision is removable by shaving a layer off. To clean the Corian surfaces after a year or two's use, the colour of the surface went from an off-white to a cream and thus a professional sanding machine and sander arrived one day.

The kitchen had a centre island preparation area. Although it looked like a mere butcher's block on wheels, in fact it had been specifically designed to house wine storage, and had four cupboards and two drawers which contained all the necessary kitchen utensils, knives, spatulas, spoons et cetera. The kitchen had a large double sink under the window on the rear wall, a dishwasher beneath, one four-ring hob, three ovens, a separate ice-making machine and a microwave which even to the end Freddie couldn't make work.

To one side, there was a breakfast area with seating for six. A built-in banquette upholstered in green leather, with cream leather piping to match the rest of the kitchen, occupied one wall and there were four barrel-shaped stools arranged around the table which was specially made in a pale hardwood. Freddie also had a massive Welsh dresser built to fit into the corner which contained more of his vast collection of dinner services.

Off the kitchen was the utility room which housed an industrial washing machine, tumble drier and the drinks fridge and from here there was a back door leading to a side passage. In this area, Freddie had built a wine cellar where in the relative cool he could keep his large stock of St. Saphorin white wine from Montreux. It also had space for dry goods like tins of cat food, tomatoes and also the Christmas cakes and puddings. On top of the tumble drier stood the Elner press iron. It was in the early days of these big pressing machines – easily half the size of the ones seen in *Prisoner Cell Block H* and often whoever happened to be using it was likened to one of the Aussie inmates. Standard routine where laundry was concerned was that I would collect all the used linen – be that sheets or Freddie or Jim's clothing – and I would load up the machine and then dry it. On a specific day, Margie Winter would come in to spend the whole afternoon ironing, using a combination of the Elner and an ordinary hand steam iron. Everything was washed in house except the big table cloths used for the dining room table which were taken out to Jeeves on Kensington High Street. Although they would be returned in perfect condition, Freddie never wanted to see the creases and so it fell to whoever was standing unoccupied when the master made his choice of table cloth to hear: "Oh, you're not doing anything. You can iron out the creases!" Once pressed, Margie would return all the items to their respective homes in drawers and cupboards. I of course would always use Jeeves' services for any dry-cleaning which Freddie's wardrobe may have required.

Only two doors in the house were meant for feline use and these were the ones in the utility room and the kitchen to both of which Jim Hutton fitted cat flaps.

As far as general domestic security for anyone else but the cats was concerned, Freddie had only the minimum that was required to cover the house and its contents for insurance purposes. He hated excessive security, not only because it gave the impression of being in a prison but also on numerous occasions, one or another of us were delayed in going out because the burglar alarm refused to set. Because the cats could not be allowed into the rooms where the alarm sensors were set, each time the alarm was activated, we had to know the whereabouts of all the cats and thus began the ritual of 'Calling In The Cats'. They would be shooed and ushered from wherever they might be hiding and collected in the kitchen. If, after roll call, one was missing the guaranteed method of rounding up the stray was to go into the garden rattling a box of munchie morsels. The prodigal pussy would then be seen bounding over a wall and into the arms of the rattler. It was then quickly whisked in to join its companions.

Since Freddie's death, however, due to perhaps some over-eager souvenir hunters, security has had to be so intensified that even a sparrow would need security clearance to land on the property.

The garden was a third-of-an acre oasis in the centre of what must be one of the most car-crowded and polluted sites in London. Earls Court Road, Warwick Road, Cromwell Road and High Street Kensington form the boundaries for a square mile which despite the congestion and traffic noise still permitted the peace and quiet we found at Garden Lodge.

The garden went through an ongoing process of change and followed Freddie's whole *raison d'être* which was to continuously create, adapt and then change and improve. When he arrived, the garden was almost a classic Edwardian affair with a brick and pillar wisteria pergola in great need of repair, large expanses of lawn edged by big shrubberies and in the middle of the lawns there were two fine magnolia trees, one by a pathway and one by the corner of the Japanese room. Over a period of time, a rose arbour was created in the rose bed, the pergola flourished once again, the shrubbery disappeared and the fishponds and Japanese gardens emerged. In the Japanese garden there were two delicate little arbours, one of which became known to us as the bus shelter. The chaos which the creation of a garden can cause is quite unbelievable. Freddie employed a Japanese gardenmaker who spent a lot of time going to quarries and selecting exactly the right rocks. These arrived at the house along with a massive crane which was used to lift them from the flat bed of the truck over the garden wall and into position. Some weighed more than a ton. It took a long time but as far as Freddie was concerned, all the time and effort was well worth it. It was his little piece of his much-loved Japan in his little corner of London.

The lime trees were pleached on the southerly back wall to create a denser privacy and the two huge plane trees on the westerly wall had to be regularly pollarded. Where once huge honeysuckle vines grew on the east wall of the garden, there ultimately sprouted a conservatory.

There was one thorny problem however as regards this conservatory. Freddie wanted to have it built against the wall of the cottages which formed Logan Mews. While he already owned the ground floor of this neighbouring building, its upper floor was owned by someone else. The garage which was the ground floor had its own door into the grounds of Garden Lodge.

To be able to build his conservatory he had therefore to wait until the other owner was prepared to sell. Because of Freddie's firm intention to build his conservatory, he was therefore at the other owner's mercy. The man could basically ask what price he wanted knowing that Freddie would have to pay. After a period of time, the man eventually sold and Freddie then had another building which he could convert and decorate and if we thought that Garden Lodge had had a massive face-lift, it was as nothing to what was about to happen at numbers 5 and 6 Logan Mews.

Robin Moore-Ede was once again commissioned as supervising interior decorator. He and Freddie had developed a very trusting rapport which extended to one occasion I remember when Robin, about to be commissioned by Dustin Hoffman, called Freddie and asked if the actor could come and see some of Robin's work at Garden Lodge. Freddie immediately obliged and laid on tea, not only for Dustin but for his wife and children as well. Freddie asked Dustin if he would do him a favour. Freddie presented him with a Japanese writing board and felt tip pen. Freddie then said, "It's his birthday," pointing to me.

Dustin then wrote on the card, Happy Birthday, drew a picture of a birthday cake with candles and signed it 'Dustin Hoffman' before handing it over to me. Sadly, it still remains amongst some of my memorabilia in the loft at Garden Lodge. But back to the Mews conversion. The way the adjoining properties existed, the bottom half of number six was Freddie's garage whereas both floors of number five and the top half of number six were residential. The cottages were surprisingly spacious. Freddie intended continuing the idea of keeping the same proportion of residential space but decided, due to the conservatory being against the outside wall, that he wanted the property's sitting room in the bottom half of number six to allow access to the conservatory.

This plan necessitated the whole of the inside of the two cottages being gutted in order to re-site the garage in the bottom half of number five.

The conservatory, the initial reason for the project, had a roof constructed of two arched gables in flexible Plexiglas with standard-glazed windows at the front and side. It was divided into two areas, one for dining and one for sitting. There were three big areas for plants plus lots of room for pots. It was a multitude of colour through-out the year with many exotic species including bougainvillea, datura and strellitzia as well as colourful geraniums, all specifically chosen so that there was always something in flower. There was always a lemon tree although not the same one. When one lemon tree died, Freddie would insist another was bought. Lemons are notoriously difficult to maintain even in their natural habitat. The furniture was cane and the cushions were covered with a colourful stripe-pattern fabric Freddie had bought in Ibiza.

Ibiza reminds me of holidays and it is perhaps surprising that Freddie never took holidays as such except on the Balearic island of Ibiza which he discovered through Roger Taylor who had a house there. Freddie loved the place and stayed either at Roger's house or at Tony Pike's hotel in the foothills just outside San Antonio Abad. No lager louts at Pikes, merely champagne louts! We would arrive on the island in a ten-seater private jet chartered from Field Aviation at Heathrow. There would be about eight of us as the other two seats would always be required for excess baggage. Even going only for a two week break, Freddie would still insist that half his entire wardrobe came with him. Just in case. I'm reminded of one occasion which wasn't too funny though. It was extremely hot on the day we flew. No one noticed that the interior of the plane was excessively hot. It wasn't until the plane was taxi-ing and taking off that we noticed that extremely hot air was being blown through the air-conditioning system. We returned to Heathrow and were told that somehow the exhaust was being partially vented through the air-conditioning ducts! We remained on the ground for three hours until the fault was fixed by which time, had we taken a scheduled flight, we would already have been by the pool at Pike's.

We were not amused in the slightest.

One of the party on the Ibiza junkets was often Graham Hamilton whom Freddie had known for many years. He and his partner Gordon Dalziel began their company Factotum to provide tailor-made chauffeur services. Nothing out of the ordinary phased either of them and they would think nothing of having to drive someone's car to the south of France while the owner went by plane. It was due to Graham's driving skills and his ability to make Freddie laugh that he knew Freddie would always ask him along to drive the People Mover which Freddie would always hire. Freddie decided that with the number of people going to Ibiza, it would be easier to transport them all at once rather than hiring individual cars and taxis. During one of the visits to Pikes Hotel, Tony Pike persuaded Freddie to go out on his powerboat which he proudly boasted was the fastest on the island. I rather think Dave Clark, who happened also to be staying at Pikes, was included in the party. It certainly was an experience. You get used to travelling on roads at sixty miles an hour but it seems very much faster on a boat. Someone might contradict me but I don't think Freddie could swim. He therefore always seemed a little uneasy on water. This occasion was no different. While the rest of us might be standing on the back seat and holding onto the cross rail, feeling the wind almost pushing us off the back of the boat, Freddie would be huddled safely in the comfortable seats protected by the windscreen in front. While the boat was at anchor off Formenterra and we all got into the crystal clear sea, Freddie remained firmly on board.

The day out was finally marred when Tony Pike presented Freddie with a bill for the outing which, because of the way he had been invited, Freddie never expected. He thought Tony was just being nice. So much for hotel proprietors. Whenever any of his friends were contemplating a stay at Pikes, he would say, "Lovely, dear. Lovely place but just watch out if he asks you to go out on that fucking boat!"

While generally not someone to bear a grudge, if Freddie got niggled by something, trivial as it might seem, he would behave like a little terrier with a huge cushion, refusing to let go until the cushion had died! He was very prone to being able to make a huge mountain out of what to us might seem an insignificant molehill.

Freddie's love of Pike's Hotel was so great that he had 'that' famous birthday party there. He chartered a plane and flew fifty of his friends from Britain to join the other three hundred guests from all around the world. The principal food at this bash was *paella*. But *paella* for four hundred? The pans were enormous and all heated by open fires. Fire figured a lot. Due to some guest's over active arm movement while holding a cigarette, some of the paper decorations caught fire which again set light to fabric hangings which had been draped down the side of the house. Everything wet was thrown on to try and douse the blaze, from buckets of ice cubes and water to champagne. Considering the spectacle, I think only twenty five per cent of the gathered guests realised anything was amiss. The rest were, frankly, far too far gone. Uncharacteristically, Freddie disappeared halfway through the party and retired to his room with a handful of friends and let the party go on without him. Although he frowned upon such reclusive behaviour in others, on this occasion even for him the crowd was too much and if you think about it, he couldn't possibly have known all those four hundred people. He just needed to give the smiling façade a break.

But anyway, back to the mews where upstairs, there were to be four bedrooms, three with an en suite bathroom and one with an adjoining toilet. The main bedroom and bathroom were three of the original upstairs rooms knocked together. He carried the marble theme of his own bathroom through to this bathroom but rather than use marble throughout, he was very interested in, and used, an applied painted marbling on the bath panels and the architraving around the doors. This bedroom also incorporated a dressing room area at its entrance. The marbler was another of Mary Austin's boyfriends by the name of Piers Cameron who later fathered her two children.

The second bedroom was decorated with wallpaper that Freddie had saved after a shopping trip in Japan many years before. It was a shade of maroon with gold pattern of Japanese inspiration. The decoration of the adjoining bathroom adhered to the Japanese theme.

Next came my room, which of all the bedrooms in the mews was the one I fell in love with. I can't think of any reason why except perhaps the colour in the bedroom which was eau-de-nil and the adjoining bathroom which had all its surfaces finished in black granite. Very Thirties, perhaps yet another inspiration from Freddie's Hollywood fascination. I just loved the black. I moved into that bedroom as soon as the mews conversion was completed. This enabled Mary to move her secretarial office into Garden Lodge where she assumed my old room. In the centre of the ceiling of the landing, a skylight was installed which flooded the whole area with light. This was just as well because Freddie had had woven a dark blue fabric of an Oriental golden design which was then backed and hung as wallpaper. Without the skylight, it would have been a very gloomy space.

There was one central staircase which led down to one side of the sitting room which was the whole of the ground floor area of number 6. Towards the back of the room, there was a small raised area where Freddie sited the dining table and six chairs. Also, within this area was the small kitchen which was decorated in the Mediterranean yellows and greens of Freddie's holiday discovery, the island of Ibiza. On one trip to Madrid, he bought a series of antique Spanish ceramic tiles which he incorporated in the mews' kitchen. It was the yellows and greens from these which he used for the washed-out and sun-faded peasant look he wanted to achieve.

It was on the same trip to Madrid that Freddie was taken by Pino Sagliocca to an antique shop in the city's centre. It was a rambling old building, one of those which is far bigger on the inside than it appears from the outside. We were guided around many rooms which contained all manner of antiques from ancient Egyptian relics through to suits of armour from mediaeval times and then to more recent nineteenth and twentieth century works, sculpture and paintings and objets d'art.

Towards the top of the building we found something that looked rather incongruous. Every now and then there was a glimpse of metal bars like a jail cell. We paid no attention and were led into what was described as a room which had been removed intact from one of the country's ancient aristocratic palaces. It was a complete wood-panelled room including the ceiling. As soon as we were all inside, someone closed a metal gate behind us. We started to worry, thinking immediately of a kidnap or some such drama until we were calmed by the shop's owner who proceeded to alter the lighting within the room and then carefully slid back three of the wall panels.

Hidden there were three of the most beautiful paintings Freddie said he had ever seen. One was very dark and exuded very dark vibes. The second I cannot remember clearly because the third remains so seared into my mind. It measured some twelve by eighteen inches and was a painting of the Madonna, in all the luminous blues and whites and golds associated with her image. Maybe it was a trick of the light but that painting really stood out.

Freddie was so taken by one of the pictures which was by the Spanish master Francisco Goya that he decided, no matter what he had to go through, he simply had to have it.

The owner of the painting was prepared to let it go for five hundred thousand pounds which Freddie was quite prepared to give. Before making final arrangements, a stumbling block arose. The Spanish government was not prepared to allow any of the country's national treasures in the form of works of art to be exported. Therefore, the only way Freddie could acquire the painting was by purchasing a property in Spain. Many solutions were suggested, including a house in Ibiza or in Barcelona but the nearest he came to buying was when someone sent him the plans and photographs of a house very near Santander near the Franco–Spanish border in the north which was one of the very few private houses outside Barcelona that had been designed by Freddie's favourite architect, the Catalan, Antoni Gaudi.

Eventually, the whole project petered out because of the huge ramifications of such an impracticable step. But there are not many people who would even think of going to the extent of buying a house just to hang a painting.

The ground floor area of number five Logan Mews was taken up by the double garage which only ever held junk. The Mercedes was always with Terry and the Rolls was very rarely used, being stored in a garage in North London, although it was eventually brought back in a very poor state – and in need of great refurbishment – to Logan Mews before Freddie's death. Behind the mews garage was Freddie's ultimate little whimsy, a fully equipped hydro spa consisting of a steam room, a pine sauna, a twelve foot long plunge pool as well as a Jacuzzi and the whole edifice was tiled in half-inch square mosaic inspired by Roman pavements and wall decorations. In the aquamarine background, designs and patterns were worked with contrasting coloured tiles, none of which of the same colour ever touched, giving the pool a blue hue which seemed not to be made by the hand of man.

The redevelopment of Logan Mews was not, however, Freddie's final design project. He had grown to love the Swiss lakeside resort of Montreux. Its anonymity suited him down to the ground, particularly in the last year or two of his life. The band was doing all its recording in Montreux and so Freddie was once again spending long periods of time in rented accommodation, in this case the Duck House. After several chats with Jim Beach, Freddie reached the conclusion that another property in yet another country wouldn't go amiss. Jim Beach looked around for him and came up with a beautiful penthouse apartment overlooking Lake Geneva.

This was one property which I never actually saw. I have seen so many plans and have heard so many descriptions of the place that I feel that I have been there. Everyone who has been there always comments on the wonderful view and of course it was this apartment building which was represented in Freddie's last birthday cake. Jim and Joe took many photographs which we delivered to Jane Asher who was a little taken aback but not daunted by the task of building a block of flats in fruitcake, marzipan and icing sugar. The apartment occupied a quarter of the top floor of the building and consisted of an assortment of bedrooms, a sitting room and dining room as well as a kitchen which Joe Fanelli loved.

Freddie plunged headlong into this new design project. He could never have only had one property. He had far too much furniture, far too many pictures and furnishings to put into one building and to a certain extent he was a hoarder. Like so many of us, he hated throwing things away. This reminds me of the occasions like Christmas and birthdays when he received so many gifts which, as they revealed themselves on being unwrapped, we would declare to be a "Loft job!" This verdict meant that under no circumstances would it be thrown away but merely that there was absolutely no place for it in any design scheme in any of his households. Instead, the gift was relegated to the capacious space in Garden Lodge's loft.

There was a delay on Freddie's moving in caused by the resolving of certain issues in the lease but this didn't stop him making elaborate plans and going on shopping sprees to furnish the place. Once again, Rupert Cavendish's shop was patronised for it was from here that the apartment's dining room antique Biedermeyer furniture came. I was also dispatched on several occasions to Sotheby's and Christie's Auction Rooms in search of furniture and paintings while Freddie pursued one of his favourite pastimes which was scouring the catalogues of all the forthcoming auctions in the world. I can evidence the fact that things are bought on the telephone at auction for once I was that person, bidding for a painting by Burgess which Freddie wanted in a New York sale.

There was an Empire suite of drawing room furniture which I bid for and secured at Sotheby's which went straight to the upholsterer and restorer for ultimate installation in the Montreux apartment. Freddie spent as much on its renovation as he did on its purchase but the end result was absolutely stunning and the furniture eventually arrived in Montreux only to be sat on once or twice.

Freddie loved catalogues because there were lots of pictures and little need to read any text unless the picture caught his eye. Freddie was not a reader. I couldn't tell you the title of any one book which Freddie ever read. His attention span wasn't long enough for him to get stuck into a novel. His boredom threshold was very, very low and his time was too precious, in his terms, to be spent reading when you could get the answer to your questions a lot easier by asking someone. Perhaps because his life wasn't 'normal', he wasn't going to derive any excitement from reading about any one else's 'normal' life.

Beds and bedding he always bought wherever he was. I remember going to Bloomingdales to buy all the bedlinen after he had secured the New York apartment. Similarly, all the beds and bedlinen were bought in Montreux for the apartment there. By the time of his last visit, the place was fully furnished although none of his projected structural alterations were ever begun.

Chapter Five

I am suddenly reminded that one of my purposes in writing this book has been to attempt to dispel some of the more outlandish rumours which have become associated with the life of this sometimes very ordinary man whose own life unintentionally touched the lives of millions. I could have written a whole book merely by dissecting all the other books which have been written and refuting the incorrect assertions and the falsehoods, whether intentional or not. Rather than be so schoolmasterly, I have decided that one of the ways to best achieve my aim is to go into some detail about Freddie's everyday life as he lived it.

In thinking about this final section, I am primarily reminded about Freddie's contradictory attraction to conflict. I don't mean confrontation but the sort of conflict which only he instigated. It seemed to be a need which permeated almost every aspect of his life. It was almost as though he needed a fight to jump-start his motor so that he could get to grips with living. Like Don Quixote, another legend, Freddie was quite capable of dreaming up windmills to tilt at. I suppose, therefore, I was his Sancho. As he always said to me, "You can never say that life with me is boring."

That much is true but, as you will now see, life with Freddie could at times be very predictable. As much as he disliked being so, he was inevitably wrapped up in a cocoon by his mere circumstances and required a confrontation of one sort or another to start the day and connect him to a real world.

Luckily, most days, all that was required was a quick flick through the newspapers. We regularly used to get the *Sun*, the *Mirror*, the *Mail*, the *Express* and the *Guardian*, the broadsheet which the house glanced at, although Joe, to give him his due, was the one who would study its columns in depth.

One of the first jobs we had in the morning was to go through the papers on the off-chance that something had slipped through without Roxy Meade from Queen's PR company – Scott Riseman Lipsey Meade – notifying us. When something unauthorised was found, Freddie would come out with some remark like, "Not that old chestnut!"

By the mid-Eighties there was little about Queen or Freddie that hadn't already been published in one format or another. On the subject of the press and its organs, Freddie never wasted too much emotional time. The papers were just something that appeared every-day. He didn't particularly follow anything that happened on the news, either in the press or on television. Very rarely did he specifi-cally ask for the television to be tuned in for the news. I think in his opinion, if a news story was important enough, television programmes would be interrupted so that the public could be kept abreast.

As far as representatives of the press were concerned, Freddie knew that if he spoke to any of them off the record as 'a friend', people like Nina Myskow or David Wigg, that nothing he said would be printed. He was also aware that if he was to give an interview to either David or Nina as well as anybody else, that they could usually not be held responsible for what was actually, ultimately printed. However logical his assessment might have been, the emotional reaction when he was mis-reported was predictably volcanic: "What do *they* know! Fuck 'em!"

On many occasions, he gave what he believed to be a reasonable interview. On one specific occasion, after much trying, David Wigg secured an interview with Freddie on the understanding that it would be centre page with a couple of decent pictures. In the end, the piece appeared as two-and-a-half columns of re-interpreted text, the reason being that the features editor had apparently decided that there wasn't enough space for the length of the original article. It was this last interview with David Wigg that deterred Freddie from giving any interviews from then on even though David had showed him the original text which Freddie approved. But that's the power of editors . . . Although Freddie logically accepted that it was not David's fault, the experience nevertheless put a spanner in the works of their friendship. Freddie never gave a newspaper interview afterwards.

With regard to photographers, rather than going out of his way to avoid the then king of the British paparazzi, Richard Young, Freddie actually had photo sessions with him. Freddie liked the photos which Richard took and considering that Richard was a dedicated member of the press corps, Freddie and he had a very good relationship. When Freddie was attending any function where photographers were present, Freddie appreciated the fact that Richard's friendly face would be at the forefront which would make him that little bit more at ease knowing that he had an ally to play to. He even invited Richard to the house specifically for a photo session and allowed Richard to include the resulting photographs of himself and his cats Oscar and Tiffany in one of Richard's exhibitions.

Critics fell into an altogether different category in Freddie's estimation. He lumped them more or less all together. He believed that all critics were failed performers. Freddie was firmly of the opinion that performers are well able to criticise themselves. The performer knows what he or she is capable of producing and they will know when that performance wasn't up to scratch. Freddie would not accept that a drama critic would see numerous performances and be able to put himself in the place of all the actors. To his mind, it was impossible – so how could a critic furnish a constructive criticism? All a critic could be left with at the end of any performance, in Freddie's opinion, was a jealous perception of a phenomenon that the critic himself was unable to achieve. Freddie lumped all critics in that category, a view with which I sometimes tend to have some sympathy. A critic/reviewer will always have to find some fault, something wrong with a work or a performance. Ninety-eight per cent of the review might be praise but there will always be that jarring criticism.

For almost everything he went to see in the performing arts, Freddie believed that most performers gave a hundred per cent and therefore anything less than a hundred per cent praise was unbecoming. He was very generous as a performer and he knew what the person on stage was putting themselves through and so therefore could appreciate the blood, sweat and tears.

By the same measure, Freddie also knew when a performer wasn't giving a hundred per cent which is why he walked out of the theatre at the interval of *Little Foxes* in New York. He remembered Elizabeth Taylor being quoted about, "I have never claimed to be a great actress. I am a great movie star . . ."

I think Freddie rather felt that if you weren't a great actress then better not to be on the stage. While saying this, he, of course, adored her as a movie star.

On this subject, as this is a very rambling section for which I crave your indulgence, there was an A-list of actresses whom he revered. Maggie Smith and Diana Rigg were almost at the top of this list because they essentially bridged all the media, something he himself started to do with his work with Montserrat. Although there were many, many other names on Freddie's A-list, those which spring to mind now are Ava Gardner whose autograph he desperately craved and which, sadly, I failed by a matter of moments to secure. She left the Crush Bar at the Royal Opera House just a few moments before I could reach her clutching my ever-present paper and pen. Another one, whose autograph I did manage to get, was Honor Blackman.

"Can you sign this for my friend Freddie," I blurted out when I saw her by chance at a theatre pub in Maida Vale where my friend Adele Anderson was performing her one-woman show. She did and he was delighted and he stored it away in his bedside cabinet with all his other treasures in all those little silver boxes.

He had a thing for little boxes, later in his life jewelled, enamelled boxes. In the bottom bedside drawers he stored the boxes that some of his Japanese porcelain had come in. Wooden boxes such as the ones used for *sake* bottles and cups. Little bits of favourite jewellery like brooches which he'd both bought and been given . . . Those personal documents and photographs that weren't in the many frames dotted around the house which he would keep near him and which he would look at frequently. A few letters and a lot of cards which he'd received over the years and which had a special significance. I suppose they must still all be there somewhere because they were all so very personal to him and who else would realise their significance?

But to return to the top of the day, if Freddie had a set time to be woken up on a specific day, one of us would take him a cup of tea, rather than a laid tray. Generally we'd find him lying in bed awake, planning his day. At this point either we would ask or he would let us know what he wanted for breakfast. This could vary from a couple of slices of toast and English marmalade to *kachori*, a sort of Indian version of scrambled eggs. Food was the only topic I ever heard him voice regarding the forbidden territory of his childhood. Other than *kachori*, there were several favourites; one was the drink *falooda* which was more like a milk shake, made of milk, rose water and a sort of red tapioca-sized confection balls which turned gelatinous when immersed in the milk; *dhansak* made with chicken, vegetables and *dal* was another favourite. I also made a few attempts at *kulfi*, the frozen ground almond dessert which is served in many Indian restaurants.

Before he became ill, he adored spicy food, be it Indian, Mexican or Chinese, realising of course that because it is spicy does not mean it's full of chillis. With his breakfast he would usually continue to drink tea. He was never really a coffee person. Occasionally he would have fruit juice but at any time during the day, not specially for breakfast.

Any mail specifically or personally addressed to him would be left by his place at the kitchen table, the first sitting on the banquette. He would open mail carefully with a knife as he loathed paper cuts. He divided up the mail into that which required Mary's attention as a secretary, copy mail from management or accountants we would file for him in paper folders which were kept in the big commode in the sitting room.

Also in this drawer we would have to keep mail from 'fans on the edge'. Let me explain . . .

On two or three specific occasions, Freddie received a series of letters and cards from 'fanatics' as opposed to fans. We had been advised by the police to keep all such mail should any of these people attempt to carry out their threats. "I'm going to get you if you don't acknowledge me . . ." was the general tenor of the contents. He would read them silently and then hand them over for us to read, saying as he did so, "Look, here's another one . . ."

It's only thinking about it now while writing this that makes me realise that it's another excess which he had to deal with in his personal life. It's something I hope none of you will have to go through. Outwardly he handled the situation very well but who knows what was going on inside? He never burdened us with the problem.

Regarding the mail which he wanted to answer personally, he would have a selection of cards which we had bought for him covering all occasions and the cards themselves ranged in taste and style from indescribably rude to those which were 'suitable for mothers'. When he was in Japan, he would always buy a huge selection of cards for his own use and keep them in his bedside drawer. We would remind him of upcoming occasions amongst his friends and family which he needed to remember. He himself had a birthday book which included dates of birthdays and anniversaries of family and close friends which he always kept meticulously up-to-date.

During or after breakfast he would inform us of his day's schedule. Terry Giddings usually arrived between ten-thirty and eleven o'clock each day. On days when Freddie had appointments which we would all have known about in advance, Terry would be in much earlier but usually we all knew that Freddie would not be out of the house before eleven o'clock.

If he wasn't going out, he would do very little. If it was a warm, sunny day he'd wander round the garden and then, at the eleventh hour, decide to invite people over to lunch. So, while one of us would get on the phone to the various people he'd want invited, the others would run out and buy the food he'd elected we were going to eat. Thor Arnold has reminded me of one luncheon occasion when Freddie demanded an *al fresco* lunch in the garden in honour of the American guests who were vacationing with us. One of the tables had been specially commissioned in sections and completed inside the kitchen, and had to be manoeuvred to get it outside. It proved impossible and so in the end, the large dining table which Freddie had brought from Stafford Terrace with the huge top of sheet glass was carried, heaved and manipulated out through the back door and on to as flat a place as we could find beneath one of the magnolia trees.

On the subject of the garden, Freddie was a very keen amateur gardener although I must admit that his idea of gardening was looking through all the garden books and deciding what plants he wanted Jim Hutton to go out and buy. Jim was a passionate gardener and only wanted to make the grounds of Logan Place beautiful for Freddie. He was, after all, the official gardener and had no reason to be ashamed of the magnificent job he did despite Freddie employing a general job-bing assistant to do the weekly tidying. But, make no mistake, Jim's was a real job. It was Jim who mowed the lawns and did the weeding. Jim who effected all Freddie's designs and schemes. Jim adored gardening. He spent hour upon hour outside in it and did everything he could to keep it looking beautiful.

Freddie and Jim once had one of their huge arguments which had something to do with the garden and Freddie said after Jim had stormed off, "Right! I'll show him. I'm *not* useless!"

I was duly dispatched to Rassell's, the Kensington nurserymen, to pick up a vast assortment of petunias in colours which wouldn't clash. Freddie had decided that he himself was going to plant two urns of these bedding plants to stand outside the French doors of the Japanese room.

Whist Jim was strategically absent, cooling off his frustration, Freddie and I spent a good two or three hours planning exactly where each plant would go almost like a battle-plan of lines of soldiers. Freddie then actually used a trowel and filled up one of the urns. But he soon got bored.

"Right, dear, that's enough. Perhaps you'd better do the next one," and off he went inside for a cup of tea. He did emerge twenty minutes later, carrying a watering can just to ensure his planting was properly watered in.

Freddie had made his point.

Back to the lunch which was one that he knew his guests would enjoy and which would vary from a simple fish pie, a favourite of Francesca Thyssen's, to a four course banquet to which he would invite as many people as were free to come. As you might have gathered, Freddie knew quite a few people who were very happy to drop what they were doing and come when beckoned. There were also others amongst his friends who were genuinely close but who would come when he really needed them. They knew the difference between "lunch" and "help!"

Freddie didn't pay for all of his friendships.

The world of entertainment is a strange milieu. You can get very close to a person in a matter of days when you're spending up to twenty hours a day in their company but because of the nature of the beast, you can then be separated for a year or two before you see each other again. Also, working in the entertainment industry is not a nine-to-five Monday-to-Friday job and therefore Freddie used the opportunities of his lunches to reunite the friendships he knew he had formed in this ever-moving arena. And, of course, being performers, musicians and artists, a lot of his friends had the time free to come when he called.

For example, there was the Actresses' Dinner . . .

I had once bought Freddie a book from Aspreys in which chronicles of dinner and lunch parties could be entered. On one side, there were the guests, the menu, the flowers, the wines and the required dress. On the other side, the table plan. This book comes in handy when you don't want to give the same guests the same meal three times in a row which, as Freddie always wanted his favourite meals each time, so often became a problem as the guests too were often the same. The Actresses' Dinner involved Freddie, Straker and amongst the guests were Anna Nicholas, Anita Dobson, Carol Woods and Debbie Bishop. It was an idea cooked up between Freddie and Peter for the camp of it . . . Having lots of actresses round one dinner table was an irresistible whim. Freddie, being Freddie, could fulfil it. I wish I had the dinner book to show you. I only made fleeting appearances in the dining room but I'm sure that everybody got on well with each other. There were gales of laughter emanating from the room into the kitchen where Joe and I were sitting. I must admit that this wasn't as impromptu an occasion as most and needed some organisation as each of the girls involved had a heavy schedule, especially Anita who was still up-to-her-neck in drink and 'Den' as Angie in *EastEnders*.

Freddie would always inspect the table to ensure that everything was as he wished. While I might have set the table as to the demands of etiquette, he would merely just make sure that all the cutlery, place settings and table furniture were where *he* thought they *should* be.

A lot changed over the course of the passing years. Earlier on, he would only have a light lunch and so our main meal would be in the evening. I suppose that was to fuel him for those many hours spent out on the town. In the last few years, this habit was turned on its head and he preferred having larger lunches either indoors or in restaurants followed by a lighter supper at home in the evening. Talking of the earlier days, for example, at the time he moved into Garden Lodge, he had a wide-ranging taste as far as food was concerned. He was always fond of stews in one form or another, whether Irish stew a la Jim Hutton with potatoes and dumplings or *boeuf bourguignon*, served often by itself or with plain boiled rice, always on a dinner plate. He loved my version of the classic *boeuf stroganoff* which I remember making for band meetings in Pembridge Road and also once in Musicland studios when Freddie was expecting Roy Thomas Baker. I had to ensure every ingredient was perfectly prepared: "Do you realise Roy knows *everything* about food!" And so I peeled the mushrooms precisely, removed the stalks exactly, chopped them absolutely evenly . . .

Lamb hotpot and *chilli con carne* he also adored and he loved unusual and different things as much as he did his mother's version of chicken pie which contained sausages and baked beans as well as chicken in a white sauce under a wonderful golden brown crust of puff pastry. He also thoroughly enjoyed fish pie, either with a potato or pastry crust and traditional steak and kidney pie. Vegetables such as fresh boiled beetroot, scattered with fresh-squeezed lemon juice and cumin. Roasted parsnips with parmesan. He loved this dish. I would boil peeled parsnips for about five minutes, then drain them and while they were still steaming roll them in a plastic bag containing flour, salt, pepper and grated parmesan before roasting them in a hot oven until crisp and golden. As far as salads were concerned, if there was a salad presented he would merely pick over it. In the hot climates where he was brought up, salads were just never on the menu where everything had to be cooked to destroy bacteria.

One thing above all, he insisted on fresh food. While he appreciated the quality of Marks and Spencer, he fully believed that it didn't bear comparison to the real thing. He adored *osso bucco, chicken dhansak, prawn creole, chilli con carne*, lamb à la Madhur Jaffrey and every Sunday of course there had to be the traditional roast – pork, lamb, beef or chicken and at Christmas absolutely, always and only turkey. Pork was always served on Boxing Day.

We always used the same butcher, Lidgates on Holland Park Avenue and I was usually the shopper, driven by Jim Hutton who enjoyed these outings to shops and supermarkets as it gave him an excuse to drive his Volvo, the third greatest love in his life – Freddie, Garden, Volvo. I got on very well with the butchers and even now when I go in, I am still recognised. We always paid cash or cheque. We never had an account.

We would always have a tasty cheddar cheese in the house because, once again before he became ill, Freddie liked an assault on his taste buds but in the last few months I suppose it was one of the symptoms of his disease that he could not tolerate intense flavours. He suffered from a kind of retching, choking feeling in his throat and from then on he would subsist on a bland diet of soups and ordinary scrambled eggs. As far as cheese was concerned, it didn't figure highly as a course on a menu, the occasional Welsh Rarebit or a lunchtime piece to snack on was as far as it got. Of course in the climates and cultures in which he had grown up, cheese was not a healthy thing to have around.

He was never over-fond of desserts. Once a week I would have a bake-in and one of his favourites was an almond and cherry cake which I found in one of my mother's old recipe books where most of the flour content was replaced by ground almonds, thereby making it an extremely moist cake. You could even store it for a week and it would still be perfectly fresh although when on the day it was baked it rarely lived to see the dawn of another.

In Freddie's household, there was always a lot of food on stand-by. Ingredients almost never went to waste as we would always find a way of using them and Freddie did not approve of throwing away food. But every so often, Freddie would find something new he wanted, ask for it at half-past-ten at night when it was unobtainable. We therefore learned and kept a stock.

He loved picky foods. On every trip to Lidgates, I would buy anything that looked vaguely interesting such as their sausage rolls of which he was a big fan. They always had something fresh, new and home-made on their counters; patés, small meat pies made of, for example, lamb and leek as well as standard quiches and cheeses. An average weekend's butcher's bill would be something in the region of £100, including, of course, bacon and sausages.

Indoor suppers tended to be anything 'light' . . . Light to Freddie meant something different from what light might mean to the rest of the world. Light also meant smaller than lunch. We often made Welsh Rarebit or a pasta, spaghetti with a little fish sauce. He was very fond of an original recipe which came out of our kitchen where we would buy three different colour pastas, white, red tomato and green spinach. We would then play around with sauces invented for each colour. The white lent itself very well to a smoked salmon, cheese and cream sauce. The green worked quite well with an ordinary *bolognaise* and the red we would team up with a *prima vera* variety, using any of the baby vegetables which were currently available, carrots, sweet-corn, mangetout. Another of his light favourites was angels' hair pasta with garlic, chilli and parsley quickly fried in olive oil and then mixed with the pasta. Delia Smith, eat your heart out! I must admit I would have been totally lost without her and her books and Freddie's culinary intake would have been greatly compromised. Towards the end of life as we knew it at Logan Place, with both Joe and Freddie ill, it fell to me to assume the chef's role as well as my other chores and duties.

Conflict for the sake of love, I've tried to tell you about that. Conflict for the sake of peace, that too. It was what Queen was all about. Conflict for the sake of life . . . This is what this section is partly about. Freddie hated yes-men; yes-persons to be PC. If you hate yes-persons, you therefore must openly invite the possibility of no-persons, people who say no. Either no, thank you or no, fuck you! Freddie liked people ultimately to be their own people and he craved friends and associates who would resist him because only in that way, through a conflict of sorts, could he realise what he really felt or thought about a situation. I think that's the reason why all of us stayed with him and he stayed with us for so long. To give an idea of the longevity of staff with Freddie, I was the junior member after seven or eight years until Terry joined the troupe.

And it was indeed a sort of *troupe* for it often felt when we went out in public that we were some top-of-the-bill variety turn.

In a way, Freddie was one of the lucky ones. Most of us take each day as it comes, taking things as they happen. Freddie, not because of *who* he was but because of the kind of person he was, mapped out and planned his whole life. Everything he wanted in absolute detail.

If he went out to lunch, it would generally be to the Italian restaurant opposite the Coleherne pub in Brompton Road. Pontevecchio has now metamorphosed into Tusk. In the days when Meridiana was open, he loved going to the talkative, airy restaurant on the site where now stands the jewellers Theo Fennell in Fulham Road. Meridiana had always been a favourite of his even when he would only go there to dine in the evening.

After lunch, if there was any shopping to be done, Harrods was a favourite stopping off point. There was always the variety of goods to catch and please his eye and all under one roof. He loved buying colognes for people and he made at least one specific expedition and bought some of each house's fragrances and gave presentation packs to everyone he knew. He always included everyone, even his cleaners, Gladys, Mary and Margie in these gestures. If he saw something he liked, he would of course buy it while out on these trips but day-to-day toiletries and soaps, bath oils, shower gels and hair shampoos would usually be in our realm to buy. He loved bath oils which gave a nice smooth feel to the skin.

If he was specifically shopping, for example, for someone's birthday present, the Lalique shop on New Bond Street was always a place where he could find something suitable. While in that area he would often stop off at Tiffany and Cartier and there was also Sotheby's to be explored. When he spent a morning at Sotheby's he would usually go to Richoux in South Audley Street and have a light lunch there, something like their Welsh Rarebit or one of their specials of the day with rice and often, if later in the afternoon, sandwiches and Earl Grey. It was a habit he had picked up when Queen were managed by John Reid whose office for a long time was next door at number forty. Always, when he left any of the Richoux establishments, he would pick up two or three of their selections of Godiva Belgian chocolates. I think he liked the packaging as much as the chocolates and when the boxes were empty, everyone having been pressganged into eating the contents, he would of course keep the boxes, some even on display. There was something about Freddie and boxes . . .

He was very keen on presentation and appreciated and understood its importance. He realised that part of the mystique of food was the way it looked. While he didn't particularly like the food which was presented as nouvelle cuisine, he adored the patterns the food made on the plates. It is after all only another expression of artistic flair.

At both Sotheby's and Christie's, Freddie found many interesting and absorbing people amongst the auction house experts. There were two people with whom he particularly got on, one being Christopher Payne from Sotheby's in the furniture department who helped Freddie acquire many pieces of his nineteenth century French furniture collection. The other was Martin Beisly from Christie's who was in charge of the Victorian paintings section. Basically, when Freddie moved into Garden Lodge, he wanted something different to put on the walls and that was when he became more and more interested in Victorian art. Before then, his taste had been much more *avant garde* by way of prints of works by Dali, Miro and Chagall.

His main reading material, particularly in the last two years, was in fact a constant diet of auction catalogues from all over the world, including New York from where I bought one day on the telephone a painting of a gypsy girl. Freddie happened to be away in Switzerland and he had given me a rough guide as to his price ceiling. It didn't take us long to work out a system of pricing in his absence and he always trusted me. Very roughly, I would be prepared to go to double the bottom estimate price. If he wanted something desperately, I would then use my discretion. You can tell when you're in the auction room whether other people bidding against you are prepared to go to the outer limits. I must admit, I loved going to the auctions. It gave me such a buzz. Freddie only went very rarely to attend the actual auction although he would always investigate at the viewing.

The system was that I would pick up catalogues of items in which he might be interested and we would look through the catalogues together and he would pick out specific lots which looked appealing. I would then go and view the pieces and mark down whether it would be worth Freddie's while coming to see them. While I was walking around I would also look for anything else which we might have missed when reading through the catalogue. I would then report back to Freddie on the condition of the items and on anything else that I had seen. He would decide whether it was worthwhile paying a visit himself. If he went, we would inspect all the items to ensure that my summary had been accurate. We would tick the pieces he wanted in the catalogue and then go off to lunch at Richoux.

He would put the matter out of his mind and try to think afresh when we returned home having put some distance between him and temptation. So many of his purchases had been impulse buys and because he had bought so much, Garden Lodge was beginning to look a little full. But that never seemed to be an argument when he saw something he really liked!

Whenever furniture was bought, I always had to have a van on stand-by almost in the street outside the auction house. Freddie hated the prospect of having to wait until the day after the auction to see his purchase. He would have already signed a blank cheque that morning which I would have taken with me and merely filled in the amount to ensure that the purchase went straight onto the van. Because the auctioneers knew Freddie and were familiar with his whims, I was able to expedite matters. The same principle applied to the buying of paintings except that with a painting, I could always carry it home myself in a taxi.

Freddie's friend Francesca Thyssen came with me on one of my first jaunts to the auctioneers when Freddie wanted me to bid for his Chagall print which used to hang above the fireplace in the sitting room at Garden Lodge. We sat right at the front under the auctioneer's desk and when we bought it I think it was the most expensive single item that I had secured for Freddie. It was over thirty thousand pounds. The only time when Freddie came along personally to an auction was for a decorative arts sale and because he was there in person, the Lalique vase which he was determined to buy went for a vastly inflated price, some thirty-five thousand pounds. But it did look lovely in situ in the sitting room window!

Freddie wasn't the only person who would send out his agent to do the bidding. Understandably, whenever a 'famous face' appears at an auction, people think that there's money to be thrown around so when someone unknown like me shows up, no one pays much attention.

The only time when he was very disappointed that I didn't come away with the goods was on yet another occasion when he was in Switzerland and he wanted me to bid for a work by the Catalan painter Joan Miro for whom, as I have already indicated, he had a great admiration. When he saw it hanging in the viewing gallery, he decided he wanted it and at that point said he would go to two hundred and thirty thousand pounds. By the time he'd left for Montreux, the ceiling had been raised to allow me to spend two hundred and fifty thousand. On the morning of the sale I had a phone call from Freddie giving his final decision, "Two hundred and eighty thousand BUT NO MORE!!"

There was a free-for-all in the bidding up to about two hundred thousand pounds which was when I entered the fray and from thereon there was only a telephone bidder and myself. The bidding increased in tens of thousands. I put in the bid at two hundred and eighty and the phone bidder immediately came back with two-ninety. I thought, "Should I? Is it worth it?"

I went to three hundred. My rival came back after a moment's hesitation at three hundred and ten and so I thought, "What the heck!" I went to three-twenty.

It took a little bit longer but the phone bid was upped to three thirty and I then dropped out.

When I told Freddie, I said that I was very sorry but that I had been unable to secure the painting. Immediately he asked, "So how much did you go?"

"You know you told me two hundred and eighty," I gulped. "I actually went to three-twenty."

"Oh," was all he said and because he was in Switzerland and I couldn't see his face, I didn't know whether it was a good or a bad 'Oh'. "Well," he concluded, "you should have gone more. You *knew* I wanted that painting!"

Whether he meant it or not, we shall never know although he had saved many thousands of pounds that day. A saving which, after all, he could spend at another auction.

Freddie was never a great shopper for clothes. Generally if Joe or I were out and about and something caught our eye clotheswise which we thought he'd like, we would buy it and present it to Freddie. Jackets, shirts, jumpers . . . We would also go to Marks and Spencer whence came most of Freddie's socks although his underwear was usually Calvin Klein. This wasn't a specific request from Freddie. It was just what Joe thought appropriate. There were, however, several occasions when Freddie shopped for clothes, notably in Ibiza when he went shopping not only for himself but for everyone else in the entourage. Black shirts with Indian patterns, bright floral shirts as well as shorts . . . A must! Also, on returning from a trip to Japan where he had bought suits and shirts both for himself and everyone else, he brought me back a wonderful red woollen jacket with black leather patches. It sounds naff but it looked sensational.

He had an assortment of suits made for him by David Chambers but in private life, Freddie was not particularly sartorially minded. He was very happy to slop around at home in a sweat shirt and track pants. Whereas he had a very clear idea of the stage image he wished to project and had always dressed that part, especially in the early days when his private life clothes were basically no different from his stage attire, he was no dandy. He never felt the need to dress in the height of fashion and he also never wanted to create a fashion. He was into comfortable clothes.

Although in his later years he would wear a suit to a restaurant or the theatre, when he went out to bars and clubs he would dress in 'the uniform' of jeans and T-shirts and leather jacket. He wore trainers mostly and was never into heavy footwear. In the early days he had always worn clogs and in the last year of his life he couldn't wear leather fitted shoes at all as they hurt his feet so much.

His restaurant tastes would encompass many foods including Chinese, Indian, Lebanese and Italian. He was very fond of the Zen group of Chinese restaurants and as far as Indian cuisine was concerned he was a regular patron of Shezan which, although now closed, was in Cheval Place at the bottom of Montpellier Square in Knightsbridge. He loved Indian food although after Shezan closed, he tended to eat Indian food as take-away only on the occasions when

Joe and I didn't cook it for him. The Lebanese restaurant on Kensington High Street attracted him because he wanted to "try something different".

We also persuaded him into enjoying Thai food which was just emerging as the coming new oriental cuisine. We made up some soups using lots of lemon grass and chillis because he loved the hot Tom Yam varieties of thin Thai soups.

He also liked La Famiglia in Chelsea off the Kings Road which had been a favourite since the early days when he and Straker and Clodagh Wallace would often eat there. In Covent Garden he was very fond of Orso's in Wellington Street and Joe Allen's in Exeter Street where Jimmy played the piano and where many of Straker's friends would gather after their West End shows.

As far as the bill at the end of the evening was concerned, Freddie generally wouldn't even carry his credit card. It would be up to either one of us to make sure that we had remembered to bring his American Express Card. He never had any other credit card. He didn't feel it necessary.

When he wanted to leave, we could generally guess by his body language that it was time to go and so I or Joe would call our waiter for the bill which we always checked and then handed over Freddie's credit card. When the card came back with the docket, after adding the service charge if necessary, then we would pass the docket and a pen to Freddie to sign. He very rarely looked at the bills himself and only then if there was some obvious discrepancy which we had found. However, he always knew to some round figure what an evening would be costing him. Despite appearing to be cavalier, he was in fact very canny.

If he stayed in during the evenings he would usually 'veg out' and watch television. He would never work his life around television and only very rarely ask that we video something for him and then it would be a programme in which he had a special interest if a friend was appearing or if the programme was a live gig, a Prince concert for example. He had one video of a live Prince concert which he forced many people to watch, sometimes over and over again.

When Freddie settled down to watch such a three hour tape, it could take either fifteen minutes in which we watched only Freddie's specifically edited highlights or six hours when he would play the same bits over and over again. It was either fast forward or play it again and again and again, Sam! These video sessions generally occurred at two or three in the morning after Freddie and entourage returned from an evening on the town. The Prince tape was immediately put on and Freddie had sole control of the remote and his guests were subjected to Freddie's enthusiasm for said artist again and again and again. I managed to avoid ever seeing it but the sound of it haunts me to this day! I was lucky in that I had the excuse of constantly getting drinks for the guests which kept me out of the sitting room.

I think Freddie admired Prince because he was so similar to when Freddie was young. Extrovert on stage, thin, dark, hugely energetic and with that charisma which turns a diminutive form into a giant. Other performers who attracted Freddie's attention were Aretha Franklin, who loomed large in his admiration stakes until she disappointed him with a concert she gave at the Victoria Apollo. I remember him frequently telling the story of how he went to the show and she sang maybe for a total of half-an-hour, perhaps forty minutes. When she went off, he was expecting her to return at least for an encore but no . . . That was it. But having said that, his appreciation of her voice never dimmed.

He very much liked black singers because also included in his pantheon of favourite stars were Michael Jackson, Dionne Warwick and Lionel Ritchie. Looking at these names, one notices that maybe they weren't all quite so black. Somewhere in between maybe . . . Perhaps because of his own background he felt a bond with them. He would listen to music at home but he would always ask one of us to put the record on because he could never – surprise, surprise – really learn how to work the sound system although a mixing board in a sound studio desk was no obstacle. That he would have mastered by the end of the first afternoon. For a man with such musical genius, even he would admit that domestic electronics phased him. That category of electronics included even the most simple kitchen microwave! Despite his star status, it was strangely obvious that neither his own record company EMI nor any others deluged him with their product and nor was he forever on to the company asking for records which other major stars have been known to do. If he wanted records which he had perhaps heard on the radio or about which someone had told him, he would ask us to go and buy them. On Freddie's behalf as well as his own interest, Joe would also go to

Tower records and pick up an armful of other people's work which he thought that Freddie might find interesting.

But, and I'm sure this is typical of many artists, Freddie was only really, ultimately interested in his own work. As a musician and a composer, his work was his life. The two, work and life, can very rarely be separated. This doesn't mean that he lived, ate and slept music. He didn't have to 'get a life'. But all the time something was unconsciously going on in his brain which would ultimately find form in a song. His work was therefore more important to him than other people's.

In an entirely different genre, he obviously admired Montserrat and the three tenors before they even became the Three Tenors. In New York, when we lived there, Joseph Papp (he of Shakespeare in the Park) had already staged Gilbert and Sullivan's *The Pirates Of Penzance* which ran for ages on Broadway. Papp came up with the idea of doing Puccini's *La Bohème*, along the same lines, in Central Park. Maureen McGovern had already been selected as Mimi and Papp then asked if Freddie would audition for the part of Rudolfo.

Three questions came immediately to Freddie's mind: firstly, the audacity of the man, asking him to audition! Secondly, Freddie couldn't convince himself that he could carry off the romantic lead in an opera. His final doubt was that he had already promised himself many years ago that he would never again do eight shows a week.

Eventually, the production came to nought and Freddie brushed the affair off and carried on with his going-out life.

Another of Freddie's favourite New York encounters was with the distinguished photographer Annie Liebowitz whose work, notably for *Rolling Stone* magazine, had become legendary in the music business. She has since become the icon for many photographers and is much exhibited. Of course, Freddie hadn't a clue as to who she was when she was brought to the apartment by their mutual friend Lisa Robinson. The four of us spent a pleasant afternoon chatting about nothing in particular which Freddie was very good at when he was relaxed. Lisa and Annie left after Lisa had persuaded him to give her an interview on television. Later that evening, 'the daughters' came round and upon asking, "What did you do today?", Freddie just mentioned that his friend Lisa and some woman photographer called Annie something . . . Lee Nolan just couldn't believe it. He out of all of us was the only one who appreciated who and what Ms Liebowitz was. He immediately demanded to know where she had sat, what she had said . . . Was Freddie going to see her again? But he was never photographed by her.

After Freddie settled down with Jim Hutton, his need to go out to the clubs and bars decreased and, of course, in the last year or so of his life he rarely went out to these pleasuredromes. However, in the days when he did, it was never Freddie on his own who left the house. On a regular basis, there would have been Freddie, Paul Prenter, Peter Straker and whoever was driving Freddie. This was the core company which was augmented again on a fairly regular basis in the early days by Kenny Everett and his entourage, Wayne Sleep, Petra von Katze and Douglas Trout, Trevor Clarke, Rudi Patterson, Yasmin Pettigrew. Later, some were replaced in favour by Gordon Dalziel and Graham Hamilton and of course there were always the visitors like Barbara Valentin and other friends from Munich and New York.

Having assembled at the house, any excess passengers who weren't in Freddie's car would take taxis which would be paid for or they would follow Freddie's limousine in their own cars. Although once, on one of its rare outings, we did get nine people in Freddie's Rolls Royce, of which he was very proud, but it was not a feat I would recommend or which was ever repeated. I should also add that four or five of the occupants were ballet dancers, therefore very supple and able to perform feats of contortion to enable them to be squeezed in. Peter Jones was driving at the time. There was room for two small ones on my lap in the front passenger seat and five managed somehow to get into the back seat. Weird!

When I first knew Freddie, his favourite haunts were the Coleherne in Earls Court and Maunckberry's Club in Jermyn Street. The Embassy Club in Bond Street then became the place to go and I can remember many happy evenings there with Stephen Hayter and Michael Fish. Legends then took over as Freddie's nightclub of choice, although he stopped going to the Coleherne after a while. I cannot quite describe the difference between a sleazy gay leather bar in New York and the sleazy atmosphere of the Coleherne in London's Earls Court except that there is a world of difference. There's sleaze and there's sleaze but the Coleherne palled quickly . . . I shall say no more.

The Copacabana in Earls Court Road opened and although it was a club as opposed to a pub, it replaced the need for the Coleherne and it became Freddie's 'local'. Although it was no more than three minutes walk from his front door, needless to say he never walked there. Or back.

Going to the upper end of these nightlife venues, our group tended to be a little more noisy and obvious. Anyone who was anybody used to go to these West End nightclubs and of course Freddie went out any night of the week, not just at weekends when perhaps an out-of-town element may have been there to gawp at passing stars. During the week, there was more room, we weren't jostled constantly and we could enjoy being ourselves and still listen and talk over the sound of the music.

However, going to places like the Copacabana was quite different. The whole attitude of the group changed. We tended to be quieter and stuck closer together as we went in so as not to draw constant attention to ourselves. We never had to queue up to pay to get in as we were always allowed in free because the owners knew that apart from the kudos of having Freddie Mercury in their club, the waived entrance fees would be more than taken care of by Freddie's bar bill. This, like the restaurant bills, was always taken care of by whoever on the Logan Place staff was in attendance.

When Freddie made it known to us that he wanted a drink, it was assumed by us that everyone in his party was to be asked if they too would like a drink. Rounds would very rarely come to less than twenty pounds and this sum refers to a time fifteen years ago. Now it would be nearer fifty pounds. Also, Freddie's drinks were never small ones. Single was not a word in his bar vocabulary. His drink would always be a large vodka tonic which we would bring to him in 'his corner' where he would always stand.

It was a fairly dark spot but afforded him a good viewing position over the rest of the club. Not many people could be in the club without at some point passing before his scrutiny. Generally, one or two people would always be with him and he never ventured on the dance floor in London. Freddie would be quite obvious if someone caught his eye and he would send someone, Paul usually, over to start talking to Freddie's intended and thus bring them into the charmed circle. It's quite strange but people never entered the realm of the inner circle unless they were invited and very few tried to storm their way in.

People's reaction to having a world famous rock star in their midst varied from club to club and from country to country. For example, in Japan he would be followed by a huge crowd, up to fifty people, but who would all keep a respectful distance, some twelve feet from their idol. Three or four people would be leading a whole trail of followers, like Halley's or the Halebop comet and its tail.

In London, of course, the whole group was also part of the famous face phenomenon. A group of maybe six people acting like one entity, not paying specific attention to anyone so as not to attract attention even though we all knew we were being looked at. Everyone in the entourage tried desperately not to acknowledge the fact and those who noticed us tried desperately to appear nonchalant, as though no one special was in their neighbourhood. It was all like a well-rehearsed play with a dynamic all its own. How to try to be anonymous at the same time knowing that you are the centre of attention. Added to this of course was the problem of keeping an eye out for any possible trouble, that rare occasion when someone would decide to try and score points by blowing Freddie's cover, storming the ramparts of privacy. But, as I said, it rarely happened and when it did, the situation was dealt with by us. Only once or twice was Freddie ever forced to leave anywhere because of unpleasantness. I only bear one tiny scar on my forearm where I was once cut by a piece of broken glass when someone was upset that Freddie wouldn't talk to them in a bar in small-town America.

Speaking of America, our life in New York was very different. Whereas the people in London led lives which tended to revolve more around Freddie, his friends in New York had their own lives to live and yet were quite happy to fit in with him whenever he came into town. People like Thor Arnold, Lee Nolan, John Murphy and Joe Scardilli. Tony King, who worked for John Lennon and Yoko Ono, and thereafter Yoko and thereafter Mick Jagger and Jerry Hall was also a constant friend in New York as he was permanently resident there, as indeed was Freddie's other constant New York friend, James Arthurs.

New York nights began generally with Freddie and I going out to eat on our own around nine o'clock. A favourite haunt of his was a small restaurant in Greenwich Village called Clyde's after which a fairly structured routine would be followed. Depending on which night of the week it was, any of Freddie's friends would know where to find him and, of course, his oxblood-coloured car would always be parked some fifty yards or so from the entrance to whichever bar or club he was in and was another beacon for them to find him.

He hated being dropped off outside any club or bar in his car. He felt it was flashy and he always preferred to walk the last few yards to the door of the place. A restaurant was a different matter and in fact he insisted on being deposited right outside the door.

Depending on the club, he would either walk straight in at the front of the queue, for example at Studio 54, whereas if we were going to somewhere like the Saint, he would insist on joining the line, particularly if he saw people he knew queuing. In New York he tried as much as possible to behave like 'an ordinary person'. His celebrity was always something of a double-edged sword.

But, try as he might, Freddie was no ordinary person. He never had been. Right from his youth at a boarding school in India, he would have had most of his needs taken care of by school servants and I can personally attest to this because I attended the same kind of school in southern India. At home in Africa, he would have had servants too and so, when he became a star, his life changed very little from what he had become accustomed to expect as normal. Freddie was used to rarely lifting a finger for his own needs. It was a completely natural state for him. Other people may have thought this behaviour strange, but he didn't and it wasn't. Also, I suppose his celebrity status itself would have naturally brought about this state of affairs. It was a lot easier therefore for Freddie to adapt when celebrity hit him.

However, I have to emphasise that he was not the sort of person to make any kind of a show. I give you the example of his cars. In England, he used a black Mercedes which, should occasion demand, was used as a 'smart' limousine or, alternatively, could look like an upmarket taxi for there are indeed many parts of the world where smart Mercedes cars are used as humble taxis. In New York, where twenty-five foot limousines are common, Freddie owned a Lincoln Towncar Sedan and indeed thought the twenty-five foot limos exceedingly common and would use them only when required to in order to get to and from a Queen gig.

The one exception to his distaste for limos was the occasion of the great outing to Jones beach on the ocean just outside Manhattan where Freddie had heard that musclebound hunks paraded. There were six of us, me, Freddie, Thor, Lee, Joe and John plus a driver. We left the apartment at half-past-six in the morning, an unearthly hour for us and usually one when we were just returning from an outing rather than going on one. However, Freddie had been told you had to get there early to secure a spot on the beach and he thought he could always have a nap once he was there.

It seemed quite strange driving down 2nd Avenue as the streets were fairly empty but it didn't stop a couple of exhibitionists on board opening the sunroof, standing up and waving to anyone they could see. Such is the madness that limos bring on! The boot (trunk for you Americans) had been loaded with picnic goodies and a cool box for the beers. Surprisingly, by the time we got there after a two hour drive it wasn't easy finding a parking space for a saloon car, let alone a twenty-five foot long stretch limo. Eventually we found a place but it still meant us having to walk down the beach to find a suitable spot. I think Freddie was somewhat disappointed with the quantity of muscles. There were some beautifully bronzed bodies but not as many of his variety as he imagined there would be. I also remember being sent off to fetch ice cream for everybody. One person had to come with me to stand in the car's space while I went off in the limo to get the ice cream. We returned to find our guardian of the car parking space being subjected to torrents of abuse from two other drivers who wanted to use the space.

It was one of the two occasions in my life when I ended up a victim of sunstroke. I didn't realise I was ill until we got back to the apartment where I found myself shivering and feeling horribly nauseous. Serves me right, I suppose.

On nightime excursions, Freddie and I would go into the New York bar or club on our own and only inside would we usually meet up with the people whose own lives dictated their own schedules. The bars could be Uncle Charlie's in Greenwich Village or The Works on the Westside or perhaps even The Eagle or The Spike, both of which were down on the lower Westside by the old piers. Most Wednesdays we went to The Roxy to rollerskate. The usual coterie would arrive and Freddie would routinely change into rollerskates. However, he would spend the whole evening sitting on the bench and would never join in the antics of the rink. Odd? When the time came to leave, he would remove his skates, put on his shoes and hand the skates back in at the counter. It was his way of 'joining in'.

Of course, many of these excursions were fuelled by artificial stimulants of which one such was a 'downer'. He was persuaded to take a quaalude by 'a friend' as we were about to enter the River Club on Manhattan's Lower West side. Everything seemed to be going fine until David Hodo, another of Freddie's friends who is the Construction Worker character in The Village People, walked round a corner only to find Freddie planted in the middle of a large black bin half-full of thrownaway beer cans, waving his arms and shouting, "Ooohh! Look! I'm trash. Trash!"

Nearly every night we ended up at the Anvil, the infamous club in the middle of the old meat market district where the trucks would still load and unload their cargoes of real beef. This was also the club where Felipe Rose, the Red Indian character in the Village People, was discovered as he danced on the bar. While the Anvil had a sleazy reputation, the music was brilliant and one could drink there until well after dawn had broken. It had a backroom but no one forced you into it and generally, the clientele and atmosphere were quite superb where anyone could feel quite at ease. Freddie also enjoyed the Anvil's cabaret, in particular the guy who dressed up and looked amazingly like the disco diva Grace Jones belting out 'Pull Up To The Bumper, Baby'! The punters always tucked bills into convenient folds of the performers' outfits. The impersonator who recreated Candi Statton's 'Don't Stop The Train' was another of Freddie's favourites.

The doorman at one of New York's clubs called The Works became Freddie's bodyguard for a time. Freddie arranged through Gerry Stickells to have this man, barrel-shaped, blond and bearded, taken on as his security for the continuation of *The Works* tour. Was that name a coincidence or what? The guy proved useless in a very short time. He had built his past up to be quite impressive but after one long night in Canada, we caught a plane down into the USA. As Freddie and I were disembarking, the cabin crew would permit the accompanying security to get to Freddie to be at his side when he left the plane and went through the terminal. We were on the point of leaving and Freddie asked one of the flight attendants whether they had seen his bodyguard. The reply was that the guy was asleep. Freddie was incensed and said, "Well, just leave him there. If he wakes up in the next city, then that's his fault!"

We left plane and the security guard behind. It was the last we saw of him. The first thing I had to do on arrival back at the hotel on the

West Coast of America was to call Gerry Stickells and ask him to arrange some new security.

The Saint was another club which Freddie frequented. It was an old theatre on the Lower East Side which was *the* state-of-the-art nightclub for gay New York. (I was able to get an honorary membership as an out-of-town resident so that Freddie's name didn't appear on the books.) Getting a membership was easy but to get the all-important locker, you had to join an ever-growing waiting list. The locker was necessary so that you could change from street clothes to fetish clothes and dancing gear as well as to stash your night's supply of drugs. A quick rundown of the acquisition of those drugs goes like this . . . Friday afternoon was time to go shopping. I would be dispatched to see our friendly neighbourhood dealer who had an apartment on the Lower West Side. The earlier I got there, the less of a queue there was.

The dealer seemed to run his retail operation like a supermarket. Through the door there was a table on which sat two workmen's expanding metal workboxes. In each of the sections he would display supplies of different pills, powders and potions, each one named and priced. The only thing that wasn't supplied was a supermarket-style mini-wire trolley. I moved further along the table, selecting my requirements which I had written on my 'shopping list' which would include enough supplies for Freddie and whoever he was partying with that weekend. Pills for this, powders for that and the potions were of the ethyl chloride variety which when doused onto a knotted corner of the ubiquitous coloured pocket kerchief and when sucked and inhaled would basically freeze the lungs and provide a huge high when dancing. Something definitely on the 'Things *not* to try' list. At the end of the table, the check-out point, the only thing missing was a till. The dealer ran through everything and told you what the damage would be and of course there were discounts for quantity and for cash. Shopping would, of course, be done alone and you would let the next person in on your way out. By Friday evening, in the summertime, the dealer would be well on the way to Fire Island and a whole other clientele.

Back at the Saint on Saturday night and duly stoked and fuelled up, the timetable which dictated the schedule of what drug to take and when was dutifully followed. Uppers were taken between eleven p.m. and four a.m. and then when the down music started on the dance floor, the downers were taken until it was time to go home, usually half past eight or nine o'clock on Sunday morning.

Sometimes, we went on to 'continuity' parties in people's private homes where at the door ecstasy tablets were handed out and where, if you did not immediately consume them, you weren't allowed the opportunity to take them later. That way the host ensured that everyone would be in the same frame of mind. I have to say that Freddie's generosity in sharing his drugs was always reciprocated by his friends who supplied him with his drinks. His New York coterie of friends never exploited him.

There was much less formality round Freddie in a New York bar and over there he never felt the need for a large group to always be around him. It was a much more relaxed atmosphere due in part to there being more celebrities per capita living in New York. The clubbers were more used to seeing a famous face in their midst and Freddie didn't feel threatened when people would good-naturedly come up to talk to him.

Meeting people as he always did in bars and clubs of course resulted in many sexual liasons and here I would like to say something about Freddie's ideas of love as I interpreted them. That there is love in all his songs is undeniable; in fact, love is what Freddie was all about and so I think it's worth a few words about how Freddie perceived love.

Take the pick-up situation outlined above, one of which involved a boy called Charles, a Quebecquois from Montreal in Canada whose smattering of English Freddie couldn't understand any more than he could Winnie Kirchberger's. Exit Charles for there was no local version of Barbara Valentin to translate for them! Although – as in the case of Charles who was flown both to New York and to London – some of these meetings were longer than mere one-night stands, the sex that these meetings engendered certainly had nothing to do with love in Freddie's mind. In fact, I don't think the words love and sex could be used in the same sentence as far as Freddie was concerned. Sexual pleasure was a physical outlet for him, a displacement activity as usefully useless as smoking or travelling. Because he was generally a hyperactive person, he always wanted to be doing something. I remember him saying that he considered sleep to be the biggest waste of time in any twenty-four hours. He hated time being wasted but he never considered sex to be a waste of time because for him the only outlet for his energies other than work was sex. He was prepared to work twenty-four hours a day when the occasion demanded and often did, but he – indeed anyone – was physically unable to do so without a break on a continuous basis.

Sex was what he did when he wasn't working. Sex was fun, sex was a good time and while doing it he didn't have to waste any of the precious emotion that otherwise went into his work.

The love he wrote about in his work was a totally different kettle of fish. Did he experience this precious emotion himself in real life? I actually don't know.

What is 'love'? I think it is something different for each person of course but I can assert that the in-love 'love' for Freddie started with him feeling comfortable in the company of someone to whom he was going to commit. He would then start to find out things about his intended, a gradual process perhaps lasting some weeks. Strangely, if he found something that was unpalatable in the person's character, he would often dismiss that information and forget it because he could balance it up with the good things he was discovering.

I don't think he ever fell 'in love' at first sight or anything like that. He loved people, sure, but each person received a different facet of the total love he bore. No one person exclusively received that total love. Ever.

I know he loved me. I know he loved Mary but in a completely different way and certainly never in the standard issue boy-meets-girl way talked about in the newspapers to try and make it easy for the public to understand.

Love is very difficult to understand.

Freddie's love started with trust. I think that was the only thing that was common to everyone he loved in whatever way. When he stopped trusting someone, he stopped loving them. Oddly, he only ever counted the good things about people, his friends. I think it's why he spent so much time with people whom we on the inside saw on the outside as having a lot of bad points. Freddie wouldn't see these.

I don't even think that Freddie ever had an idealised view of love. Those first wonderful feelings most of us get from falling in love, Freddie would get from a song that he'd written. The love he wrote about and therefore achieved in that song would be the requiting he required to be able to go on loving. He got so much love from his friends and this was commuted into the emotion which Freddie needed in order to write about love in his songs. His main emotional outlet was the writing. Conflict was again a part of this relationship for someone who stood up to him, said 'No' but who went on loving him, often gave him the impetus he needed to create. Of course, when he had created in a song the feeling of perfect love, why risk not being able to recreate it in real life when by keeping all the different loves and sex in different compartments, he would remain invulnerable? He knew he could so easily be let down as had happened so often.

Freddie needed love as much as the next person but, to emphasise, he had to know that the love came from a source he could trust. Because of his unconventional upbringing, he didn't start off with conventional love. Not having his relatives and parents around for so much of his childhood, constantly being there and loving him consistently, he perceived love in a different way from those with contrary family backgrounds. Most people, in fact. No doubt his parents loved him from afar. He wasn't to know that that wasn't normal but he compensated for the distance involved by seeking out love from sources he always knew were going to be there. Sources of his own creation. Within his control.

He got his love in non-sexual ways and in non-sexual situations. He loved his friends. It was that simple. An easy way to understand this was that whereas sex was fun, loving one person singly and solely to the exclusion of others could and had hurt. In his experience either lovers had left him of their own volition or he had worked it so that he made the lovers leave him. There is indeed a huge difference between lust and love and these feelings should not be confused with 'that loving feeling' of which the Righteous Brothers sang. That 'feeling' was one which I contend that Freddie never had in the first place to eventually lose. It's a phenomenon which is particularly relevant to gay men. Gay men don't necessarily have to have love and sex from the same person in the same, ongoing relationship. Gay men find that they can derive all the love they can possibly need from their good friends.

Sex . . .

Well, as Boy George said, "I'd really rather have a cup of tea."

Earl Grey was Freddie's preference but unlike George, Freddie was always ready for both sex and tea, with the tea, preferably, coming afterwards.

The importance of friends was one reason why he was so incredibly generous to them all and why parties and entertaining his friends were so important to him. Gifts and gift giving were ways for Freddie to repay the friendship he received.

For one birthday party he threw, forty people sat down at the same table created from several separate tables in the sitting room at Garden Lodge. Although it was his birthday and people brought him presents, he in turn gave all his guests presents. I was dispatched to Tiffanys in Bond Street and picked up an assortment of gifts suitable for both men and women, costing about fifty pounds each. I think that here it is useful to stress that at no time on any occasion, including the wonderful Hat Party, was there anyone remotely resembling a dwarf carrying anything remotely resembling a bowl of cocaine. There. Bang. Another myth exploded.

At another festive occasion, this time one of his famed Christmas lunches, everyone present received a glittering brooch from Butler and Wilson, Straker's being, I remember, a fizzing champagne glass, so there are many bits of Freddie still around in people's lives. The small treasures that he gave and took such delight in giving are in fact huge treasures to those of us who cherish them still. I received an Afghan-like dog in the form of a lapel brooch.

And speaking of Christmases, wherever he was in the world, whether New York, Munich or London, he was always one for the traditional. He insisted on a Christmas tree although very rarely when abroad did he manage to secure the size of the ones we had in Garden Lodge. He had a certain ideal view of what Christmas should be. Whether Zoroastrians celebrate Christmas I don't know but Freddie had picked up the notion somewhere along the line. Christmas as he celebrated it was a very British thing and he was drawn to what he perceived were traditional British roots.

His active part and involvement in the proceedings was telling everybody else what to do and where to put things and how to hang decorations. At Garden Lodge, Jim always arranged the table centrepiece and kept it a secret until the last minute. A mixture of seasonal flowers and fir cones and Christmas baubles – *Blue Peter* and its yoghurt pots, loo roll cores and sticky-back plastic had nothing on what Jim Hutton came up with.

Not that Freddie would even wrap presents himself. Most of them came pre-wrapped and packaged from the shop because Cartier,

Tiffany and Lalique do that kind of thing. Christmas cards he chose from the selection which I would go out and buy but he would always write the cards himself. He would go through his own address book and write the envelopes although these would frequently not be posted as inside many of them he would also include a cheque. It was how we in the household always received our Christmas bonuses.

The cast list for Christmas day's lunch would start being prepared at the beginning of December with a basic list being added to, subtracted from and generally changed and swapped around daily. It almost became a tradition that on Christmas Eve he would have open house; Mike Moran would, latterly, always be there to play the piano and everyone would gather to sing carols.

Talk of British tradition! What could be more Victorian than carols round the piano? Freddie used to enjoy the carol singing I think almost as much as all the other parts of Christmas together. I remember one year, he was overjoyed when Stephanie Beacham and her children were there, all singing carols . . . This communal singing business he always thoroughly enjoyed, often holding impromptu choral harmony sessions, especially when in the company of Straker and Kenny Everett. Whether this enjoyment came from his time at his English boarding school at Panchgani in India, who knows?

Christmastime was always a poignant anniversary regarding Freddie's friendship with Kenny Everett. Kenny had been extremely influential in 'breaking' 'Bohemian Rhapsody' on Capital Radio in 1975, introducing the seven-minute single to a nation accustomed only to the three-and-a-half minute sound bite. It seems incredible and rather farcical now to remember that this intense friendship between two highly emotional people broke up because of a confrontation over drug use. It wasn't even a head-to-head argument. There was no one-on-one row. It was 'relayed' to Freddie (by some kind friend, of course) that Kenny thought that Freddie was quite happy using anybody else's drugs without providing any himself. When Freddie heard this, he couldn't believe his ears because it was his own feeling that the boot was in fact on the other foot and that it was Kenny who was always appropriating anyone else's 'stash' other than his own. Freddie's opinion was similarly 'relayed' back to Kenny and the situation then arose, which I think everyone must have encountered, where it becomes impossible to patch up a hole that never was. Polarisation ensued, pride took over and the rest is conjecture but they never spoke again after Christmas 1980. Drug induced paranoia? What? My personal feeling is that it's just the way some friendships go. How the newspapers thought that Kenny was one of the last of Freddie's best friends to speak to him before he died, I really wouldn't like to say.

At some point in the Christmas week he would go over and see his parents and family and take their presents but they would never be involved in any of his Christmas schedule at Garden Lodge. Freddie never mixed friends and relatives, even to the point where when his parents were invited to Garden Lodge, Joe and I had to go out. Mary would be asked to stay. His parents had grown to like her, having been introduced to her so many years before when he and Mary were sharing a flat and it helped to square the view of normality which he wished to give to his parents. Normality in the strictest sense of the word. Not necessarily 'straight' as in heterosexual but merely to allay any fears they might have had for him, to assure them that there was an ongoing secure continuity in his life and that no harm was coming to him.

Christmas Day began at about eleven at night on Christmas Eve. After his carol session, Freddie and troupe would go to the Copacabana which gave me a chance to get on and prepare the vegetables for the next day's banquet for upwards of about twenty people.

For me Christmas Day would start at about nine in the morning, getting the turkey (or turkeys depending on numbers) into the oven (or ovens depending on numbers). All the traditional vegetables and trimmings were prepared, including home-made stuffing and bread sauce. We made three varieties of stuffing, one of sausage meat, sage and onion, then one of tomato, mushroom and rice and finally the traditional chestnut, of course. Then there were the accessories, Brussels sprouts, a carrot-and-pea *macedoine*, mashed swede, mashed butternut squash, roast parsnips, roast potatoes, chipolata sausages rolled in bacon and lashings of home-made gravy!

All very Famous Five, really.

I would have made the puddings and cakes in September or October when they're traditionally supposed to be made. I must admit, Freddie did enjoy fresh, home-made food. Whenever Freddie was going into the studio, we would make an assortment of sandwiches for him, although it was Joe's speciality of home-made sausage rolls which Freddie carried in with special pride and handed round to everyone, eating perhaps only one himself.

Christmas lunch would start without an appetiser at about two o'clock. Guests would definitely include Mary and her current beau, Jim Hutton, Peter Straker, Trevor Clarke and then it could also include Rudi Patterson, Graham Hamilton, Gordon Dalziel, Dave Clark with his friend John Christie, Yasmin Pettigrew, James Arthurs and his friend Jim, Paul Prenter when he was alive and around and of course Joe and myself.

It wasn't a necessity to watch the real Queen's message to the Commonwealth and so after a leisurely lunch, the fun began. One of Freddie's little foibles was that everybody who came to lunch brought a gift for everyone else who was there. It was a thoroughly sweet gesture for in that way no one would ever feel left out and everyone would have the same amount of presents to open except Freddie who had millions more than anyone else! The sitting room looked like a war zone of waste paper and great care was taken when throwing the paper away that nothing remained hidden inside. One walked through a sea of discarded glitter, ribbons and wrappings.

From about five o'clock onwards, other people would begin to drop by just to wish a Happy Christmas. Generally the company would break into smaller groups in all the rooms on the ground floor and intermingle and catch up on what had been happening in their lives since last they'd seen each other. Freddie's Christmases were meeting places for people who often didn't see each other from one year's end to the next. Geography, work patterns. Showbusiness knows no constant structure other than impermanence.

The Christmas decorations remained in place for the full twelve days of Christmas and were dismantled on January 6. New Year's Eve was always celebrated by Freddie but in the last few years a pattern emerged where we used to spend the New Year at Gordon and Graham's apartment high up in Quadrangle Tower in the Water Garden complex. He started to go to Gordon and Graham's traditional Scottish celebration when Freddie decided he no longer wanted to go to the clubs. A great deal of fun was always had.

I remember one occasion when we brought the evening meal with us and Joe was let loose in the boys' kitchen to dish up some amazing chilli prawns and rice; huge tiger prawns. The party would consist of Freddie and Jim, Gordon and Graham, Mary Austin and whoever she wanted to bring, Joe Fanelli and his current beau and myself. I remember another occasion when we had Freddie in stitches when two friends of Joe Fanelli's turned up. Tony Evans, together with a friend of his and ably assisted by we boys from Garden Lodge, performed a Bananarama routine, they being the big girl band of the moment, the vastly more talented forerunners of today's Spice Girls. I think everyone surprised each other at how easily we seemed to recall the dance and movement routine. I pitied the neighbours that night.

Prior to these Hogmanay nights, Heaven was a regular New Year's Eve haunt. A group of people would be rounded up at Garden Lodge at about nine o'clock for a champagne supper and then the well-lubricated party would sally forth in time to arrive at the club for midnight. Fortunately, Freddie never had to worry about parking and nor would he ever have to worry about being turned away by the security bouncers on any door.

Easter was always another excuse for Freddie to buy presents. He really did get the most intense enjoyment out of giving things to people. Of course he never needed to wait for an occasion but the occasion made him feel better about his indulgent excess. Other people's birthdays of course were prime examples of these convenient moments.

For any of us really close to him, the birthday present would consist of something special which he'd gone out and bought, perhaps as part of a bulk purchase but always with a specific person in mind. This was always accompanied by a card with a cheque inside it. One friend of Joe's, Donald McKenzie, whom Freddie liked a lot, was very taken aback when Freddie presented him with an antique Lalique vase, knowing that Freddie had bought it just a short while earlier at auction.

Gifts, for Freddie, meant first and foremost the thought . . . So many people would say to him, "Oh, what can we buy you? You've already got everything and whatever you want you can just go out and buy!"

On the contrary. Freddie on more than one occasion was incredibly bowled over by a gift that might have very little monetary value but the thought put behind it would stand out a mile and make it priceless. Anybody who knew Freddie knew of his pet adorations, 'pet' meaning either cats or fish, or 'pet' meaning adorations like Lalique and fine porcelain and art. So often he was speechless when he opened gifts from, maybe, one of the cleaners who had put a lot more thought into her gift than someone with a vastly higher income.

If it was any of our birthdays – Jim's, Joe's or mine, even Mary's – Freddie would invariably decide to 'give' us a party. Many of Freddie's friends recall a telephone call from him saying, "It's Jim's birthday next week and I'm having a party and I want you to come . . ."

How much say we had in our own guest list was of course limited to being able to invite a friend or two but the parties were always wonderful affairs. Inevitably, they were crowned by some masterpiece of confection in the shape of whatever our current fancy might have been, interpreted and created by amongst other *pâtissières*, Jane Asher and Kim Brown (nee Osborne) and Diana Moseley's sister, Fiona.

Kim once made a wonderful cake in the shape and form of Garden Lodge and another specific cake I remember for one of my birthdays was in the form of a stage set of *Aida* with a pair of singers on it with numerous orchestra members in a pit in front of it. The last birthday cake which we had made for Freddie was of his Swiss apartment building, made by Jane Asher.

Another legendary and totally eye-catching feature of Freddie's parties were the prawn trees which we occasionally wheeled out from the kitchen. Very simply, they were cones made of inch-diameter chicken wire with individual whole prawns poked through with bodies facing out. It was almost something Salvador Dali might have come up with. The tiers of pink prawns were occasionally interspersed with springs of fresh green parsley.

Another birthday of mine which I remember was in New York. It started on a Thursday evening and didn't really finish until we got home on Sunday night, Monday morning. One long round of bars, restaurants, drinks . . . and of course friends. My present on that occasion in 1981 was a solid gold Cartier screw-bracelet. Cartier was often visited to provide presents. Although Freddie himself never wore a watch, it was as though he would make anything he had to do fit in to the number of hours available. If he had appointments at specific times, there would be others around who had watches to ensure he would arrive on time. Otherwise, lunchtime was when he felt hungry. If he had planned a dinner at home with friends at a certain time. He would always be ready for it as there were clocks all over the place, although never a timepiece on his wrist.

He developed a dislike of giving watches to lovers. After the second time he gave one, the current lover, like the predecessor, soon became an 'ex'. He felt that any relationship was cursed as soon as he made a present of a watch. On one occasion, he had picked up a lorry driver, to whom he had famously quipped, "What's the queen from Queen doing with a queen from Queens?" although whether or not the young man in question really was from the New York borough of Queens is quite another matter. On the journey back to the man's apartment, he passed Cartier which had already opened. Freddie went in and bought a clock for the trucker. However, I must emphasise that he didn't buy every stray trick a gift. It just happened that Cartier on the aforementioned occasion was on the way. It was the first time I could remember someone having been bought their present before the sex had been enjoyed!

I think the only special occasion dinner to which absolutely none of Freddie's friends was invited was one of his parents' wedding anniversaries which he gave at Garden Lodge before he had moved in. Just his family and Mary of course, who looked very good in a scarlet Bruce Oldfield couture which I had helped her pick out from a large selection and which Freddie bought for her.

I feel I must also point out that Freddie's drivers were also an integral part of his life and our household. In New York it was a man who was nicknamed 'Lori' as his surname was Anderson and in London, in the time I knew Freddie, he had three drivers who always acted as his security bodyguards as well.

The first was Peter Jones, nicknamed Gemma, of course, who remained with Freddie for quite a few years, including the beginning of the Munich period. After he and Freddie parted company, which was not a very amicable split, Freddie gave Peter Jones every opportunity to redeem himself. Basically, the way I remember it, Peter lost his international licence in Munich after a drink-driving conviction and then lost his licence again in England. Peter never officially informed Freddie. He simply didn't ring in. If only he had rung in, Freddie would have kept him on doing other security work. Freddie loathed sacking people and would have always found an alternative. Because Peter never communicated over a period of two weeks, and because Freddie discovered the truth of the situation from other sources, the questions of honesty and loyalty became involved and Freddie was unable to exercise his prerogative of mercy. It then became acrimonious and Peter suffered as much as Freddie, who went through the tortures of the damned in parting company so unnecessarily.

Then Gary Hampshire, on a well-earned sabbatical from the John Reid experience, drove Freddie and after Gary returned to Reid, Terry Giddings was employed from a security company run by two brothers whose services the Queen machine had often employed.

Terry Giddings was a gentle giant, whose love for his vivacious wife Sharon and his children was something tangible and deeply moving. When he spoke of his children, his son Luke at the time, he fairly oozed paternal pride which I would have dearly like to have bottled. I could have made a fortune. On the occasions when Freddie wasn't going to use Terry he would let him know in advance but Terry still often found occasion to come over to Garden Lodge with his young son, Terry's *doppelganger*, for Luke was a dead blond ringer for his dad. Freddie adored playing with Luke who was after all 'a model' having appeared in several commercials.

Although Freddie certainly never wanted any children of his own, he adored certain children of other people's, especially when they went home with their parents after tea. He had a wonderful relationship with his only godson, Rheinhold Mack's son John Frederick. One thing Freddie demanded of children was respect for their elders and unquestioning obedience, perhaps mirroring his own childhood and upbringing. Continued unruly behaviour really disturbed him and although he hated the idea of Garden Lodge being treated like a museum, it had in reality not been designed for boisterous children to go exploring in. Yet he loved the attitude of a child like Luke Giddings, an East-End boy with boundless curiosity because Luke knew how to behave and to ask questions. If told once, "Now don't play around with that," Luke would duly stop and never repeat the bad behaviour.

But back to drivers and driving. Freddie had drivers because he hated the thought of driving and as far as he was concerned there were drivers who were good at driving just as there were cooks who were good at cooking and each allowed him the luxury of not having to do so but instead to write and perform music, which is what he himself was good at.

He did once have a couple of driving lessons as I'm sure he must at one time have at least tried once to boil an egg but he loathed the very idea of either occupation. I think as far as Freddie was concerned, driving was a waste of time. Rather than thinking of the road and the route, he felt there were better ways of occupying his mind. Also, I think he was too impatient a character to have made a driver. Mind you, I could well imagine him being the master of road rage now! And of course, the nearest Freddie ever caught in the way of public transport was a taxi. But the likelihood of his ever carrying enough money to pay for even a bus was nil.

As far as needing to carry cash, there were few places he went where he ever needed cash. Only twice in the twelve years I knew him did I ever accompany him to the cinema, one film being *Raiders Of The Lost Ark* which we saw in a movie theatre in Manhattan. I paid. He was thrilled at popcorn being thrown through the air from one group of friends to another and although it meant that he couldn't hear some of the dialogue, he loved hearing the audience cheering out loud, a phenomenon one would expect from live theatre rather than a movie house. Partway through the second half of the movie, a fly very obviously crawls into the mouth of one of the actors playing a German soldier giving orders. For some reason, Spielberg, a man whom Freddie greatly admired, decided that the scene should not be edited. When Freddie and I saw it, some couple of rows in front of us, a large black New Yorker leapt to his feet and screamed aloud, "A fly! That man jus' ate that fly!"

Freddie was floored. He was in stitches of laughter.

The second movie we saw I should have realised was going to be a disaster. It was in Munich that a group of about ten of us including Barbara Valentin and Winnie Kirchberger went to see *Die Unendlicher Geschichte* (The Never-ending Story as it had been originally titled). The story had lasted approximately ten minutes when Freddie turned to me and said, "I'm getting out of here. This is ridiculous!"

Freddie never dreamt that even though he was seeing the film dubbed into German in Munich that it would at least not have English sub-titles. I think he became extremely frustrated. Although he had a very rudimentary grasp of German, it upset him that there were obviously a good few jokes which he didn't understand and he could see the rest of his friends laughing. Going to extremes, he might even have been a teensy bit paranoid, thinking that they might just have been laughing at him not understanding. That apart, Freddie's boredom threshold was so low that to sit in his seat for an hour-and-a-half watching something that bored him was an impossibility. There were very few things through which he sat all the way and, thus, he was always extremely particular about what he would go out in public to see. Generally it would only be to something where particular friends of his were involved, although on one or two occasions he specifically went to see something because he wanted to see it. Because he had been told so many good things about such and such a play by his friends in the profession, he would trust their judgements and opinions.

Films therefore he watched mainly on the television screen. He would never ask us to rent out movies for him to play at home. He did have a few pre-recorded films and some which he had specifically asked us to record for him from the television. Two of the most played were *Some Like It Hot* and George Cukor's *The Women*, a screenplay which he had almost memorised by heart. *Imitation Of Life* with Lana Turner was a special favourite. He loved the title. Curiously apt for a man like Freddie whose own life was in so many ways merely a reflection of other people's real lives. I can remember him on at least a couple of occasions being in tears at the end of the movie where Susan Kohner who played Juanita Moore's errant daughter arrives too late for Juanita's funeral and tries to jump on the white coffin in the horse-drawn hearse.

Too much for a pop star in his own front room.

Although this might sound superficial and dismissable, I have to emphasise that this was the everyday life I am trying to describe and which was, as such, incredibly ordinary. I am sure many people will recognise this situation from their own lives. Freddie's was no different. While Freddie was moved by this specific scene I have just outlined, he never lost sight of the fact that he was being successfully manipulated by the director and the writers. Although it was, after all, only a movie, it was also only what he himself did so consummately in his own film-making on the videos as I hope I have already shown.

He never made any specific plan to watch a movie which was coming up on TV. What could happen was that either Joe or I would see in the *TV Times* that there was a Marlene Dietrich season and when we told Freddie, he would ask us to video all of them for him as he knew he might not be in the mood to watch them as they were broadcast. However, he adored Dietrich and would quite soon get around to seeing the recordings, usually with Straker who was Freddie's movie-watching side-kick. Freddie would whimsically decide that Tuesday afternoon would be movie time and ring up Straker who, if he were free, would come over and be Freddie's date. Instead of a popcorn and Coca-Cola date, it would be more likely champagne and caviar canapés. Incidentally, it was because of his adoration of Marlene that Freddie jumped at the idea of George Hurrell photographing the band for *The Works*. Hurrell had legendarily portrayed Dietrich and many of her contemporaries.

Overall, the movies he tended to watch were black and white. I think he admired the strength of the big women stars in Hollywood when they started to command big studio salaries, the likes of Norma Shearer, Joan Crawford, Bette Davis, Dietrich, Rita Hayworth, Lana Turner . . . The Hollywood Immortals. In New York, he was always impressed that he lived only just around the corner from Greta Garbo.

The male stars just never seemed to figure as highly in Freddie's pantheon . . . Much has been made of Freddie's apparent desperation to get near Burt Reynolds. I do seem to remember once or twice Freddie passing a comment along the lines of, "He looks quite good."

But as to Freddie going out of his way to meet Mr Reynolds, that was never the case. There. Another little myth exploded. And on the subject of exploding myths, neither did Freddie ever have anything more to do with Rudolf Nureyev than sharing a stage one night in Barcelona. There is no way Freddie could have kept quiet about sleeping with Rudolf had he done so and, anyway, neither was the other's type!

It has also been said that Freddie met part of Rock Hudson in a backroom bar called the Gloryhole in Los Angeles. Yes, Freddie went into the bar once to my knowledge but had no intention of going any further than the bar. Wild exhibitionism in public was definitely not for him. As far as I'm aware, he never even met Rock Hudson in polite society. Once again, had he done so, make no mistake, we would have *all* known about it. Although he didn't broadcast gossip, he could never refrain from telling close friends any tales about himself which would titillate them.

Let me shoot something else out of the sky – namely the press's statements that John Murphy was another of Freddie's ex-lovers. Freddie and John did have a very close relationship but I don't think it ever got anywhere near going to bed with each other. As far as I'm concerned, it certainly wasn't John from whom Freddie contracted

HIV. For most of the time I knew John, he was very happy with his lover Jim W. King.

I think Freddie acquired a lot of his acknowledged video inspiration from the black and white movies he loved. They reflected the heyday of Hollywood movie stars. The stars were the movies. Perhaps now, without the stars, there is too much demanded of the actors who have to compete with the special effects. In Freddie's videos, the band are the movie stars and nothing detracts from them, special effects or no.

It has been well-documented that Freddie went often to the movies as a child and at school and it is not inconceivable that the films took the place of his family who were not close at hand for a great part of his growing up. It must have given him a great haven of escape from the realities of school life and having to make his own way. Freddie learned at an early age what a star was. Perhaps it was then that he decided he was going to become one. Interesting that he grew up at the same time that Elvis Presley, the eponymous pop star, had just established a huge career in movies, soon to be followed by Cliff Richard in England and later The Beatles. Although Freddie never aspired to film stardom in the same way, it was because he knew that it had already been done so successfully by his true heroes, Presley, Lennon, etc. and he never, never thought of himself as an actor, even in his videos. Although he would have never been able to learn the lines, it was in the same vein as driving a car and cooking . . . there were others who did it so much better. He was a musician and the best musician. He enjoyed films made by people who were the best film makers.

He was never scared of getting involved in a project where he was confident in his own knowledge and ability but would always step back from any area of work where he had the slightest doubt about his ability to deliver.

He had exactly the same approach towards his friends and the people with whom he associated. He became a very good judge of character. Maybe it had come with practice for there had been several relationships both of love and friendship which had ended very, very badly which taught him these lessons. Two of the people I'm thinking of were Bill Reid and Paul Prenter. I don't think that Bill Reid ever loved Freddie in the way that I know Jim Hutton did and when Freddie ended the relationship, perhaps Bill saw the golden goose taking flight.

Paul Prenter was a different matter. Freddie felt so let down when Paul sold his story to the *Sun* newspaper. Freddie had really gone out of his way because of his belief in their friendship to keep it afloat when things were going badly wrong for Paul. Paul was also a close friend as well as an employee and Freddie's instinct was the same with both employees and friends and lovers. He never wanted to end these relationships. He found calling it a day very difficult. The relationship with Freddie and any of his employees – because all employees became friends – was very difficult for both parties. Imagine a line, one end being employee and the other, friend. The dividing line separating the two ends which were always there changed by the minute. Sometimes, Freddie needed a friend rather than an employee and at other times, it was the employee Freddie needed to do what he wanted rather than to offer an opinion. To be able to do both was like walking a tightrope over ever-changing battle lines.

As far as employees were concerned, more often than not employeeship came out of friendship. Beginning with Mary, with whom he lived for six or seven years and who became employed by him. Joe Fanelli, who was his lover for a couple of years, became an employee. Jim Hutton, whom Freddie finally persuaded to give up his job as a barber at The Savoy, became an employee and in this way friendships and lovers both past and present were able to be maintained. People retained at least a semblance of independence.

Of course the main motivation for Freddie's generosity in this matter was his own guilt. He always felt that he had disrupted people's lives so much. In Joe's case, Freddie had invited him to England in 1978 and away from his life, family and friends in Springfield, Massachusetts, and when Freddie fell out of love with Joe, he wouldn't have dreamed of seeing Joe displaced in any way. Freddie was always involved every year in extending Joe's alien's residency status. In fairness, it was the same with Mary. Her expectations had, after all, been destroyed just by Freddie admitting his gayness and he never ever wanted to hurt her. But, don't get me wrong, I am not saying that Freddie bought friendship. I am one of the lucky people whom Freddie allowed to get close to him and no amount of money could explain the feelings that any of the people close to him felt.

It's so hard to explain feelings. Intense loyalty mixed with love, admiration . . . I would have done anything he could have asked of me, but he never asked. He never expected. Anybody involved with him was held as if by a magnet, the magnetism of his personality, his spirit . . . Him. Sitting at home, curled up watching television, it's very difficult to imagine the man on stage. You knew that he would have been unable to remain quiet and introspective for any length of time. He knew that there were two Freddie Mercurys. The one curled up on the couch watching *Countdown* and the one perched on that one's shoulder. There was the person and there was the showman, each vying with the other to move the physical carcass around.

Generally the showman won. Deep down inside it's what Freddie always wanted. He had always been a showman. In its latter stages, the disease killed the showman. The showman went first and without the showman, the person was unable to continue. Freddie was no longer in a position where he could hold his head up and know he could defend himself. When the showman died, there was nothing left to fight for. The final decision was his alone. His whole life had been brought about by what he had done. He had always planned on being a star. How he did so, he felt was not his concern. He had both the hardware and the software and Freddie, metaphorically, wrote his own programs.

As has been made clear to me, I think I can speak for all his friends and say that every single one of us took great pride in knowing him. There was no expectation on his behalf when he lavished friends with the gifts he bought. Because their friendship flowed back to him anyway, that was his dividend and the dividend always came. Friendship and loyalty meant more to him than anything money could buy and he was always the first to be loyal.

This loyalty could have a very protective manifestation. One example of this quality also illustrates that Freddie could argue with friends, sometimes fall out for a while but the underlying friendship still remained. I remember one evening when one of the company was a young man who had been seeing John Reid. In private, he had told a third person all the gory details of his friendship with Reid. Without thinking, the third party began to gossip and tittle-tattle, revealing some of these juicy titbits. When Freddie heard what this young man was saying, he turned and snapped at him, "What do *you* know about! Just fucking shut up and mind your own business. In fact, fuck off!"

This incident occurred even after the fiasco of the failed joint birthday celebration at Pikes in Ibiza which caused a lot of friction between Freddie and John Reid. Freddie was no fickle friend. I can't think of one short-term friendship he had. When you were Freddie's friend, that meant for life. Unless of course Freddie's character assessment proved false. Although he loved gossiping himself, 'dishing' as he called it, he never liked to hear vicious gossip about friends of his from friends of his. Those who did, ran their friendship with him very close to the wind and there were several who capsized.

Freddie's attitudes to his professional advisors was much on the same basis as his friendships. He was very loyal to men like John Libson his accountant, Jim Beach, Queen's manager and always to those like Robin Moore-Ede who worked artistically with him on his houses. The accounts office came to him rather than the other way round, as did the Queen Management. Appointments would be made and John Libson and Amin Salih would come to the house laden with accountancy paperwork. In fact they were prepared to go further than the house, for on many occasions Freddie would fly them and Robin Moore-Ede to wherever he was in the world. I remember one time specifically when they came to Munich for meetings in the Hilton Hotel, Robin laden with plans of work at Garden Lodge. Even though Freddie wasn't in England, he was never out of touch. Although Freddie perhaps didn't understand the finer details of accountancy and financial matters, he had a very clear knowledge of the overall picture. However, I very much doubt that he would have ever met his bank manager or that that person would have been the same bank manager whom Freddie would have had to have seen to get his first mortgage.

Mary was the link between Freddie and the institutions, acting both as private secretary and company secretary for Freddie's companies between him and the accountants who would also have organised insurances etc. Freddie trusted Mary above anyone else where his finances were concerned. When Freddie needed cash for whatever reasons, he would sign a cheque presented to him by Mary who would then go off to Coutts Bank in Kensington High Street and draw the money.

As has been previously revealed, Freddie for many years had his own accountant rather than merely relying on Queen's accountants for his personal business and as we know, John Libson ultimately became one of the two executors of Freddie's estate. Although there were many occasions when Freddie, either directly or via John Libson, must have been approached to invest money in other businesses and projects such as Shezan restaurant in Cheval Place, he never diversified his financial interests in anything other than Queen and their projects. Even Goose Productions, Freddie's company which had recorded Peter Straker in the past, had long since ceased to function as a record company.

Freddie was never a person to turn down advice out of hand and trusted good judgement as is seen by his choice of executors. After all, there were so many other good friends he might have chosen but knowing he was leaving a working empire behind, rather than burden people less expert in the ways of international high finance and the complicated ins and outs of the record business, he chose to rely on the professionals.

One of the things he hated most was being called Fred. I just mention it because none of his immediate friends ever called him Fred. The straights, people like the road crew, tended to call him Fred because to them he was, 'just one of the blokes'. However, the name never fell kindly on Freddie's ears even though in his passport his name was Frederick Mercury, profession Musician. He never considered himself as anything else. He even once famously turned down a million dollars to appear in and write the music for an advertisement for Freixenet, the Spanish sparkling wine. He did not see himself as either an actor or a writer-for-hire.

As far as his management was concerned, whether personal, financial or business, he obviously felt more secure dealing with people he knew and upon whom he looked as friends. He always saw the value of management. While I was there, I saw the situation develop from Jim Beach being employed as the band's business manager with Paul Prenter as the day-to-day personal manager to Jim Beach becoming the band's manager. It took Freddie and the band as a whole quite a while to trust Jim completely. Considering what they had been through in the past with the Sheffield and Trident deal, they'd had their fingers burnt once and they weren't about to again.

To a large extent, it was John Reid who had shown Queen how to manage themselves and Freddie learned a great deal from Reid and all the people who worked at South Audley Street. It was a business legacy which Freddie never forgot. Queen saw and understood how their own management company had to be set up – i.e. with proper PR, press representation, office management and co-ordinated fan club functions.

Queen Productions, when it finally fledged in Pembridge Road with Jim Beach in the John Reid role, was almost a carbon copy of John Reid Enterprises ten years before. In the meantime Queen had learned of the dangers in managing themselves and of what they should look out for and I think they were all four quite relieved when they relinquished their own management into trusted hands. Freddie trusted Jim and Paul Prenter to staff Queen Productions entirely as they saw fit and never interfered in any way. It is surely some testament to those employed at Queen Productions that people like Julie Glover and Sally Hyatt, who even now when Queen as a performing and recording entity no longer exists, are still employed by the individual ex-band members.

In both his former and his latter years Freddie regarded record companies and their representatives as a necessary blot on the landscape of his career. Freddie loved writing music. He hated having to prove to people sitting behind desks that the music was good. I have to point out that even in the twelve years I was with Freddie, we both saw the record business change dramatically. As far as I'm aware, the only British record executive with whom Freddie became friends was Ken East and his wife, the inimitable Dolly, who had been chief executive both at Decca and EMI. Freddie had formed a good relationship with Bhaskar Menon at Capitol but he very rarely spoke to any of the departmental staff at EMI. Freddie, it has to be said, was not a great communicator with 'the little people', as Leona Helmsley once famously uttered.

This *détente* in Freddie's relationship with his record company was a great turnabout for at the beginning of his career he was greatly fond of men like Sir Joseph Lockwood who headed EMI and whose vision, like Freddie's, was so gratifyingly eclectic. I suppose, come to think of it, it's all down to Sir Joseph Lockwood that I can even write this book because without him there would have been no Freddie at the Ballet Gala and I might now be assistant wardrobe master at The Royal Ballet.

Freddie began to feel very alienated from the record companies when managing directors turned out to be younger than him. Also, when punk started to become so big, he felt that it was music that didn't sound as he judged music was supposed to sound. Freddie understandably was not thrilled when other bands became temporarily more important than Queen at EMI, for he could never forget one of his proudest boasts which was that in one particular year, Queen on its own had provided EMI with a quarter of its revenue.

To this day, EMI Publishing still looks after the collection of the royalties of the catalogue owned by Freddie's company, Mercury Songs. I think Freddie looked upon EMI Publishing rather as he would his bank. It was where you got money. EMI simply became Freddie's hole-in-the-wall.

He would meet up with PR people like Phil Symes and Roxy Meade both of whom he liked a lot. It's another example of trust in a relationship. He knew that these people, in a way, had his life in their hands and it was right to ensure their loyalty. However, the meetings were usually not to plan something but to discuss events which had already happened. Phil and Roxy would always have an outline of PR strategy from Jim Beach and they would more often than not be present at any band interviews. Freddie however preferred not to have PR people present at his interviews, in fact he liked to be interviewed alone, just him and the interviewer in a closed room. This had been the situation when he met Judy Wade for an interview which appeared in the *Sun* on February 8, 1984. Because Freddie was naturally not a deceitful, deceptive or dissembling person, he always told more of the truth than was necessary and alone in a room with a reporter, there was no one there to keep an eye on what he was saying and to restrain him. When the interview appeared, it was half the length that he imagined it would be. When confronted, Judy Wade said that it would have been impossible to have printed the whole text. She said she was holding back for his benefit not for hers. Admissions such as, "I'm just going for a line I'll be back in half-a-minute," would not have done anyone any good. However, she was fully prepared to underline in her second sentence that admission of being a fully 'out' gay man, although this does now lay the later myth which was popular which claimed that Freddie had never admitted his gayness.

Where his own projects were concerned, such as the launch of *Mr. Bad Guy* or *Barcelona*, Freddie would say what sort of events he would agree to appear at in conversation with Jim Beach who would then go to Phil or Roxy who would come up with a plan which all three would submit to Freddie for his approval and input at a meeting at Freddie's house. They would then explain to him what certain events he had not specified but which they had suggested he might do over and above what he himself had first envisaged. As I've said, Freddie never spurned advice. He might not have taken it but he always listened.

I've already dealt with Freddie's relationship with his parents and his sister, with whom he was always very guarded as he wanted to protect them from things which they either would not understand or would not accept. Also, he felt the less they knew, the less they could tell. Let me explain. He never wanted his parents to be door-stepped or trapped by a member of the media who might badger them with questions which they were afraid of answering. If they knew nothing, they could in all honesty and integrity say nothing. The Bulsaras were a very traditional Parsee family and Freddie instinctively knew the limits to which his family could go in being modern. He was very sensitive to them and never wanted them compromised. Also, by maintaining a distance from them, he was also able to protect himself from some of their censure.

Strangely, Freddie was very ageist in his way. Things had to be brand new or antique. Same with people. He wasn't one for getting on with or meeting his friends' parents. Having said that, he did send my mother the most massive, beautiful bouquet of flowers when she was taken into hospital but he had no interest in people's families as a matter of everyday moment. It was almost as though he had no other relations than his immediate nuclear family and even their presence often proved too much for him to be able to handle. Talking to him it was almost as though he had never had a childhood. It was never a topic he talked about and he never referred to life other than as a late teenager in London and even then very little about the time he spent at Art School.

Life seemed to have begun at Victoria Road, London W8, for there, away from his family, he could at last start to be himself.

It was as though he had only ever been a butterfly. He had never been a chrysalis and certainly had no repeatable memory of the caterpillar days. He would have hated being an old man and this was one reason, I think, why he never reacted more strongly when he discovered he had Aids. And, as far as the idea of children was concerned, Freddie only had one real opinion, "Fried or boiled?"

While he had very strong opinions about Mick Jagger and Elton and The Who still performing at such advanced ages, I rather think that however much he would have disapproved he would not have been able to stop himself and escape doing the same thing. As it was, he was spared at least the indignity of appearing as mutton dressed as lamb. He never looked his age except when very ill and certainly, 'til that point, had aged so much better than any of his peers.

His view of women was that he really liked them but he always liked them more if they had that certain capacity to be 'just one of the boys'. He didn't specifically categorise human beings as men, women, children . . . He saw them all as people who he liked or didn't like to be with. He gave no special dispensations to man, woman or child for either gender or age. He never preferred to be in the company more of men than women. That just wasn't an issue.

I feel, oddly, that somehow there ought to be more which has to be said on this subject but there really isn't anything more to tell. Freddie was what he was and therefore what he was in some respects prescribed the company he kept but provided that the company entertained him in whatever frame of mind he was currently enjoying, Freddie set no specific store as to who that company was in the way of gender or sexual preference. He assumed that everyone he associated with was an open book and had no hang-ups or no-go areas in their personality. Because he couldn't be normal with his family, he had to be normal with his friends. And he was normal. Not tortured, not stressed, not torn . . . He was never anything but absolutely what he thought of as normal.

As to his other friends, significantly and in no special order, his friendship with Dave Clark started with a professional relationship, namely Freddie's involvement with recording the soundtrack for Dave's show *Time*. Freddie had always thought a lot of Dave because of Dave's own business acumen in the way he had managed his recording career. Dave had a real business brain, had never had a manager and Freddie admired that enormously. Dave was a real self-made man. One of the originals from the Sixties, especially in rock'n'roll. And what's more, Dave had not only kept the money he'd made but he'd amassed more and more and Freddie did find that praiseworthy. On several occasions Freddie said that had he had a brain more like Dave Clark's, he would have been so much richer. However, for Freddie, given his circumstances, it was enough for him to know that he wasn't being ripped off. Being lied to, being stolen from and being taken advantage of . . . these were his nightmares and worst fears in both his business and personal life.

But from Freddie's first association with Dave Clark developed their particular friendship. For Freddie it was an opportunity to talk with someone who was 'in his position', having to live a life constrained by his job and, therefore, by his celebrity. They could talk as equals and indeed they behaved as such. If anything, Freddie found life easier to cope with than Dave and this was what Dave found so interesting about Freddie; that Freddie was a modern, up-dated version of him. They did grow very close in Freddie's last year as Dave was one of the few people whom Freddie permitted to see him deteriorating. Dave would sit with Freddie while the blood and plasma transfusions were being administered and that was a long, arduous and stressful process, believe me.

It was through Dave that Freddie was able to enjoy what he counted as one of the most momentous evenings of his life – an invitation to dinner *chez* Lord and Lady Olivier. That's Olivier as in Laurence and Joan. Because of the excitement, none of us at the house ever really found out what went on. That he had a wonderful time was not in doubt but he couldn't repeat any of the conversations or say who did what or when although I don't think there was a lot of dancing on tables.

However, for Freddie, who must have listened at school to many of this famous actor's recordings of Shakespeare plays, it was a night to remember. Perhaps because it was such a special night, he wanted to keep it private, personal to him alone. The more people you tell, the faster the specialness falls away.

A lot of Freddie's friends were turned away in the last year or two. It must have been very difficult for them to know what was going on and yet at the same time be unable to mention it as they were not supposed to know because Freddie hadn't confided in them directly. It's a testament to all of them that they still respected Freddie's friendship and said nothing publicly to anyone, so proving that Freddie was generally a pretty good judge of character even though they must all have felt slighted at being kept at arm's length.

It would be more than fair to say that Freddie had love affairs with cities and countries as much as he ever did with people. The very early Eighties was definitely his New York period, followed from 1983 to 1987 by his German period, most notably Munich. Prior to New York, I suppose one could say that the world was his playpen as he spent the years before my working with him travelling round the world both recording and touring. He worked a lot more in the years before I joined him, work as defined by the number of days and hours on stage or in the studio.

In New York, other than Thor Arnold, Freddie's immediate 'family' included Lee Nolan, John Murphy and Joe Scardilli who deserve to have more said about them. Although they all knew each other separately in the way of casual friendship, it was Freddie who cemented the mutual bond and made their individual relationships so much more important. Tall and dark-haired, Lee worked as a waiter in an Italian restaurant. We were all much of an age, mid-twenties, early-thirties. Lee was always full of life and very much the joker. He came from out-of-town but had settled into the gay Manhattan lifestyle of the Eighties, he was always ready for a party. Joe and John were already firm friends as they often worked together as cabin crew for American Airlines. Because of their work schedule, their joining Freddie's little parties was more intermittent but when they were in town, they joined in with gusto.

So came about the existence of Mother's Club in New York, a tight-knit group of like-minded men, all breathing the heady air of liberation which was an overpowering aroma in the New York of the era. For a man like Freddie, brought up in repressive boarding schools and families and having had his wings clipped for so long for the sake of Queen, this was a space in which Mercury could really go into orbit. I have never seen any repetition of the intimacy of his relationship with Thor and Lee. To Freddie, these were two very special people and Freddie always had to mark specialness, like a big cat marking its territory. There were always little presents bought to celebrate and somehow make real this group solidarity. Probably unconsciously, the giving of a gift to a friend meant for Freddie that what existed only as a feeling was made physical reality. On one occasion, for each of them Freddie had bought small silver pill boxes from Tiffany's so that each of us had our own place to stash the happy pills which stoked our weekends on the town.

The Munich years were characterised by two friendships, one with Winnie Kirchberger and the other with Barbara Valentin. We were staying at the Munich Hilton and one night Freddie had gone out with a very pleasant man called Horst who eventually became Joe Fanelli's boyfriend and it was from Horst that Freddie got the brown cowboy hat that he was sometimes seen wearing.

A couple of nights later, Freddie met up with Winnie in one of the gay bars, probably the New York. The following day, we were due to return to England and I'll never forget Freddie saying to me, "Well then, which one should I choose for when I come back?" So, the topic of conversation on the flight on the way back to London was the settling of the pros and cons of whether Winnie or Horst?

With Barbara Valentin on the other hand, there was no choice involved. Freddie and Barbara had many things in common from the word go including a mutual sense of fun. Life was also much easier with Barbara because of her command of English. There were many long nights when we would stay up drinking and laughing, sampling the many delights which were quite substantially available in Munich.

Freddie liked Barbara's attitude towards being a star, for in Germany Barbara was at the zenith of her celebrity. Freddie loved the way she would deal with her adoring public even after the point where her tolerance would give out and on the umpteenth approach, she would simply snap, "Fuck off! You're a nobody!"

There were many occasions when Freddie would have loved to have behaved with the same high-handed regality but he could never bring himself to do so.

Freddie loved Barbara's straightforwardness although unlike Freddie, Barbara expected to be treated like a star whenever she was out in public. And yet, conversely, like Freddie, who was actually an internationally recognised star, when Barbara was outside her own country, she didn't expect or look for star treatment. Their relationship worked so well and was close enough that they decided to buy an apartment together in Munich. Initially, when the place was a shell, Freddie was horrified to see the evidence of the down-and-outs who had been camping there. His comment was, "They must recognise something. There's tramps living here even before us tarts move in!"

In the event, Freddie never actually lived there although Barbara fulfilled a huge role in Freddie's life at that time. Being a star, she, like Dave Clark at a later date, could understand what Freddie went through in his day-to-day life. She was always there for Freddie and understandably was very hurt when Freddie turned his back on her. Whether the events had happened or not, Freddie became very disillusioned when with more and more frequency articles were appearing in the German press's gossip columns such as in the *Evening*

Times about the relationship between him and Barbara. One of the load-bearing factors which worked against Barbara at this point was that in the past she had often commented that she knew the gossip columnist concerned.

After one article claiming to have knowledge of him and Barbara getting married, Freddie decided that enough was enough and fuelled by others whispering in his ear, he concluded that it could only be Barbara who was providing the information.

There were those who said that because her own star was on the wane, this being three or four years after they had first met, Barbara was hitching her fortunes now to Freddie's. There were always people around Freddie who were not content to merely wait to take advantage of situations but who actually created circumstances themselves in order to get closer to Freddie. It was a situation which had surrounded him ever since he became famous. There were always people behind the scenes trying to manipulate Freddie's life and then claiming the credit. Not that Freddie was ever easily manipulated but it was like the old adage about saying something often enough, the words become believable. He couldn't bear people close to him gossiping about him.

Winnie won the toss in the game of pros and cons and became the significant other. I think Freddie was rather drawn to being involved in Sebastian Stub'n, Stub'n being the Bavarian term for a neighbourhood restaurant serving typically Bavarian food which was Winnie's business. Dishes like *Schweinhax'n* (pigs' ankles), *Kartoffelknudel* (Freddie described these as, 'Fucking footballs'), various *Bratwurst* and the inevitable cabbage. Generally, what Winnie provided was hot, filling and tasty and Winnie himself was dark-haired with a moustache, some five-feet-ten in height and somewhat chunky in the usual Freddie mould.

How this relationship ever really got off the ground I think must be down to Barbara Valentin in that Freddie had about as much German vocabulary as Winnie had English. By that you can deduce that the relationship was largely based on sex. They both made as much effort as the other – like, none – to learn each other's languages so the eventuality was much 'pidgin' and waving of arms from both parties. Freddie was an expert at waving his arms.

But the relationship lasted with Barbara as the indispensable go-between and interpreter, throughout the Munich period. While

Freddie was officially contactable via Musicland or via me at The Munich Hilton or the Arabellahaus Hotel, it wasn't long before he had moved into Winnie's apartment. The relationship ended because Freddie's in-loveness with Munich was waning and being replaced by his passion for his new house in London and, concomitantly, with Jim Hutton. All Freddie's lovers had very unsophisticated roots. All had country origins but Freddie's own acquired sophistication, he also being a country boy although he would be loathe to admit it, always rubbed off in varying degrees.

Peter Straker was a huge part of Freddie's life for a very long time. They were already great friends before I started working for Queen and Peter was the first of Freddie's longtime friends who I met. Peter was a laugh. He also was present through all Freddie's various emotional and life situations. He was someone, being an artist himself although not in the same league as Freddie, who could understand and share the pressures. Peter was a shoulder for Freddie to cry on, an arm to comfort him and a companion to share the good times. There were many occasions that Freddie, Peter and myself solved the problems of the world from dusk to dawn. I can see us now sitting in Garden Lodge. Freddie would be on the three seater sofa, Peter would be generally in the arm chair near the kitchen door and I would be in the one on the opposite side.

I often wonder, now, why we sat in this position when it would be me who went to the kitchen to get the champagne from the fridge to fill the glasses. When it got to the point of the vodka and the brandy, I would leave the bottles on the coffee table for us each to fill our own. To help lubricate our thoughts, here is an idea of the drinks on hand – two or three bottles of champagne, Cristal for special occasions, Moet for every day, half a bottle of brandy, Remy Martin, a bottle of vodka, Stolichnaya, all the various mixers, tonic for Freddie, Coca-Cola for me as well as the ubiquitous ice bucket.

A typical subject which would start these evenings might be Fergie's bows, for example. Everyone had an opinion. A monumental crisis could be made out of the fact that the newly ennobled Duchess of York wore a bow on everything. The old saying, 'Making a mountain out of a molehill' had nothing on us but in the course of an hour or so, we would have solved the purely hypothetical problem which was to us as real and important as the next glass of champagne and thus the madcap Duchess would end the evening thoroughly de-bowed.

Nothing of earth-shattering importance was ever talked about. Nothing of real significance. If a serious topic was introduced by anyone, it would have lasted about five minutes before being discarded. These nights were not the nights for serious conversation. On another occasion, the subject of the evening was a new song Freddie was tinkering with in which he wanted to introduce the sound of a thigh being slapped. We spent, the three of us, two or three hours slapping our thighs to absolutely no avail. However, when we awoke the following morning it was to bruised thighs and palms that really stung.

Straker helped relieve the pressure for Freddie. He was always there with a ready laugh. On a deeper level, it was as though they had a brotherly conflict as the fundament of their relationship. There was a competitive streak in both of them. While they never came to blows over petty disagreements – because they cared too much for each other for that – there was a sort of one-upmanship which characterised their life together. Freddie's contacts with his rock – he hated being thought of as a pop star – cronies and Peter's ongoing ability to be able to introduce Freddie to ever more famous members of the acting and theatre fraternities proved of great interest to us on the periphery of their relationship.

In the twelve years I knew Freddie it was only Peter who had this relationship with him. A lot of the friendships which Freddie made in the latter part of his life were through Peter who effected Freddie's introduction to Susannah York, Pam Ferris, Anita Dobson, Stephanie Beacham, Anna Nicholas and the list goes on.

It does seem strange that in his final year both Barbara Valentin and Peter Straker who were amongst the most important figures in his life were sidelined. There are reasons that I know of for this. There could be many more.

The first is that Freddie really did not want people he was close to watching his deterioration. He didn't want to put people he loved through the pain of watching him die and being unable to do anything about it. He had spent many wonderful hours with these people going out enjoying themselves, giving them a great time and he didn't want to have these people seeing him frail and tired. These people also reminded him of what his life used to be like, a life which he could no longer enjoy.

If you look at the people whom he marginalised, they were all part of what I have to call Freddie's 'crazy' life. Freddie was also, understandably, envious because his friends, his co-players in his good life scenario, were able to carry on enjoying their own lives. It would have been the final compromise for him to have had them change their lifestyles for his sake and, indeed, there was no reason why they should have done so even had he asked. Earlier on in this 'crazy' life, another victim of Freddie's censure had been Wayne Sleep whose personality, Freddie considered, changed like Jekyll's to Hyde's when Wayne had drunk too much. Freddie didn't like the person whom Wayne, drunk, became and so . . . Another one bites the dust.

Freddie, in the event, had the willpower to do as he was told by his doctors. No smoking, no drinking and certainly no recreational diversions. He was not interested any longer in people who wanted to indulge themselves in these ways at his expense in his house. He never wanted anyone to do something for which he would owe them. He did not wish to feel beholden to his friends. He wanted a clean slate and, of course, would never even have believed that anyone would have wanted to change their behaviour for him.

Mike Moran was a man with whom Freddie began a working relationship which developed into a very close friendship. Freddie recognised him as a consummate musician in the same way that he regarded Peter Straker's talent as a vocalist. Freddie met Mike on the Dave Clark *Time* project and they got on so well that the bond overflowed the parameters of *Time* itself! Mike Moran receives a large amount of credit for the *Barcelona* album and also a credit on the last Queen album, *Innuendo* where he collaborated with Freddie in the studio on a couple of tracks.

Their friendship blossomed and Freddie would spend a lot of time with Mike in Mike's house in Hertfordshire. 'The Great Pretender' was recorded in Mike's studio and Freddie was so proud of that. I always got the impression that Mike would do anything for Freddie and they were founder members of their mutual admiration society. Mike was involved in every single project after the completion of *Time*. He was involved in the video for *Barcelona*, and all of Freddie's appearances to do with *Barcelona*, including the Ku night, La Nit in Barcelona itself and in general became a sort of musical zimmer frame as Freddie's illness wore on. Mike understood the way Freddie's mind worked and they developed such a rapport that it let Freddie relax a little more and not have to shoulder the worry about his newest opus on his own.

While not detracting from Freddie's original ideas and moving genius, Mike does not receive, in my opinion, the credit he is due. Mike was able to develop the warp and woof of Freddie's weave into the most beautiful carpet. I'm sure if they had met professionally earlier, Freddie would have worked with Mike earlier and therefore for longer.

Freddie never claimed to be a great pianist. In fact, he absolutely dreaded 'Bohemian Rhapsody' in performance in case he got the run up the piano wrong. Whereas, Mike Moran, playing just three notes on a keyboard can make those three notes sound like a masterpiece. Mike never tried to claim more than what he was officially credited for but to a large extent it was he who kept Freddie working. He always encouraged Freddie to do that little bit more.

Mike became one of Freddie's extended family immediately. Freddie grew very fond of Mike's wife Linda and he thoroughly enjoyed going to their house. It was always an outing, well worth the distance and the effort as he grew more and more home-bound.

Some of the final relationships he made were, willy nilly, with medical personnel. In his earlier life he dreaded visiting doctors and in general had been a very healthy person. Indeed, he would have had to have been so to have coped with the incredibly gruelling tours which Queen undertook. He always passed with flying colours the physical examinations required by insurance companies to validate the policies which covered the tours. He saw himself duty and honour-bound to be so healthy because for Freddie not to have been able to sing at a twenty thousand seater venue would have lost a lot of people a lot of money. His visits, therefore, to his doctor, Gordon Atkinson, in Shepherd Market had been much more social events than medical forays.

However, in the last year or two, some of the most surprising – to me at any rate – relationships sprang up between the various doctors and the nursing staff whom Freddie encountered. One of the most frequent was Graham Moyle, the link between Freddie and his GP, Gordon Atkinson, and the hospital. Graham was the in-house physician at the Chelsea and Westminster Hospital who was in charge of Freddie's case. The two men got on very well together. Two consummate professionals.

It was almost unthinkable that he could have been so relaxed and at ease with these comparative strangers but of course he had no secrets and nor could he have had secrets from them. He knew there was no point in maintaining his usual façade. They knew what the outcome of his life was going to be. The only thing that none of the team could say was exactly when . . .

Even with us, Freddie always maintained an air which he hoped was communicating the impression that everything was fine and that it was business as usual. With the doctors and nurses whom he knew had his life in their hands, he could afford to let the guard drop totally. I can understand his thinking. It was as though a huge weight had been taken off his shoulders when he was with them and he need pretend no longer. He actually looked forward to them coming.

Freddie had regular visits from various specialists – an oncologist, a dermatologist and the consultant in overall charge of his case, Brian Gazzard. Freddie also had a special relationship with the sister who came from the Chelsea and Westminster Hospital specifically to give him his blood transfusions. As I will explain more fully later, Joe and I had been taught how to administer all the other drugs but, because of the high risk potential of a blood transfusion, it was decided that a trained nurse be in attendance. Since then, of course, I have learned what are the necessary precautions and the possible dangers of incorrect administration. It can be too fast, too slow . . .

I think it would be helpful for people to understand better what gruelling processes these transfusions were. As the transfusion commences, the patient has to be checked very carefully for reactions. The familiar observations (the 'obs'), temperature, pulse and blood pressure are taken at regular intervals. Every five minutes for fifteen minutes to begin with, then every fifteen minutes for the first hour, then half-hourly until the end of the transfusion which normally for one unit of blood will take four hours. Although very careful checks are made to ensure compatibility of the blood, there is always a chance that there might be something not quite right and a patient can go into anaphalactic shock. Freddie would usually have three units transfused and so it's a fairly simple calculation to realise that these were twelve-hour days he went through. His very weakness, which was the reason for the transfusion in the first place, was initially exacerbated because all the checking which had to be done as each unit of blood was given meant that he was unable even to doze for longer than a few minutes at a time.

Even in the early days of these visits, Aids was not something that a lot was known about but Freddie was able to ask them questions and get answers which he couldn't do with friends and family. When you are very, very ill it is quite understandable that your illness rather takes over. It, perforce, becomes your life and so if there is no one in your life who can answer your more than pertinent questions, it becomes a pleasure, something you can look forward to, to have someone with you who can help you out and with whom you can really share. Joe, obviously for his own reasons as well, dedicated a huge amount of his time to find out more about the disease. Freddie was always kept appraised of new developments in the many research programmes which were featured in the medical and scientific magazines which Joe steeped himself in. A vast amount had, by necessity, to have been learned by the medical profession in an extremely short period of time.

I cannot end this chapter without including an account of Freddie's relationships with both the band and with Jim Beach . . . With the latter, he had a very good working relationship. Jim had been a young lawyer with Harbottle & Lewis in the very early days of Queen's existence. Jim was probably the only lawyer in London at that time who played in a jazz band and who at least therefore understood something of the soul of a musician. Jim was then brought in, once the band was managing themselves, to look after their business affairs, i.e. touring and recording contracts etc. Once the band's 'manage-themselves' phase had passed, Jim became Queen's full-time manager. During this period, the band were tending to do more solo projects and so Jim became more and more involved with the individual members of the band as he represented them as individuals as well as, collectively, Queen.

Although Jim may have a reputation in the music business of being, shall I say, a little brusque, he is also very well-known for getting what he wants. Getting his own way in negotiations. Freddie knew that Jim Beach was going to secure the best deals possible and therefore a certain amount of trust and mutual respect developed between the two. They grew quite close as this made for a much better working relationship and as I have pointed out, Freddie always needed to make a friend of a business contact. Freddie always took great pleasure in picking out specific gifts for Jim and his wife Claudia. Over time, Freddie got a great insight into Jim's appreciation of English water colours.

Jim also showed Freddie the respectable side of 'the high life' by organising visits to restaurants like Freddie Giradet's restaurant in Lausanne which was at one point the most exclusive in the world. Freddie learned to appreciate the fine wines of Switzerland including what was to become his favourite, St. Saphorin, of which on one occasion he imported twelve cases via Peter Pugson's wine company. Whereas Freddie had no competition in his knowledge of the more rakish high spots of '*le beau monde*', Jim had a discerning cultural palate born from a substantial English upbringing which Freddie recognised. Freddie knew that he could learn a lot from Jim Beach and, as usual, took advantage accordingly. Freddie was very happy to let his career be guided by Jim Beach provided that his own input was paramount. Freddie always had the final veto.

In my time with Freddie, he always had a very good working relationship with John Deacon but it never seemed to follow on in their personal, offstage relationship perhaps because of John's family commitments and family life being miles apart from Freddie's idea of a social life. I do know that Freddie had a lot of respect and was very fond of John. Both Roger and Brian were much more rock superstar models. In Queen's heyday, Roger held as many headlines as Freddie, Roger's arm being easier to twist to go to 'the parties' where he was 'seen'. It was only in the latter years that Brian also started carving a niche for himself in the tabloid press and that can be almost solely ascribed to Anita Dobson's positive influence. Freddie, distinctly, did not like being 'seen' in public at the 'right' places. His concentration was much too focused on his own performance to even think about, for example, going up to the Royal Box at Live Aid. He was not one of nature's liggers.

The band would go out socially together when they were, for example, recording and occasionally they would go out to a nightclub together but usually their relationships stayed within the work aspect and very rarely strayed outside. If any of the band as individuals had a party, the other members of Queen were invited and would attend but there was never a regular social relationship between the members of Queen like, once a week, let's all go out and eat . . . I have an idea that things developed in this way after the advent of Paul Prenter because after this, Freddie had someone on tap who could always accompany him to the bars and clubs. When Freddie had someone permanently in his life, he would be more likely to socialise with the other band members because he wouldn't be looking for a sex partner for the night.

To conclude this section, I have decided to recount what I can class as my personal memories of five of the most significant moments of my life with Freddie. I list them in no particular order except the final episode, which I count the most and unforgettably important. There was a photo session in Ibiza which for some reason sticks out in my mind, a hasty packing of bags in New York, the launch of the *Barcelona* album at the Royal Opera House, Covent Garden, the gala concert attended by HRH Prince Andrew and then there was the fifth . . .

The photo session in Ibiza took place at the same time as the Ku concert. The shoot happened in the grounds of the hotel in which Montserrat was staying on the newly developed port area. Both Freddie and Montserrat were to be presented with replicas of the ship Santa Maria by the organisation which was in charge of the quin-centennial celebrations regarding Columbus' discovery of the New World. Freddie took four or five different outfits because he couldn't make up his mind what to wear. His were a combination ranging from the very informal – white jeans and various brightly coloured shirts – to the formal, duck-egg blue and green suits. One he'd bought in Japan and the others had been made by David Chambers. There were a variety of shirts which all accessorised the suits varying from strongly and brightly coloured to white. Five different ties completed the wardrobe. Just goes to show a lot of hard work goes in to achieve the casual, thrown-together look. Hardly a case of, "I just picked the first thing I found in the wardrobe!"

It was to be one of the more casual shoots which had been set up to provide photographs for the promotion of the *Barcelona* album and single and also to give this Columbus Group some focus of identity.

As usual, Freddie was nervous as he always was on any occasion when he was to meet Montserrat. It was something I always found strange. It would take him only moments to get over any nervousness he might have felt but it was always the same scenario. His nerves would show in his talkativeness in the car going to the rendezvous and this'd happened each time he went to a photo session, a record-ing session . . . anything. But he was adept at making the atmosphere immediately as relaxed and happy as possible although it was always a bit of a performance and inevitably, at the end of any such get-together, he would say, "Well I wasn't really worried about it in the first place," which was really his way of saying to himself, "What *was* I so worried about?"

It was the setting, the Spanish sunshine ... The formal pictures which were this session's precursor had been taken by Terry O'Neill and were used specifically for the *Barcelona* album cover and while it was an enjoyable enough session, it was indoors and was a formal photo shoot. The Ibiza one was so much more relaxed. Montserrat had brought various floral patterned frocks in many colours but the ones they settled on were brown flower patterns on a white background. If Montserrat is known for another passion other than her family and her music it is shopping! Something both Freddie and she had in common and a subject about which they would always compare notes. Rooms had been arranged for Freddie in order that make-up and hair could be done easily. Montserrat was staying there anyway.

It was such a happy day. It was fairly early by Freddie's standards. It was only champagne that flowed. It just glows in my memory as a very happy day.

The incident concerning the hasty packing of bags occurred early one morning in New York. Just prior to this episode, Queen had been touring in South America and had finally arrived in Venezuela. Just before the tour started Freddie found himself very much attracted to a barman called Richard in The Works on the Upper West Side but for all Freddie's efforts, the man remained immune to the Mercury charm offensive. Out of sight, out of mind was never really one of the phrases which summed up Freddie's attitude. Out of sight, to the back of the mind was more apt. In Caracas, Freddie found himself much drawn to a swarthy Latino called, I think, Eduardo who kept Freddie occupied for a couple of nights. Just as we were about to leave Caracas, Freddie promised Eduardo a trip to New York so that he could come and see Freddie. Due to Eduardo's commitments, he wasn't able to make the trip for a couple of days until the following weekend and this delay eventually proved to be his downfall.

On arriving back in New York, battle plans were drawn up by The Master. Richard from The Works was going to capitulate. Only total surrender would suffice. A visit to The Works had become a regular event on our nightly schedule and on each visit Freddie and Richard were beginning to get on better and their friendship developed. On the Friday night, Eduardo duly arrived as planned and we went out to eat. Eduardo announced that he was feeling very, very tired. He had been working all week and had come straight to the plane from work. Freddie told him, "That's fine, dear. Get the car to take you back to the hotel and I'll just go for a little drink and I'll be back soon."

Well, this little drink took us of course to The Works. At this point, I really believe that Freddie fully intended to return to Eduardo at the Hotel because he wasn't a hundred per cent sure what would happen with Richard but Richard picked this night to call Freddie's bluff and accept his invitation to come home with him. Suddenly, *panic*!!

There was no way that Freddie was going to let Richard get away which was a distinct possibility had Freddie deterred him and postponed the date. But what could he do? I suppose the easiest thing was to book another room at the Berkshire Place but Freddie's mind didn't work like that. He figured he was already paying out a thousand dollars a night for the suite he had so why should he pay out more? Eventually, at four or five in the morning, we came up with the following plan. As Eduardo had a return ticket, I was deputed to book him on the first flight back to Caracas. Then, back at the suite in the Berkshire Place, while Freddie and Richard were uncontrollably giggling in the kitchen, I had to go and wake Eduardo in the bedroom with the flimsiest of excuses. My script read that Freddie had met up with friends and had gone to Connecticut because of some work that was going to be happening. Eduardo hadn't unpacked too much and so after his bags were together, I escorted him downstairs to Freddie's waiting car which took him back to the airport.

I had never in one way felt so bad about the job in hand in my life although on the other hand, I couldn't help laughing to myself at the sheer farce of the situation. Talk about bedroom doors banging. It was a scenario worthy of Neil Simon as the master wrote in *California* or *Plaza Suite*. It could have been this little stint in the kitchen which gave Freddie the idea for the kitchen in Garden Lodge because he had the same style of kitchen cabinet built and installed, the ones made by Boffi in lacquered oxblood.

I have to observe that the said Richard's surname might have played some small part in this episode. His surname was Dick and Richard predictably became known as Dick-Dick. He and Freddie had great fun together while their passion lasted but it was no great love affair.

And poor Eduardo!

I have to mention here the odd habit which developed during private, non-Queen travel of always missing a flight we had quite seriously booked with all intentions of catching it. All very well except that our partying schedule usually outlasted the curfew which we would have to have stuck to in order to have caught the flight. I don't think we ever caught the first flight we had booked. My first job on returning to the hotel early in the morning was always to rearrange the flight plans.

The third event in my litany concerns the launch of the *Barcelona* album in Britain which took place one lunchtime in the Crush Bar at the Royal Opera House in Covent Garden. Montserrat had flown in just for the day and we collected her en route from the Inn On The Park where she had booked in to change her clothes. Once again, the event might have been a military manoeuvre. Timing was all-important.

I think the occasion was important for me because the Opera House was where I was working when I first met Freddie but this time, I wasn't merely a backstage worker I was one of the causes of the event that was taking place front-of-house. I had worked at the Opera House for four years and very rarely in that time had I experienced anything to match the feeling I had when I walked with Freddie and Montserrat up the famous red-carpeted stairs to the Crush Bar with flash bulbs popping at our every step. It's so hard to describe this feeling but I wish everybody could feel it at least once in their lives. I felt that I had come a very long way.

I think it was a landmark day for Freddie too. It was as though the Opera establishment had opened its ranks a little to let him in. I don't think he would have ever deemed that they'd accepted him but it was a huge step for Mercury even though only a small step for opera.

Inside the Crush Bar, the scenario was like King Arthur and Queen Guinevere being shown to The Round Table where both of them fielded questions hurled at them by the assembled press. There was TV footage taken of the event and considering where and what the occasion was, both Freddie and Montserrat took it in their stride.

It was as though Freddie had just 'popped in' to a sitting room. He looked quite relaxed in the pale blue suit. I suppose this press launch was a wonderful apex to a project which had started as something which, when finished, had it never even reached the ears of the public would not have mattered to Freddie. This was his totally selfish project which he did only for himself but now he had the eventual added bonus that his public would have a chance to share his pleasure.

The Crush Bar seems to feature in my high points of Freddie's life as much as it did in his own. For me, I suppose, there was always that added extra dimension of my perspective over time. Then I was invisible and backstage, now I was sharing a feted and celebrated company in the spotlight. The only occasion on which I and my co-workers had in the past been acknowledged on stage was on the occasion of the Queen's Silver Jubilee when after the curtain call all the backstage staff were summoned on stage to be applauded not only by the house but by seventeen members of the British Royal Family whom we met afterwards on stage behind the curtain. Upon shaking hands with Her Majesty, she asked benignly, "And what do you do here?"

Time stopped still. The Royal Family departed and we were left milling around on stage bathed in a really tangible euphoria. We in turn were just about to leave when Princess Margaret returned to the stage and asked, "Has anyone seen my mother?"

Her Royal Highness was then escorted to the back of the stage where Her Majesty was regaling the assembled stage hands with stories of horse racing. It really was a most fantastic event.

Mine and Freddie's combined royal event concerned Prince Andrew whom I had met several times before as he was a regular visitor to the opera and the ballet as was I, both being friends of the principal dancer Wayne Eagling. Freddie and I were part of a group that attended a big gala night at The Royal Opera House. Freddie's biggest quandary this night wasn't what he should wear but what he should do to entertain himself between the end of the gala and making his entrance, fashionably late, to the party afterwards in the Crush Bar.

The fashionably late bit was accounted for by Freddie's leaving the Opera House and driving round the block a couple of times before making the suitably grand entrance. It was in the summer, strawberries and cream were much in evidence and Freddie was introduced via Wayne Eagling to Prince Andrew. It was their first meeting. To break the ice, Prince Andrew was absolutely charming and fished out the end of Freddie's silk scarf which had draped itself accidentally into Freddie's glass of champagne.

Andrew wrung out the sodden scarf and they both laughed. They continued chatting for a while during which time HRH finished his plate of strawberries and cream. Freddie noticed HRH's discomfort at being unable to politely rid himself of his plate. At this point, Freddie turned round to me and said, "Phoebe, get rid of that plate!"

Prince Andrew looked a little taken aback and said, "Did you just call him Phoebe? I know him as Peter."

At this point, it was Freddie's turn to look taken aback. I think all he could utter was, "Oh!"

I duly relieved HRH of his empty pudding plate. It was true that Freddie invited Prince Andrew to Heaven along with others of the company after the party but HRH declined. Freddie and troop duly left for Heaven. I believe it was on this occasion that one of the ballerinas lay down and cavorted in the empty coffin which was a feature in one of the leather bars at Heaven, much to the chagrin of other patrons. You somehow got the impression that no one was supposed to enjoy themselves in these sorts of clubs. You weren't supposed to be seen to be having a good time.

Through Wayne Eagling, Freddie had attended the performances of quite a few ballets. Of everything he saw, his favourite was Kenneth MacMillan's masterpiece for the male dancer, *Mayerling*. Traditional ballets almost always centre around the ballerina and this was the first full length ballet which demanded an inordinate amount of stamina from the male principal. While Wayne wasn't the first cast as Crown Prince Rudolf, as far as Freddie and I were concerned, his was the best portrayal. Freddie even seriously considered sponsoring a run of performances of *Mayerling* but as soon as ballet officialdom entered into private patronage, it became too involved and centred upon him and he lost interest.

We were lucky at Covent Garden because I knew one of the box office staff and so should Freddie decide that there was something he wanted to see at the last moment, tickets were not a problem. In those days, prior to computer ticketing, a block of ten of the best seats in the house were always left available should any VIP require seats. These seats were kept on hold until the last minute when the box office knew they would always be able to get rid of them. These seats were generally front row of the grand tier, best seats in the house. This means of acquiring seats is definitely no longer available, thanks to the inevitable computer.

Which brings me on to my number five on the significant moment list. This next and last just goes to show that like life, my time with Freddie was not always a bed of roses. This is more a chain of events than a single situation and it is as sad a memory as it is an important one, although the outcome brought about an incredible strengthening of our relationship.

It concerns one of the most important tenets of Freddie's life, the question of trust. And I have to say, my own life, for trust is a two-way street. In hindsight, the build-up to this situation occurred over quite a long period but in essence I began to feel an unsettling shift in our relationship. I can't put my finger on the moment and so I can't say when the process started but I remember it building up to a moment when after much soul-searching I told Freddie in the middle of 1989 that I thought it was better that I left Garden Lodge.

At the time, as it was happening, I didn't know what was going wrong but it finally occurred to me that there was so much that I wasn't being told, I was beginning to feel very marginalised in the household.

There were bits of information which I was hearing which under ordinary circumstances I would have been privy to. I felt like the untried apprentice about whom someone once joked, "They're just like mushrooms. Feed 'em shit 'n' keep 'em in the dark!"

To be specific, I was being deliberately kept in the dark about Freddie's appointments at the hospital or with the doctor. Nothing of life-or-death importance but Freddie's whereabouts was information I would have usually known and been told about both by Freddie as well as by Joe and Jim, because everyone in the house would always assume that the others knew equally what any single person knew. As far as we 'staff' were concerned, although Freddie hated the ultimate confrontations that could arise in a household such as his, he would let petty situations develop and simmer and would rather enjoy watching them brew. It was one of his ways of controlling the drama, rather like his way in business in general. If relationships were too hunky dory and too cosy between all of 'us', he would often get to feel left out, as though there was some big conspiracy against him being hatched. Being the master puppeteer, he always knew that it could fall to him to pour oil on the ruffled waters and to emerge the ostensibly sympathetic shoulder to cry on at the opportune moment. A master.

At that point, I really could not understand why I was being excluded from being told this medical information. I have to re-emphasise here that Freddie was doing his utmost to play the health question very close to his chest. I had no alternative but to come to the blind conclusion that whatever Freddie was suffering from, it was indeed very serious. I suppose, deep in the back of my mind, I had suspected that Freddie had Aids but the forward parts of the mind, the positive-thinking parts, tell one the opposite story. That he hadn't . . .

But, then, what had he got?

This unbearable situation continued and looked like doing so as I was unable to summon up the boldness or find the right moment to approach Freddie and ask him privately what it was that was the matter with him. In the end, I went through Joe, Jim and Mary. I just had to tell them, "Look . . . There is no point in my being here if I don't know what's going on, I cannot plan anything in my own life and I simply shouldn't be here."

It transpired that Freddie suspected that it had been through me that certain information as to the state and causes of his health problems were being leaked to the press and to others. Freddie had heard something which had come back to him via an eighth or ninth party which could only have come from a source within Garden Lodge, something to do with a visit to a hospital which he had made earlier on in the year and which should have been entirely confidential.

Joe and Jim reacted to my unease by being conciliatory . . . "Are you sure that's what you want to do? Are you really sure?" Things like that.

I was absolutely sure. What I was even more than sure of was that I was so unhappy that I really needed to leave. After all that we had been through together over the past ten years and the relationships we had all built up, I felt that it was being eroded for some mystery that I was being kept away from. It was distressing and cruel. As I had hoped, the message got to Freddie and he came down into the kitchen one day not long after, before Terry had come in for the morning and when Joe and Jim had either gone – or been sent – out, I'm not sure which. He was sitting down at the kitchen table and I was by the moveable butcher's block in the middle of the kitchen and he said, "What's all this rubbish about you going?"

So, I tried to explain what I was feeling and he actually told me what it was he thought had been going on. As far as he was aware, he thought that I had been telling one of my best friends outside the inner circle what was going on in the house and that this had become the subject of gossip.

Once his suspicions were all out in the open, I knew immediately that there was a glimmer of hope in salvaging the situation because, very basically, I knew that I had not and would never have blab-mouthed so carelessly. It was not in my nature. I knew if I could spend ten minutes trying to explain and convince Freddie of this, things would be okay.

We talked. I told him, "Okay, maybe when I started work with the band, because everything was so new and wonderful and glamorous, of course I told my friends what a wonderful life it was. But," I continued, "after all the years of knowing you, I fully appreciate what your privacy means to you and you know I would never invade it. You know I would do anything for you, anything you asked . . ."

It must have been about this moment in the conversation that Freddie must have had a change of heart. He turned to me and said, "Well, you know I'm very sick. But that's the end of the conversation. There's just no more to say."

He didn't have to say anything else. I had already lost some friends to Aids so I understood fully what he was saying. It was 1989, after all. Freddie, also, knew that he had no need to elaborate.

The tension eased visibly, immediately, but I was still not a hundred per cent sure that I should be staying. Obviously, something was leaking out of the house and however much I racked my brains, I couldn't be sure of every single word that I'd ever said to every single person about my life. I even began to doubt myself.

I know that I never ever told one single person about Freddie's illness, not even my best friends, not even when they pestered me about their suspicions, for the topic was almost common gossip on every street corner because of the continual press speculation. As far as I'm concerned, it is the prerogative of any person suffering from any illness to tell only whomsoever they wish. It is no one else's place to pass on any private information like this and the right to impart such information is only the right of the sufferer. I knew, however, that my constant lie, which I told when pressed about Freddie's health, would catch up with me eventually but I persisted with what seemed like a mantra, "No, he's fine, he's just a bit under the weather." Or, "Just a liver complaint, dear."

I knew that true friends would be there when the time came and would understand why I felt I had to lie. One of my regrets, however, is that Freddie never knew the amount and depth of concern which was being expressed for him by people in all walks of life and at all times of day. I knew but I could never tell him that I knew that they knew because he never wanted the subject broached.

A short while after this conversation, time enough for both Freddie and I to acclimatise to a new state of openness, Freddie asked me whether or not I still wanted to leave. It was an incredible request from a man who had spent his life avoiding such confrontations. It says something about the relationship we had that he found himself able to ask.

I replied, "Well, you don't really need me here."

"But I do need you," he said. "I want you to stay." At that point, I was very overcome with emotion. I then felt really guilty that I had made Freddie do this. I didn't know whether to laugh or to cry. We merely hugged.

I then took on more of the responsibilities of caring for him and suddenly the grey lowering skies of the last few months lifted as far as my relationship with him was concerned.

Not long after this episode, I remember a day which for me represents the final cementing of our ultimate relationship. It was late Spring in 1991, the magnolia blossom on the trees was in full bloom. I was suffering yet another attack of gout, this time in my ankle. I had first developed gout some years before. For people who've never experienced this ailment, I won't even try to explain the pain and its intensity. The day in question was one of those when Freddie had decided he wanted to sit out in the garden and due to my illness, I wasn't able to get very far without the aid of a walking stick. Freddie arranged for two of the big wicker chairs from the conservatory to be brought out into the garden, along with one of the accompanying stools, and placed beneath the magnolias. It must have made quite a picture, both of us invalids sitting in the capacious armchairs, each with our afflicted foot supported on the footstool, the sunlight playing down through the leaves and flowers above us. He had an arrangement of magazines put out and drinks so that we wouldn't have to move anywhere. We spent a couple of hours there, talking about nothing in particular. However, after three hours, he got bored with the idyllic setting and its carefully arranged props and went back inside.

I have to say that it was not until after he died that I found out how the information which had so threatened the integrity of my relationship with Freddie was getting out of the house. The gossip was being passed on, without doubt, and the unwitting carrier turned out to be Joe. I think, totally unknowingly, when Joe went to the gym every day, he was going as much as to a social club as for a workout. In amongst his acquaintances at the gym was someone who was later discovered to be a reporter for the *Daily Mirror*. So, while Joe was having conversations with his friends, information was being gleaned from what he was saying and, from between the lines, elaborated upon as it was passed on like a horrible game of Chinese whispers.

Chapter Six

Sometime in September 1991, Joe and I had been given British Telecom pagers so that we could keep in constant touch all the time we weren't together in the house. For example I might be out shopping and Joe could be at the gym and we could maintain the secure knowledge of being in touch should anything untoward happen at home and we were needed immediately. The pagers were never actually needed but for our peace of mind and for Freddie's, they were worth their weight in gold. He was visibly deteriorating. Just a little piece of plastic with a couple of microchips made all the difference.

From about the end of September onwards, it must be remembered that Freddie's eyesight was failing. It was why he hadn't been going out quite so frequently. At Bonhams one day, where there was a flight of white marble steps leading to the street in Montpellier Square, he missed his footing and only just in time grabbed hold of my arm. It was the first time he realised that he couldn't gauge the tread of the step. His sense of perspective had gone. I suppose it takes something unexpected like this incident for a person to be pulled up sharply and forced to evaluate the extent to which their own physical decline had progressed. For Freddie, part of the great joy of being alive was being able to see. This was a major setback in his will to carry on. He knew he was never going to beat his disease but he was determined to fight it with all his strength.

Freddie had flown back from Switzerland on Saturday, November 9, 1991, having made up his mind that he was no longer going to take any of the drugs that were keeping him alive. He was not going to have any more of the Gancyclovir, Septrin and all the others. He accepted that he would have to continue to take the painkillers. Up until this point, he had been on Dihydrocodeine (DF118) but the doctors, after discussion, considered he would be better off having Diamorphine as he needed it. After the first dose, Freddie found that he was extremely nauseous and so an anti-emetic was also prescribed. Again, Joe and I were taught the amounts and frequency of the doses. The anti-emetic worked up to a point but right until the end, Freddie had difficulty tolerating the morphine.

Some months prior to this date, Freddie had been admitted as an overnight patient to the Cromwell Hospital in Cromwell Road just around the corner in order to have a Hickman line implanted. This simple operation involved a canula being inserted into a vein in the neck. Then the rubber tube at the head of the canula is implanted under the skin and emerges through the skin on the upper left pectoral to which can then be attached an infusion valve. The only physical evidence of the presence of this canula is a tiny scar on the lower part of the neck in the clavicle region. This insertion facilitated easier administration of the medications. It solved the problem of having a nurse on hand to insert venflons every time access to a vein was required. At this time, such access was at least twice a day. No patient's vein system could tolerate this invasion for long. This Hickman line access point could remain in situ for any amount of time up to a year. Extreme care was needed where hygiene was concerned as any stray infection had an open access to the body. Such stray infections could cause radical reactions even in a matter of seconds.

Without unwarranted blowing of our trumpets, I think great credit is due to Joe and myself for keeping the access line clean. It can never be fully sterile once it has been opened. In later experience, I came across patients whose lines didn't remain in place for more than two or three weeks at a time due to infection. When you consider that Freddie's bed was literally crawling with cats and that all this was taking place in a domestic – not a hospital – environment, he was very lucky.

There was talk of connecting Freddie's Hickman line to a Diamorphine pump but Freddie vetoed this because of the nausea this drug left him with. Towards the end, he asked for the Diamorphine less and less and at the end relied solely on orally ingested analgesics.

The reason he stopped the life-sustaining drugs was that he had been made a prisoner within the walls of Garden Lodge by virtue of the fact that the press were now outside the gate permanently, thus preventing his ever leaving the house or his friends gaining entrance to the house without being pestered.

For the first week or so following this decision, it seemed to make no difference to his condition. He was obviously getting weaker because one of the drugs that he was taking was to boost his appetite and after declining it he was eating and drinking a lot less. He'd still be able to take scrambled egg, occasionally rice – fried of course not boiled – and he'd drink water and Earl Grey tea with milk. He'd only ever had hot lemon and honey when he knew he would be singing or when he'd had a cold or bad throat. We used to make up fresh fruit drinks with the juicing machine and tried to get his taste buds going with fresh pineapple or mango juice. He loved fresh fruit salad and we always ensured there was a large variety of fresh fruit like star fruit, kiwi fruit, cape gooseberries and passion fruit in the house. All the exotic varieties.

He was determined that while getting weaker, it should be business as usual as far as possible. This was carried out from the grand bed which, as previously mentioned, had been made specifically for the room and in which he would spend a great deal of his time surrounded by his beloved cats.

Freddie had many cats throughout his life and it is no mere silliness when I emphasise that he placed as much importance on these beloved animals as on any human in his life. Tom and Jerry were the start of Freddie's live-in feline loves. They lived with him and Mary at 100 Holland Road and then moved with him to Stafford Terrace but ended their lives in Mary Austin's flat on the corner of the terrace. With Tony Bastin came Oscar, the big ginger tom who became the tribe's patriarch but yet who, in the end, must have felt so intimidated and thus displaced by the continual arrival of the latter youngsters, he inevitably left the nest and effectively went to live with someone else on the other side of the Garden Lodge wall. Then the long-haired blue point Tiffany, a gift from Mary and the only one of Freddie's cats apart from little Lily not brought in from the Blue Cross sanctuary. While Freddie adored Tiffany, he hated the idea of such constant in-breeding with any animal, Tiffany being a case in blue-point where some of her vital organs failed because of her in-bred lineage.

Delilah – his favourite cat of all – and Goliath came next. While some might think this an odd pairing of names, Freddie took great pride in telling everyone that he wasn't going to fall into the expected trap of calling his great black new love, Samson. Actually, Goliath wasn't a very apt name because the cat in question never grew very big. But he made up for this by being incredibly loving and dribbled his adoration at the slightest excuse. After that came Miko, who was a tri-coloured tabby. She arrived after one of Freddie's Japanese shopping sprees and was duly christened.

Next was a cat found by Jim and dubbed Romeo, a white-faced masked tabby. Why Romeo? Who knows? Last but not least was Lily, a mainly white cat with a touch of the tarbrush, little patches of black dappling the petals of the lily. One way of telling that Delilah was Freddie's favourite was that she was the large one who did only as she pleased. He was so enamoured of his feline brood that Freddie commissioned paintings of every single one of them from Ann Ortman, one of which of Oscar he sent to be auctioned at one of the Queen fan club conventions.

Freddie only ever personally fed his cats from the dinner table or by means of running snacks, elevenses or afternoon refreshment available at whim in the form of dried nugget food. Otherwise it was one of our jobs to feed the feline *ménage*. In the mornings they would get tinned food, either Sheba or Whiskas. In the evening they would get fresh food, poached fish or chicken. Something strange about the animals – if Freddie had scrambled egg for breakfast, each of them would enjoy being given a little egg, a little sausage but on two or three occasions we tried to entice them with their own fresh-cooked scrambled egg with a little sausage or bacon and they turned their noses up at the slightest hint. Obviously it was the illicit thrill of the dinner table which was the great lure.

One thing that did annoy him was if any of the cats ever 'sprayed' on the soft furnishings. He could never understand why when they had all the gardens and as much roaming space as possible that they felt the need to protect and mark their territory indoors as well but I suppose that there was little wonder when you consider how many males and females there were in the 'family' at any one time. However, you would often find either Joe, Jim, Mary or myself scrubbing at the moiré silk which had suffered a fresh stain and Tiffany's object of defecation, namely the kitchen toaster, just had to be thrown away when she refused to be deterred, the turd in question being quite vile.

This time it was *me* who was not amused!

Considering their environment however, I suppose they were

reasonably well-adjusted animals. The cats of course had their own Christmas presents. Freddie would send Jim out to complete Christmas stockings for all of them so that each cat might find a couple of cat-nip toys, some little nibbles and various other little 'cat things' each Christmas morning.

While living in Munich, Freddie was actually given a kitten but he knew because of his peripatetic existence, it would be very unfair on the animal for him to keep it. He therefore asked two friends of his, a young Irishman called Patrick who was living with a waiter nick-named Polder in Winnie's restaurant, to be foster parents. That way, the cat, immediately called Dorothy, would always have a home but Freddie could have free acess at any time. Freddie never had cats anywhere other than where he knew his real home was. Deep down, he knew that home was where the cats were.

One thing that I didn't miss on leaving Garden Lodge was the constant barrage of telephone calls. There were six of us around the house during the course of the day. Multiply one average person's telephone calls by six and then add a factor of increase to cater for Freddie being a star of worldwide artistic and business significance and perhaps you have some idea of the bells, Esmerelda, the bells! The one instrument whose bell was not connected was the one at the side of Freddie's bed. The phone system in Garden Lodge was based on an office or hotel switchboard system where any extension could pick up an incoming call although internal calls could be made by dialling a specific extension.

We could always call Freddie on the internal line which would activate the bell but no external calls were heard. Every extension other than the main receiver in the kitchen was of the old-fashioned, dial-face variety. He felt they worked better! His natural curiosity always rose to the surface. If he had been in the sitting room and the telephone had been answered in the kitchen, he couldn't resist asking, "Who was that? Should I have spoken to them? What did they want?"

It must have really got to him not being able to answer the phone because he loved the telephone. But not answering it personally was the only way he could protect himself from the unnecessary and sometimes distressing intrusions of the outside world. All Freddie's telephone calls were screened. They always had been. While Joe or I would answer the phone, we had a list of people whom we knew he didn't need or want to talk to. We were able, through the internal exchange system, to check with Freddie whether the caller was someone he wanted to talk to.

As September drew into October, if he felt like a change of scenery, he'd make his way downstairs in one of his many dressing gowns to sit for an hour or so in the sitting room. Someone would always be with him just to ensure his safety. He tended to get out of bed less after 'the decision' but it still didn't stop him looking at Sotheby's and Christie's auction sale catalogues, his usual reading material. I would get up at about eight o'clock in the morning, cross the garden and go into the main house from my bedroom in the mews and wait for him to wake up. We'd set up an intercom between his room and the kitchen although if he needed anything at any other time, he'd use the telephone system to call us in whichever room we happened to be. However, it was easier for him just to press the intercom's buzzer.

I'd take him a cup of tea and, if he felt like it, sit and chat about how he was feeling, whether there was anything he wanted done, anything that came into his mind. At that point, I'd also try to persuade him to take some nourishment. A slice of toast, maybe. But, more often than not, it was refused. He used to get annoyed with me as I continually badgered him to try and eat something because while we always had a large stock of various food items in the house, you could guarantee that when he *did* want something to eat it would be something we didn't have. As far as he was concerned, there was no point in eating any more.

That he was going to die he had only to acknowledge once when he came off the drugs and there was no need to speak of it again. Similarly, although he was not at all without faith, he never spoke about what was going to happen to him after death. He was of the opinion that that was a question one worried about during the years of life. With the closeness of the inevitable, there was little point in thinking about it. Whatever was going to happen was going to happen and he knew he didn't have long to worry about it. In my later experience and having had time to reflect myself, it seems that life does prepare a person for death. When the end is in sight, you think back, not forward. You think about what you have done, on the good times.

So, conversations were not deep and meaningful. Just easy communication to pass the time. I'd rearrange the pillows and cushions and then leave him propped up in bed watching the television screen. The television was mainly left on because it was company which wouldn't talk back and which he didn't have to entertain. At this point, the company he enjoyed most was that of Oscar, Delilah, Goliath, Romeo, Miko and Lily. He would never refuse them entry to his bedroom, unlike us humans when the mood took him. I'd spend the next few hours hovering in the kitchen because that was the easiest place for Freddie to get in touch with anyone if he wanted anything. The kitchen was also the place for fulfilling the housekeeping role that I was employed to do, making sure that everything was in its place for his next visit downstairs. How often had he walked into a room and rather than say, "Oh, that looks good!" instead would say, "Where's the ashtray!"

He was always very particular and to the last noticed every new scratch and stain. He pronounced famously about Mary Pike, one of his cleaners, "If she'd been around in Louis The Fourteenth's time, there wouldn't be any antiques today!"

In her undoubted eager thoroughness, Mary was famous for taking chips and chunks out of the most expensive of Freddie's antique furniture with her most modern vacuum cleaner.

We may have had to tolerate it, but we were *never* amused!

As I've said before, everything had its place in Freddie's life.

As beautiful as the kitchen was, all that ox-blood, black, white and green, I often felt a need to get out. Anywhere. It wasn't that I was going to be disloyal to this man who was always so very loyal to his friends and I wasn't going to run out on him now but I often felt the need just to breathe empty air.

Once refreshed, it would, however, be a real joy when the buzzer on the kitchen intercom sounded because it was a sign that Freddie wanted something, that the lethargy had lifted for a while. I always ran upstairs hoping that the summons was to do with food and occasionally I was rewarded, though most of the food was fed into the mouth of whichever cat happened to be with him.

This whole cycle of waiting for his finger to find the buzzer would carry on throughout the day. I would probably see him maybe a dozen times from perhaps two minutes to an hour. In between summonses, I would often go upstairs and peek round the bedroom door just to check he was all right. Often he'd be dozing which led me to believe that his nights must have been very, very long. I'd stay in the main house until about ten-thirty, eleven o'clock, checking on him one last time before I would go to bed.

Very rarely would he call for either Joe or myself during the night. Although he could be a tyrant, a demanding, unreasonable prima donna, underneath the façade he had one of the softest, kindest hearts imaginable. He realised the need for our rest so that we would be able to take care of him as he knew we wanted to during the day.

Thinking back, his nights must have followed the same pattern as his days, that of dozing and waking and having all the time in the world to think of what was happening to his body as a result of his decision to abandon the drugs. He had always made a point of finding out what each drug was for and what it would do. That way, he had his own control over the course of his illness. There were times when the doctor suggested something, but it would always be Freddie's choice as to whether the treatment was carried out.

Throughout his life, Freddie realised more and more the need for personal control after taking into account the times when his inexperience and naiveté had let him down in his younger days. I don't think being in charge had ever been more important to him than in his last weeks.

Having taken his decision, I have to stress that in no way had he ever considered suicide. That was something that other people might have done. Instead of seeing suicide as the ultimate choice, Freddie would have seen it as a loss of control. In his ideal world, he would have gone to a clinic to be put down, with an injection like his beloved Tiffany.

I find any description of both my own feelings and the atmosphere in the house during these last two weeks of Freddie's life very difficult to express and however I contrive to relate them will not do the reality full justice. The situation brought about contradictory feelings. Not only did we not know how long Freddie's dying would take but we also, perhaps selfishly, didn't know for how much longer we ourselves could keep up the brave smiling faces.

But Freddie was determined that life was to continue as normal. Every day we went shopping. Every day, Joe went to the gym. Every day, Jim worked in the garden. Every day the cleaners came in but they never went anywhere near Freddie's bedroom.

It was as though the house was encased beneath a huge, invisible glass bell jar, like the ones that covered the works of Victorian clocks.

I heard clocks everywhere in the house, ticking away, ticking away, each minute being part of a countdown whose length we didn't know. Each tick counting away the moments of Freddie's life. Everything outside the glass jar carried on as normal but we inside, it seemed, had always to be active, always straightening a book, replacing an ashtray, plumping a cushion, anything which might indicate that Freddie was expected to come downstairs again momentarily and he would see that his house was still perfect, just as he wanted it.

I couldn't tell you from one day to the next what the weather was. I just went out into it whether it be cloudy, sunny, freezing cold . . . Nothing really mattered. It must have been on the Tuesday night before he died that I had my talk with him. The doctors had told each of us that we had to enable him to let go, that in order to make it easier for people to die, they had to be told that it was okay by those they were about to leave behind.

I was lying on the bed with Freddie and he was asking how things were in the house, if things were straight and tidy. "I feel so tired, wondering whether I will ever see any of it again. Trying to visualise what's going on. I'm so isolated up here. All of a sudden it feels a huge house."

I sensed this was the only chance I would have to carry out the doctor's advice. "Everything's fine," I said. "Just as you'd like it, like always. And we're fine too. We're coping. Don't worry about us. If you feel it's time to go, we're behind you all the way. Don't worry about us. Don't feel you're leaving us. Everything's fine."

We just sat quietly, silently for an hour or two and then he dozed.

This, the final week of Freddie's life saw several sets of visitors. His family, Bomi and Jer, his parents and his sister Kash with her husband Roger and their two children, arrived early in that week for afternoon tea. While directing events from the bed, with superhuman effort he was able to entertain them for some two or three hours. This was still Freddie protecting them, making them believe that there was nothing for them to worry about. We brought up the tea which included home-made sandwiches and shop-bought cakes. Little did any of us know that this would be the last time that they would see Freddie alive. Although they wanted to return later in the week, Freddie categorically denied himself and them another meeting. He didn't want to put them through further suffering by them seeing him as bad as he was. Was there anything more for him to say to them?

Elton John arrived one day and stayed for about forty minutes and this time he arrived in his Bentley and pulled up at the front door. So often in the past, he'd kept his visits secret by driving in his Mini and parking in the Mews. His reply to the press's questions was that, "I've come to see my friend."

He was due to leave for work engagements in Paris. Before he left, he gave me a series of telephone numbers where he could be contacted.

Brian and Anita came and on another occasion Roger and Debbie. Both visits were fairly short. Without them knowing it, Freddie was saying goodbye. Dave Clark was fairly frequently at the house. Freddie took comfort at his being there, realising that this gave us some respite from the continual care and observation.

Dr. Atkinson made his usual regular calls throughout the week, every other day, to monitor the deterioration in Freddie's health. At this point, we were led to believe that Freddie still had maybe two to three weeks left. Terry Giddings still came most days even though there was no possibility now of Freddie ever going anywhere . . . Terry was very concerned.

Even though she was seven months pregnant and had little Richard at home, Mary still tried to get to the house daily for a short visit in order to continue her work. Freddie had determined that business was still to be as usual.

Which brings us to Friday, November 22, 1991.

On Thursday, the day before, Freddie asked that we get Jim Beach on the telephone and then informed us that he had arranged for Jim to come over and see him. We realised it must be for something quite serious because of Freddie's general health. Jim had kept in touch with Gordon Atkinson as much as he had with us or Freddie at the house, so that he was always abreast with the reality of the situation. Jim thus arrived at about ten o'clock in the morning and went straight up to Freddie's bedroom. At one point, Joe went up and provided them with what appeared to be much needed refreshments.

At about three-thirty, after a long meeting of five-and-a-half hours, which showed that Freddie was still entirely capable of rational thought, Jim Beach came downstairs and informed us of the basic content of the previous hours' discussions. Freddie and he had decided that it was time to release a statement with regards to Freddie's Aids status. Obviously, this came as a great shock to us as we waited in the kitchen. Jim Beach explained the reasons behind this announcement and gave us the chance to put our point of view. None of us knew exactly how to react at that point. After all the years of having to keep this huge secret to ourselves, it was now going to be broadcast to the world. After discussion, we accepted the reasons behind it. A lot of good could come out of Freddie admitting to having the disease while still alive. His circumstances and celebrity could be used as a basis for the benefit of other sufferers and those affected by the disease. It would show that anyone was at risk.

It was explained to us that the full effect would be much diluted should his health status be revealed after his death.

You have to realise that I had been consistently lying to my closest friends for these past years. For the full information to be now released as an official press statement made a public liar of me.

Freddie had thought about releasing a statement at various times during recent years but was always held back by his feelings and concern towards us and his family, the people closest to him. He wanted to protect us as much as himself from the glare and scrutiny that going public would have created. He didn't want anybody to have to walk down the street with people pointing at them and talking behind their backs. Also, due to the recent revelations to him from both Joe Fanelli and Jim Hutton about their own health, he did not want Garden Lodge to be branded a House of Death and life for all the residents within made intolerable.

Roxy Meade, the Queen press officer, was instructed to release the statement on Friday evening. Jim Beach had hoped to avoid the tabloid press capitalising on the news because these newspapers had devoted so much space in the previous months, printing and speculating on rumours of Freddie's ill-health. Jim had hoped the Sunday broadsheets would carry the news more responsibly.

After checking the prognosis for Freddie with Doctor Atkinson, Jim Beach left on a previously arranged trip to Los Angeles to deal with band business.

Since the previous Monday, Joe, Jim and I had been operating on a rota we had worked out so that Freddie had someone with him twenty-four hours a day. This included one of us being with him all night. Freddie would be in the bed and the one on duty would be on top of the bed at his side. We actually did very little but at least we were there to hold his hand when he woke. He would lie awake often for an hour or more but not need conversation. The physical presence of another human being was enough. Should we be asleep when he awoke, he would never wake us.

It had been my turn on duty on the Friday night, following the press announcement and that's when Freddie explained to me his reasoning behind the timing of the announcement. He had a fairly peaceful night as though a weight had been lifted from his shoulders. In the morning, I left his bedroom when Joe got up so that I could have a short nap before Saturday's merry-go-round. Jim went and bought all the papers and there was Freddie splashed across the front pages. We turned the television on downstairs and there he was too. We took some of the papers up to him but they were left unread on the bed. Freddie appeared withdrawn, as though he knew what was about to happen. The press's speculation over and embellishments upon his statement no longer concerned him.

I actually saw very little of Freddie on Saturday due to my having been with him all the previous night. I went to bed at my usual time and it was Jim's turn on the rota. At half-past-five in the morning on Sunday, the phone extension by my bed rang. I could tell it was an internal call by the ringing sound.

This particular dawn call was from Joe. He sounded very anxious and asked me to come straight over to Freddie's room. I didn't have the courage to ask if he was dead. I just put the phone down and threw some clothes on.

When I got to Freddie's room, I found Freddie had slipped into a coma. He had had an attack of rigors. He was lying very stiffly, his head at an awkward angle and his eyes were staring into the corner of the room behind him. There were no signs that he was aware of our presence, even though we tried talking to him and gently shaking him.

We were confused. While we'd been preparing ourselves for anything out of the ordinary, we were not actually at all prepared for this turn of events. We called Dr Atkinson who told us he would be with us as soon as he could. I called Mary and let her know what had happened. She came over to the house later in the morning, at about ten-thirty, and we left her to spend a short time with Freddie before having to return to her little son Richard.

Dr. Atkinson arrived and, after we'd unburdened all our fears, he tried his best to calm us down and explained to us that Freddie could carry on in this state for a further few days. He spent quite a lot of time assuring us that Freddie wasn't like this due to anything we had or hadn't done and that there was nothing more medically that we could do for him. All that was left was for us to be there with him.

Freddie's family also called. One thing which still plays on my conscience, even now, is that I couldn't let them come to see him that afternoon. I explained to them that Freddie was not having a good day but maybe early in the following week he would feel better. I didn't know then that I would be calling them four hours later to say that Freddie had passed away.

Dave Clark was called and immediately made his way over to the house and by the end of the afternoon, we had also been joined by Terry Giddings. In the house by then were Freddie and Dave Clark upstairs, Jim, Joe, Terry, Gordon Atkinson and myself downstairs in the kitchen. At about a quarter-to-seven, Dr. Atkinson said that there was nothing more he could do for the moment and so would go and have dinner and return afterwards. As Joe escorted Dr. Atkinson through the garden and thence out into the Mews, Dave Clark came downstairs and asked Jim and I to go upstairs to help Freddie to the lavatory.

We were pleased and surprised that Freddie had been able to ask to help to be relieved. While Freddie was clinically bed-bound, he was proud to the end that as far as he was concerned he wasn't. In that final week we would manoeuvre him to the edge of the bed and then supporting him with our arms like a human zimmer-frame, we would get him to the lavatory and back. Therefore, to his own satisfaction, he was *not* bed-bound!

When we got to his bedside and started to move him, we found that nature had taken its course. In the process of making him comfortable again, both Jim and I noticed that he wasn't breathing.

It was about a quarter-to-seven.

My first reaction was to try and get Doctor Atkinson back who had only just left. From the house, I called over to Joe in the Mews on the phone as Gordon Atkinson was already driving away in his car. Although Joe's running out into Logan Mews alerted the press to something going on, Joe managed to stop Gordon and brought him back inside. Gordon immediately came up to Freddie's bedroom where he pronounced Freddie dead and certified the time as being twelve minutes to seven.

Chapter Seven

From that moment it seemed to fall to me to be in charge of the situation. It was as though a bomb had dropped and everyone was in a daze. Even as I looked round, everything appeared as though we were in a fog and I was the only one able to move.

A frantic round of telephoning began. The first and most important call was to Mary. The second call was to Freddie's mother and father. It was so difficult informing his parents of what had happened. I had earlier put them off visiting once more. It was after those two calls that I had to try and trace Jim Beach at one of his many meetings in Los Angeles. Jim's role as manager had now been superseded by that of Freddie's executor, along with John Libson whose home phone number we had never been given. Even though it was Sunday, Queen business didn't stop. In the conversations I had with Jim Beach over the next hour when I'd finally got hold of him, it became obvious that timing was of paramount importance.

Timing and the manipulation of events seems to have been an integral element in this whole story and now it was decided that it couldn't be seen that Freddie's body was being sneaked out of the house. Doing so might appear that we were trying to cover up the fact of his death. A statement had therefore to be released to the press before the departure of Freddie's body could be carried out with the likelihood of any dignity at all. That's why the press announcement was released at midnight, giving me time to make the necessary arrangements.

Some two weeks previously, when Freddie had made 'the decision', I had broached the subject of how we would remove Freddie from the besieged house with my father who, coincidentally, was and is the general manager of the funeral directors John Nodes. We had therefore already laid plans to replace the usual fibre-glass coffin-shaped container with a proper coffin in case the press somehow managed to get photographs of his leaving. After I'd arranged the midnight departure, I think it was Terry Giddings who informed the local police of what had happened and asked their advice as to how to deal with the press outside the house.

The funeral directors' van pulled up and reversed into the mews to the front door of the house. Joe was up in the bedroom when I led my father, Leslie, and his four coffin-bearers with their burden up the narrow main staircase to Freddie's bedroom. It was more than surreal. To feel all that Freddie had achieved in life, which was mirrored in the house, and witnessing the arrival of his coffin surrounded by men dressed in sombre black was unreal. Joe and I stood to one side, our backs against the French windows leading out onto the small front balcony.

We couldn't take our eyes off Freddie. We watched with tears brimming as the men manoeuvred Freddie's body into the black protective bag, the use of which being mandatory in the case of every death which has occurred from a communicable disease. It wasn't a shock as such because I had read about it, seen this type of activity on television and in the cinema but when it is happening to you and one of your loved ones it jars. For me it was the moment of finality. Once he was zipped up inside the bodybag, there was just no way he was ever coming out. And it was the last time I saw him. Although as it was happening, I realised and accepted that this had to happen, I really didn't want to see it happening and as a last memory of my friend, it was not the most pleasant. What was sweet was seeing the little teddy bear that Jim Hutton had placed with Freddie being put into the bag with him.

"What the eye doesn't see, the heart doesn't grieve over," is one clichéd situation that I now wish I could have experienced at that point. I really didn't want to witness all this. Who would? I remember holding Joe's hand. He was shaking. I was nearest the bed. He was on my left and I could see out of the corner of my eye that he was shaking. I reached out and squeezed his hand to let him know he wasn't there on his own.

The bag was placed tenderly and carefully in the coffin and when they were ready I led the pallbearers down the stairs. For the first time, one of Freddie's aims of lining up all the doors in the main house and the Mews so that you could look in a straight line from one end of the property to another came into good effect. He always used to say, "Take the money and run!" and indeed, with this configuration of rooms, he was able to make his last exit swiftly and unencumbered. Or, in the manner of the announcement which always used to come at the end of every Elvis Presley concert, "Ladies and Gentlemen, Mister Mercury has left the building!"

With the invaluable aid of the police who had arrived in force with barricades to keep the press at bay, the van pulled away from the Mews and into Logan Place. When the van got to the end of the street, due to the one-way traffic system it had to turn right. The police created a road block for five minutes, thus preventing any of the press from following the van and discovering where Freddie's body was being taken.

One of the strangest calls to the house that evening had been from Freddie's great friend Barbara Valentin, the German actress with whom he spent many happy hours. She had telephoned to ask how Freddie was although she had no idea that he was dying. She had just felt that it was the time to ring. It came as a terrible shock to her to find that she had called perhaps an hour too late. I sensed the same reaction to the news from all the calls that I had to make including those to his friends Thor Arnold and Lee Nolan in San Diego. Bad news always travels fast and soon we were being inundated with calls from all over the world. The rest of the band were informed by Julie Glover, the Queen Productions secretary and Jim Beach's trusted right hand.

Because of Freddie's wish to be cremated and my previous experience when I was very young of having helped my father, I knew that we had to have two doctors' signatures on the death certificate and so one of the calls was to Doctor Graham Moyle who had looked after Freddie through much of his illness. Even though there were a few people in the house, it felt incredibly empty.

The creator of these surroundings was no longer here.

I don't think any of us felt particularly tired and I know it was gone four o'clock Monday morning before I got to bed.

It fell to me to sign the certificate registering his death at Chelsea Registry Office which I did the following day. I then went to the head office of John Nodes and Sons to complete the more formal details of Freddie's funeral. I knew from the family, whose responsibility the body of the unmarried Freddie now was, that the funeral according to Parsee tradition had to be as soon after death as possible. After speaking with them, I found out what their requirements were and then it was up to my father Leslie and myself to organise the fine tuning.

We had to find a slot in the schedule of the West London Crematorium where we could reserve an hour for the service. Usually, cremations are only allotted half-an-hour. The earliest available was Wednesday morning. Through talking with Freddie's mother and father, I found out what time they would need for their religious services to be observed and it was arranged that Freddie's body would be brought to Ladbroke Grove late on the Tuesday night where only close blood family would be permitted to attend.

While Freddie had been a public figure for the last twenty-five years, for the first twenty of his life he had belonged to his family. I felt it only right that his family be involved as much as possible with the arrangements for his funeral. It was, after all, the last chance they would have of reacquainting themselves.

It was a strange feeling, assuming the mantle of control at this extremely emotional time but someone had to be in control, as dispassionate and cool-headed as possible, considering the mass of press gathered outside in Logan Place who had been there in strength since the previous Friday evening when the spokesperson had issued a statement on Freddie's behalf that he was suffering from Aids. For two weeks prior to that announcement, the press had been outside twenty-four hours a day. By day, there were about ten and by night, a minimum of three. However, at the time of his death, there must have been between thirty and forty.

The funeral had been arranged for Wednesday. The remainder of the Monday and all of Tuesday of that week, while we all walked around in a dreamlike state, we were kept busy by the non-stop ringing of the gate bell and the enormous amount of floral tributes arriving. Included in my job was the ringing round and arranging of who was to ride in which car to the funeral and every now and then increasing the number of the floral hearses as more and more flowers arrived. All the flowers went to the crematorium although, after the funeral, I arranged for all the suitable bouquets to be sent on to hospitals and hospices where more people could get some joy from them.

The day of the funeral, I felt that my whole world had stopped. For years Freddie and I had lived in each other's pockets and so I felt that a part of me had died too.

My job was over. I knew that there was absolutely nothing more that I could physically have done for Freddie. It had been his decision to bring his life to a close by refusing any further medication to keep him alive. He had never let the disease totally dictate his life and when he felt his control slipping, he made a conscious decision to retake it.

Ultimate control.

Quite simply, he got things done and those things were always done the way he wanted.

The day of the funeral, Wednesday, November 27, 1991, dawned. It was a dull damp, late autumn morning and everything in the garden would have looked drab except that the lawns at Garden Lodge were awash with unseasonal colours. The floral tributes to Freddie which had been arriving for the last three days were doubled up in some places. Inside Garden Lodge, a small group of Freddie's friends had gathered to accompany him on his last outing. We left the house in a cortege of three limousines augmented by a couple of private cars in a procession which was led by five floral hearses. Freddie always liked things done in style.

I was in the car with Joe Fanelli and Jim Hutton. My mind was preoccupied with the course of events which had led up to this moment and for what was to happen over the next hour or so. I remember looking out of the car window and seeing people stop and stare as the cortege passed by and I wondered if they had any idea of whose funeral procession it was that they were witnessing. The column of cars arrived at the crematorium literally moments before the hearse bearing Freddie's casket, on top of which was a small paper flower, a last gift to Uncle Freddie from his young niece, Natalie.

The timing of the hearse's arrival at the crematorium chapel for the ten o'clock ceremony was immaculate, just like a military operation or, perhaps more appropriately, one of Freddie's gigs. His body was carried into the chapel to the strains of Aretha Franklin's 'You've Got A Friend' and the ensuing Zoroastrian service was a continuation of one that had begun at eight-thirty that morning by the two white-robed Parsee priests in the chapel of rest at the Funeral Directors John Nodes and Sons in Ladbroke Grove.

Several members of Freddie's immediate family had attended this earlier ceremony and although Freddie himself had not been an adherent of any religion in his adult life, his wish to be cremated fitted in very well with the wishes of his family whose Zoroastrian faith he respected. Freddie had been far from being actively opposed to anyone's religion or faith. The things that offended him were the trappings and hypocrisy involved in the various clerical and institutional aspects of established religion.

Gathered in the funeral chapel of the West London Crematorium were both branches of Freddie's family, the one bound by ties of blood and the other bound by friendship. At the end of the service, Freddie's body exited this world with Montserrat Caballe's voice singing 'D'amor Sull' Ali Rosee' from Verdi's opera *Il Trovatore*. Freddie was never one to be conventional so I thought this was a fitting *adieu* and that Freddie would have approved.

While funerals are generally quiet, private affairs, the mass of press, photographers and onlookers on the bank opposite the chapel reminded us that the person to whom we had just said our final goodbyes had been no ordinary mortal.

Back at Garden Lodge, a small group of Freddie's friends – the band, their consorts, Jim Beach, Gordon Atkinson, Graham Moyle, Terry Giddings, Mary, Jim, Joe, Dave Clark and I – who had attended the funeral, had gathered to celebrate his life with champagne. I felt he would have been proud of his send-off and that my discharging my last obligations had been up to his expectations. One of my jobs had been to always make sure he looked presentable whenever he left the house and I don't think he would have complained this time.

Epilogue

Just for Freddie, there follows an up-dating of the cast featured in this book. To my knowledge, Freddie, this is reasonably accurate. I thought it might amuse you . . . without abusing too many sensitivities.

A

HRH The Prince Andrew   *Married and divorced, now deskbound in a dockyard.*

Thor Arnold   *Still nursing. Now relocated in San Diego.*

James Arthurs   *Still a businessman living in Connecticut.*

Debbie Ash   *Still an actress.*

Jane Asher   *Now* huge *in cakes, McVitie's biscuits and most branches of Sainsbury.*

Gordon Atkinson   *Still generally practising. In Mayfair.*

Mary Austin   *Single parent, mother of two. Currently still residing in Chaillot . . . sorry, Garden Lodge.*

B

Tony Bastin   *Dead.*

Jim and Claudia Beach   *Queen's manager and his wife. Still. But also, now, one of Freddie's two executors. Jim, that is and, therefore now, effectively, the fourth member of Queen. The succession was assured.*

Rupert Bevan   *Still gilding picture frames and restoring furniture at Putney Bridge.*

Stephanie Beacham   *Still actressing.*

Martin Beisly   *Senior director at Christie's specialising in Victorian pictures.*

Debbie Bishop   *Acting and singing.*

David Bowie   *Composer, musician and performer. Now a public company.*

Bryn Bridenthal   *Earth calling Bryn.*

Dieter Briet   *Wind-surfed over the horizon.*
Briony Brind   *I think she's retired.*
John Brough   *Probably a record producer by now.*
Kim Brown   *Now a widow, working at EMI. Pete sadly died, like Freddie, far too young.*
Michael Brown   *Still wardrobe master for the currently homeless Royal Ballet.*
Jackie Brownell   *Sorry. Lost contact.*
Bomi and Jer Bulsara   *More than ever his parents.*
Jo Burt   *Jo, are you still strumming?*

C

Carlos Caballe   *Still managing his expanding stable of talent.*
Montserrat Caballe   *Still your own diva, Freddie.*
Montsy Caballe   *Fine.*
Piers Cameron   *Living happily with a long-time friend of mine.*
Rupert Cavendish   *Still ensconced in his Empire empire.*
Annie Challis   *Rod Stewart's assistant.*
David Chambers   *Don't know.*
Charles the Canadian   *I hope you're well, Charles.*
John Christie   *I still get Christmas cards.*
Dave Clark   *Still misses you.*
Trevor Clarke   *Holding his own.*
Roger and Kashmira Cooke   *Looking after your parents.*
Carolyn Cowan   *Now a very good photographer.*

D

Gordon Dalziel   *Blonder than ever.*
Jo Dare   *Don't know.*
John Deacon   *Glad it's all over.*
Derek Deane   *Director of English National Ballet.*
Denny   *Still cutting?*
Jim Devenney   *Come in, Jim.*
Richard Dick   *I hope he's still around.*
Anita Dobson   *As Elvis said, Taking Care of Business.*
Rudi Dolezal   *Queen are a big loss.*

E

Wayne Eagling   *Director of Dutch National Ballet.*

Ken and Dolly East   *Gone down under.*
Eduardo the Venezualan   *I still feel guilty.*
Gordon Elsbury   *Don't know.*
Kenny Everett   *Dead.*

F

Joe Fanelli   *Dead.*
Pam Ferris   *She was wonderful in Roald Dahl's* Matilda.
Tony Fields   *Saw him in a movie the other day.*
Michael Fish   *In deepest Brixton. No, not the prison.*
Leslie Freestone   *Still working. Will never retire.*

G

Brian Gazzard   *Now a very eminent authority on HIV/Aids.*
David Geffen   *Now makes films as well. As what.*
Bob Geldof   *Just as famous as ever.*
Boy George   *Has become a wonderful writer using that razor-sharp wit.*
Terry, Sharon and Luke Giddings   *Alive and well. Terry now drives
    proper company directors.*
Julie Glover   *Works full-time for Brian May now.*
Harvey Goldsmith   *Still promoting. Now really, really famous.*
Bruce Gowers   *Don't know.*
Richard Gray   *Looked happy and well at your photographic exhibition at
    the Royal Albert Hall.*

H

Tony Hadley   *He really thought a lot of you.*
Graham Hamilton   *Semper factotum.*
Gary Hampshire   *Still with John Reid. Still.*
Sarah Harrison   *Living in France with Gerard Manchon.*
Stephen Hayter   *Dead.*
Peter Hince (Ratty)   *Now a very, very good photographer.*
Jennifer Holliday   *Probably somewhere on tour in the USA.*
George Hurrell   *We think he's still around.*
Jim Hutton   *Alive and well and happy and living in Ireland.*
Sally Hyatt   *Working now for Roger Taylor.*

J

Michael Jackson   *Still touring. Taken to fatherhood like a duck to water.*

Elton John   *Still touring. Now one of the outer knights.*
Peter Jones   *Off the map.*

K

Petre von Katze   *Yes . . .*
Trip Khalaf   *Haven't heard in a long time.*
Tony King   *Now working with Prince Rupert Loewenstein.*
Winnie Kirchberger   *Dead.*

L

Debbie Leng   *Happy with Roger and Rufus Tiger and Tiger Lily.*
Carl Lewis   *Now has a seriously wonderful collection of crystal.*
John Libson   *Still accounting but now your second executor.*
Sir Joseph Lockwood   *Dead.*

M

Rheinhold Mack, Ingrid and John Frederick   *America didn't quite work out.*
David Mallet   *From what I know, he's still directing.*
Fred Mandel   *Not a dicky bird.*
Diego Maradona   *Became the 'hand of god'.*
Brian May   *Can't lose the recording bug.*
Donald McKenzie   *Still bogged down with Joe's estate.*
Roxy Meade   *Got out. Happy with child.*
Bhaskar Menon   *Gives a lot of interviews.*
Robin Moore-Ede   *Who knows?*
Mike and Linda Moran   *I don't hear.*
Peter Morgan   *Haven't a clue. Care less.*
Diana Moseley   *She's still working hard.*
Graham Moyle   *Still researching into HIV/Aids.*
Russell Mulcahay   *Moved up a rung. Feature film director.*
Nina Myskow   *Still in touch.*

N

Anna Nicholas   *Still trouping.*
Lee Nolan   *Happy, waitering in San Diego.*
Gary Numan   *Occasional sightings.*
David Nutter   *Does he direct the 'X' Files? Please inform.*

O
Terry O'Neill   *Still snap-snapping away.*

P
Elaine Page   *Conquered Broadway as Norma Desmond.*
Rudi Patterson   *Alive and well.*
Christopher Payne   *Often on the telly.*
Yasmin Pettigrew   *Graduated a degree course.*
Mary Pike   *Still around.*
Tony Pike   *Still there.*
Paul Prenter   *Dead.*

R
Kurt Raab (Rebecca)   *Dead.*
Bill Reid   *Last heard of, was very sick.*
John Reid   *Calmed down.*
Tim Rice   *Now Our Lord. Oscar winner.*
Cliff Richard   *Appeared as Heathcliff after upstaging Wimbledon.*
Dave Richards   *Bought Mountain Studios.*
Howard Rose   *Haven't heard.*
Hannes Rossacher   *Still hard at work.*

S
Pino Sagliocco   *Presumably still gigging.*
Amin Salih   *Presumably still doing sums.*
Joe Scardilli   *Last time I saw him he was doing okay.*
Jane Seymour   *Medicine woman.*
Wayne Sleep   *Hoofing away.*
Lord Snowdon   *Watch the birdie.*
Gladys Spier   *Still with us.*
Billy Squier   *Fine. Has become a script writer.*
Rod Stewart   *Going for respectability in a very big way.*
Gerry and Sylvia Stickells   *We're looking forward to his photo book.*
Peter Straker   *Still alive and Brel.*
Phil Symes   *Once again doing Queen's PR.*
Barbara Szabo   *No know.*

T
Gail Taphouse   *Still on* pointe.

Mr Tavener   *Still the only gentleman builder.*
Chris Taylor (Crystal)   *Alive and well and gardening in Australia.*
Domique Taylor   *Still a very brave and beautiful lady.*
Elizabeth Taylor   *She was a star at your Memorial and a true survivor.*
Gavin Taylor   *No idea.*
Roger Taylor   *Another one who can't get rid of the recording bug.*
Baroness Francesca von Thyssen   *Moved up a rung or two. Now an Arch-Duchess. Lovely as ever.*
Douglas Trout   *Still crimping?*

V

Barbara Valentin   *Life has never been the same.*
Vince the Barman   *The one that got away. Lucky?*
Paul Vincent   *I dunno.*

W

Clodagh Wallace   *Still managing.*
Misa Watanabe   *I wonder if she's accrued the other half of Japan, yet?*
David Wigg   *Still hacking for the Daily Distress.*
Margie Winter   *Still about.*
Stefan Wissnet   *Don't know.*
Carol Woods   *Back in New York.*

Y

Susannah York   *Still lovely.*
Richard Young   *Older and wiser. Oh, well, perhaps . . .*

Z

Brian Zellis (Jobby)   *Alive and kicking but out of the business.*